GEOMETRICAL JUSTICE

Legal decisions continue to mystify: why was this person sentenced to 20 years in prison, but that person to just 10 years for the same crime? Why did one person sue for civil damages, but another let the matter drop? Legal rules are supposed to answer these questions, but their answers are radically incomplete. Wouldn't it be wonderful to have a theory that predicted and explained legal decisions?

Drawing on Donald Black's theoretical ideas, *Geometrical Justice: The Death Penalty in America* addresses these issues, focusing specifically on who is sentenced to death and executed in the United States. The book explains why some murders are more serious than others and how the social characteristics of defendants, victims, and jurors affect case outcomes. Building on the most rigorous data in the field, the authors reveal wide discrepancies in capital punishment – why one person lives, but another person dies.

Geometrical Justice will be of interest to those engaged in criminal justice, criminology, and socio-legal studies, as well as students taking courses on sentencing, corrections, and capital punishment.

Scott Phillips is a professor of sociology and criminology at the University of Denver, USA.

Mark Cooney is a professor of sociology at the University of Georgia, USA.

GEOMETRICAL JUSTICE

The Death Penalty in America

Scott Phillips and Mark Cooney

Routledge
Taylor & Francis Group

LONDON AND NEW YORK

Cover image: Mark Cooney

First published 2022
by Routledge
4 Park Square, Milton Park, Abingdon, Oxon OX14 4RN

and by Routledge
605 Third Avenue, New York, NY 10158

Routledge is an imprint of the Taylor & Francis Group, an informa business

Library of Congress Cataloging-in-Publication Data
A catalog record for this title has been requested

ISBN: 9781032009902 (hbk)
ISBN: 9781032009865 (pbk)
ISBN: 9781003176633 (ebk)

DOI: 10.4324/9781003176633

Typeset in Bembo
by Newgen Publishing UK

To Kathleen, Caroline, and Ryan – I love you – SP
To my son, Nicolas, and daughter, Zara, two wonderful beings – MC

CONTENTS

FIGURES

TABLES

AUTHOR BIOS

Scott Phillips is a professor in the Department of Sociology and Criminology at the University of Denver. He has written extensively about two topics: Donald Black's geometrical theories and the American death penalty. His research has been published in social science journals and law reviews, including *American Sociological Review*, *Criminology*, *Law and Society Review*, and the *Harvard Civil Rights – Civil Liberties Law Review*. His research has also been covered in major media outlets, including the *Houston Chronicle*, *The Dallas Morning News*, *USA Today*, and *The New York Times*.

Mark Cooney holds law degrees from University College Dublin and Harvard Law School and a Ph.D. in sociology from University of Virginia. A professor of sociology and adjunct professor of law at the University of Georgia, he has authored numerous publications in the sociology of law, violence, and conflict. His most recent book is *Execution by Family: A Theory of Honor Violence* (Routledge 2019).

PREFACE

Imagine a world without science. A world with no understanding of how life forms, why objects fall to earth, how substances combine to form other substances, or when the human brain becomes fully developed. A world without cars, heated homes, telephones, electricity, computers, affordable clothing, books, trains, refrigerators, abundant food, bridges, shopping malls, airports, or craft beer. In such a world, we humans would be far fewer in number, our health would be markedly worse, and we would be immeasurably poorer. Science, like most things, can be used for good or evil, to create and to destroy. In practice, science has enhanced life far more than it has undermined it. Science has improved the lot of humankind beyond recognition, and continues to do so.

Despite the obvious benefits of science, many intellectuals continue to resist it, especially when applied to humans. Their objection is not to a science of the body – which gives us modern medicine – but to a science of the person. Some of the so-called human sciences, such as sociology and anthropology, have increasingly become anti-sciences.

We have seen this up close. We are sociologists of law who study the relationship between law and its social environment. The late 1960s saw the launching of a scientific legal sociology, born from the realization that traditional legal thinking based on rules has a limited ability to explain the handling of real-life cases. Not all rule violations that could result in an arrest do so, for example, and not all arrests result from rule violations. Thus began the search for the sociological sources of legal outcomes. That search resulted in a theory of law developed by Donald Black in his pathbreaking 1976 book, *The Behavior of Law*. Black's theory of law argues that the outcome of a case depends on its social geometry – the location, direction, and distance of the case in social space. Did a respected member of the community drink too much and accidentally run over someone just released from prison? Or did a person who was just released from prison drink too much and accidentally run over a respected member of the community? Did a man punch a stranger? Or did he punch his wife? The same act can produce very different outcomes depending on the relative social status of the parties and the relationship between them. Although Black's geometrical theory of law promised substantial scientific dividends – to explain why the outcomes of factually similar cases can be so different – many legal sociologists eventually ignored it. They turned instead to a humanistic approach that emphasized the subjectivity of legal actors and the unpredictability of their actions. That approach has produced some important empirical findings but, understandably, no general theory.

In the meantime, the scientific approach has not stood still. Black and others added to the theory of law. The most important extension is articulated in Black's 2011 book, *Moral Time*. This newer theory takes a step backward to move forward. Why is an act forbidden by law in the first place? And why are some acts more serious offenses than others? His answer is that law forbids certain changes in social space or movements of social time, and the greater and faster the movement of social time the more serious the transgression. This body of work is known as Blackian theory, social geometry theory, or geometrical theory. It remains the only comprehensive theory of who brings and who wins legal cases.

We believe it is time to return to a fully scientific legal sociology, one that prizes theory that is general, simple, and, above all, tested against the evidence. In this book, we provide the most complete description to date of the geometrical theory of law and we test it using the best information available anywhere on the handling of legal cases: death penalty data.

One might reasonably ask whether the world needs another book on capital punishment. Existing books cover a myriad of topics, including historical, economic, philosophical, legal, and autobiographical aspects of the death penalty. The book you hold in your hand is different. We make no claims about the rights or wrongs of the death penalty, how often innocent people are sentenced to death, or whether the death penalty saves more lives than it sacrifices. Instead, we ask whether geometrical theory predicts the most consequential decision the legal system ever makes: sentencing a human being to death. Why are some defendants sentenced to die and executed? Why are other defendants – whose crimes were equally violent – spared? The answers to these questions will, we hope, be of interest to legal sociologists, lawyers, death penalty specialists, and indeed everyone concerned with the reality of legal justice.

Given the quality of the death penalty data, the stakes are high for the scientific approach to law and geometrical theory in particular. If the theory fails when confronted with such rigorous data, it is probably time to fold up its tent and start prospecting elsewhere for something richer. If, on the other hand, its predictions are upheld, we can be more confident that we possess an important theory, one that is accessible to lawyers and non-lawyers alike. Which is to be? Will we be moved to abandon geometrical theory or, rather, to acknowledge that the theory enhances our collective ability to understand an institution that touches the life of every person on the planet? Is justice geometrical?

We have two audiences in mind for this book: students and scholars. We want the text to be accessible to non-specialists interested in death penalty justice such as undergraduates, graduate students, and law students. At the same time, we aim to convince our academic colleagues that our quantitative analyses of two large data sets are valid. To accomplish these divergent goals, we have divided each chapter into two parts. The main body of the chapters tells a story that is supported by real cases, hypothetical cases, and easily understood statistics. For the more specialized reader, we have placed the technical details of our methodology, analyses, and findings in chapter appendices.

ACKNOWLEDGMENTS

In writing this book, we have incurred many debts, intellectual and personal. We are grateful to Daniel Boches, Callie Burt, Bradley Campbell, Paul Colomy, and Cathy Durso for their insightful comments on previous drafts. We also received helpful feedback from our students: Scott's 2021 *Conflict and the Law* class in the Department of Sociology and Criminology at the University of Denver and Mark's 2021 *Sociology of Law* classes in the Department of Sociology and the School of Law at the University of Georgia. Scott's former students at Rice University, Breck Garrett and Ivan Zapata, did an excellent job collecting more than 3,000 newspaper articles about Houston homicides. Mark's student Mahima Patel did sterling work organizing the large body of materials on the Houston cases we describe at the beginning of several chapters.

We are especially grateful to Donald Black whose brilliant work inspired this volume. However, since we wanted to test his theory at arm's length, we have not consulted Donald about the contents of this work.

For friendship and support, Scott wishes to thank his wife Kathleen, his children Caroline and Ryan, his parents Dorothy and Phillip, his mother-in-law Nancy, his friends Miko and Justin, and his mentors Mark and Paul.

Mark gratefully acknowledges the continuing love and support of his spouse Mary, his adult children Nicolas and Zara, and his siblings Susan, Rachel, John, and Patricia.

PROLOGUE

The death penalty has long fascinated writers and scholars. Quite apart from the voluminous research literature found in social science journals and law reviews, a substantial array of books has appeared on the subject. Some books review the moral debate surrounding execution (van den Haag and Conrad 1983). Others discuss the legal doctrines that regulate capital punishment (Steiker and Steiker 2016; Rivkind et al. 2016). Even more common are reviews of policy issues (Bedau 1964; Paternoster, Brame, and Bacon 2008; Acker, Bohm, and Lanier 2014; Bohm 2017; Baumgartner et al. 2018). A sub-genre chronicles the personal narratives of activists (Prejean 1993), prison wardens (Cabana 1996), and lawyers (Dow 2005). Other authors have explored the history of capital punishment (Banner 2002), botched executions (Sarat 2014), wrongful convictions (Radelet, Bedau, and Putnam 1992), the persistence of the American death penalty (Garland 2010), racial discrimination (Baldus, Woodworth, and Pulaski 1990), the execution process (Johnson 1998), the decline of the American death penalty (Baumgartner, DeBoef, and Boydstun 2008), and international perspectives (Hood and Hoyle 2008; Johnson and Zimring 2009).

Our interest lies in the question of when the death penalty will be imposed in individual cases. A byzantine set of rules and procedures govern such cases. They differ from one jurisdiction to another, but share one thing in common: they fail to explain who actually receives a sentence of death – how justice operates in practice. Most defendants who could be sentenced to death are not. Moreover, most condemned defendants are never executed. And some defendants who do not appear to be eligible for the death penalty are nonetheless dispatched to death row and executed. This limitation is not confined to capital cases. The rules and principles found in constitutions, legislation, precedents, and regulations are an imperfect guide to how law operates in practice. Regardless

DOI: 10.4324/9781003176633-1

of the topic – robbery or breach of contract, rape or trespass, fraud or medical negligence, insider trading or a disputed will – breaking a written law, even when detected, does not automatically lead to a legal case being filed, pursued, or won. Conversely, not breaking a law is no guarantee that a legal case will not be brought or even succeed.

Now, there is more to law than handling disputes. Law discharges several other functions. It sets the basic rules of society, establishing the branches of government and the relationship between them. It concretizes broad notions of morality and fair dealing into rules about equality of treatment and due process of law. It facilitates transactions. Indeed, that is what many lawyers spend most of their days doing – drawing up contracts, establishing trusts, conveying property, making wills, forming or dissolving corporations, making property transfers run smoothly. But most people have little occasion to question the Constitution or the idea of the rule of law. They might only contact a lawyer when they buy a house or make a will. Yet virtually everybody has some contact with police – as a speeding motorist, a witness to an accident, or a victim of a crime – and many have had more sustained dealings with prosecutors, courts, judges, and juries. For the great majority of people, law consists of conflicts and the response to them.

The handling of cases is central to law, then, and to understand it better we need to look beyond the written rules. To do so, we must start from the beginning: law is a system created by people for people. The human element is therefore crucial. That brings us to sociology, a body of knowledge that has long highlighted the gap between the law on the books (what should happen) and the law in action (what actually happens). What does sociology teach us about the law in action?

The Sociology of Law

Sociology is the study of social life. The new discipline of sociology emerged out of the profound transformation that human societies began to undergo some 200 years ago as they evolved from an agrarian social order that had survived for several thousand years to a new and unchartered industrial civilization. Sweeping changes came about. People moved from villages filled with familiar faces to towns and cities populated by strangers. Families became smaller and less central to the lives of their members. Religion retreated from the public sphere, becoming a private matter. A scientific understanding of the world developed, and its technological offshoots boosted prosperity enormously. Individualism began to replace communalism. The old hierarchy based on land gave way to one based on capital. Corporations grew in size, number, and influence. The state expanded and came to regulate more aspects of life. With these and other large-scale changes occurring around them, intellectuals naturally began to ask fundamental questions about the nature of society: What is it? Where is it going? What holds it together? A new science was born.

Forerunners

From its earliest days, sociology displayed an interest in law. The three most important theorists who largely defined sociology's mission – Karl Marx, Max Weber, and Emile Durkheim – each thought deeply about law's social dimensions (see, e.g., Treviño 1996: chapters 4–6; Deflem 2008: 24–55).[1] In doing so, they focused on macro-sociological questions, in particular, the place of the legal system in modern society. They emphasized diverse roles for law, consistent with their divergent social philosophies. Marx saw law as an institution created by capitalism that, in turn, supports capitalism, a product and a pillar. Weber considered law to be a product and a pillar of the rationalization of society (i.e., the drive to make social life orderly, predictable, and rule-bound). For Durkheim, law was a product and a pillar of the values that hold societies together. Durkheim alone went on to formulate testable relationships between law and its social environment.[2] But neither he nor his fellow theorists paid any systematic attention to variation in individual case outcomes, such as who gets arrested and who gets convicted, or who sues and who wins in court.

The American Legal Realists, a loose-knit group of academics and judges, were the first to draw sustained attention to the social dimension of cases. Toward the end of the 1920s, thinkers such as Karl Llewellyn, Underhill Moore, Fred Rodell, and Jerome Frank came to emphasize the unpredictability of legal decisions, our limited ability to foretell the outcome of cases. As Llewellyn (1931: 1241) wrote in an influential essay, "there is less possibility of accurate prediction of what courts will do than the traditional rules would lead us to suppose." Jerome Frank (1949: viii–ix), a federal judge, helpfully distinguished between two branches of Realism: rule skepticism and fact skepticism. Rule skeptics stress the ambiguity of legal rules: looking at the same statutes and cases, skillful lawyers can virtually always come up with arguments for either side of a case that are equally compelling. On top of that, juries may apply rules in an idiosyncratic fashion and judges may overturn even the best-established rules when they think it appropriate. Fact-skeptics, by contrast, emphasize the unpredictability of fact-finding. Frank made the simple but powerful point that most legal disputes do not turn on contested points of law. Instead, they revolve around disputes about the facts. On what date did the parties verbally agree for delivery of the contracted goods? Who threw the first punch? Did she consent to the sexual encounter? Police officers, prosecutors, judges, and juries must typically choose between competing stories of what happened. In their construction of the facts, imponderables play a large part. Which party will prove to be more convincing? Will vital witnesses turn up? Will they be intimidated by the occasion or, rather, deliver their testimony in a convincing manner? Will the opposing lawyer manage to undermine their credibility on cross-examination? Will the decision-maker harbor unconscious prejudice for or against the witness? None of this, Frank argued, can be predicted in advance, and none of it ensures that the decision-makers reconstruct what happened accurately. Frank (1949: 14) summarized his position in a simple formulation: "facts are guesses."

The Legal Realists were well named as they looked beyond the narrow confines of the classroom and the courtroom and injected a much-needed dose of sociological reality into thinking about law. They recognized that we cannot understand law by looking at the formal rules alone. But their questions were better than their answers. They were experts at highlighting the human side of cases, but they were less adept at developing a theory of the human side. Frank (1949: 111), for example, felt that "the personality of the judge is the pivotal factor in law administration." However, he was not optimistic that "those jungles of the mind which we are just beginning to discover will soon be reduced to a high state of civilized order" (113). Nor were any of the other Realists successful in coming up with generalizations that could be tested with data.

A second stream of inquiry came from anthropology. Working in small scale, less-developed societies, anthropologists became interested in how societies could be orderly in the absence or unavailability of the state (see, e.g., Bohannan 1967). In the 1930s, Llewelyn teamed up with the anthropologist E. Adamson Hoebel (1941) and conducted interviews with elderly members of the Cheyenne nation, eliciting information about how they had handled "trouble cases" when they were still an independent people. By the time the next generation of anthropologists began their research, virtually all societies had been fully incorporated into a state. New questions arose about the role of legal institutions in small communities far removed from the political center. Did people ignore the law or use it? How did their courts compare to those of more developed legal systems (e.g., Collier 1973; Nader and Todd 1978)? Max Gluckman (1967), for example, observed judges deciding cases among the Lozi of Zambia, noting the considerable emphasis they placed, in contrast to Western judges, on preserving relationships, a pattern he attributed to the multiplex or socially close ties between the parties. Laura Nader (1990) analyzed how the active pursuit of legal grievances by the residents of Talea, a Zapotec town in Oaxaca, Mexico, was nonetheless compatible with a considerable degree of community harmony. Valuable as these and other anthropologists' insights were, they fell short of a general theory of law.

Law and Society

Legal Realism eventually petered out and legal anthropology remained a small specialized discipline. However, the 1960s saw a surge of interest in the social life of law. A professional organization, the Law and Society Association, was founded in 1964 to foster scholarly inquiry. Two years later came the establishment of a journal – *Law & Society Review* – that remains the leading publication in the field. Law and Society is now a broad field that welcomes scholars from multiple disciplines, including sociology, anthropology, criminology, economics, political science, history, communications, and law. This ecumenism allows multiple voices to be heard, but it comes with a price: the field lacks a coherent core. Law and Society has come to encompass pretty much anything that touches upon any of law's social dimension (see, e.g., Abel 2010). Consider just a few of the questions law and society scholars have posed:

- Why do people obey the law (Tyler 1990; Papachristos, Meares, and Fagan 2012; Nagin and Telep 2017)?
- Can the law effect significant social change, such as the desegregation of schools, the promotion of gender pay equity, or "LGBT rights" (Rosenberg 1991; McCann 1994; Keck 2009)?
- By what mechanisms do laws come to be enacted and spread across the countries of the world (see, e.g., Boyle 2002; Halliday and Carruthers 2009; Frank, Camp, and Bayliss 2010)?
- How has the legal profession come to be socially structured (Abel and Lewis 1988–1989; Galanter and Palay 1991; Heinz et al. 2005)?
- In what ways does the plurality of legal rules and social norms found within and across modern societies combine and conflict at the local, national, and international levels (e.g., Merry 2006; Berman 2012; Valverde 2012)?
- How do organizations interpret and implement new legal rules, such as those prohibiting employment discrimination (e.g., Edelman 1992; Edelman, Uggen, and Urlanger 1999; Dobbin 2009)?
- How do legal ideas affect people's everyday understandings of the world (e.g., Ewick and Silbey 1998; Nieslen 2004; Chua and Engel 2019)?
- What can social theorists tell us about the role of law in modern society (e.g., Deflem 1996; Treviño 2007; van Krieken 2019)?
- What effects does regime change have on the rule of law, conceptions of justice, and criminal behavior (Dezalay and Garth 2002; Karsted and LaFree 2006; Savelsberg and McElrath 2014)?
- Does the legal system perpetuate racial inequality and, if so, how (e.g., Pager 2007; Alexander 2010; Rothstein 2017)?
- What adverse familial, occupational, civic, and social collateral consequences do legal punishments have (e.g., Manza and Uggen 2006; Western 2006; Comfort 2007)?
- How and how often does the legal system convict innocent people (see, e.g., Gross 2008; Garrett 2011; Zalman and Carrano 2014)?

Some of these questions treat law as an independent variable – law impacts something else (e.g., how law affects people, organizations, or social change). Others approach law as a dependent variable – something else impacts law (e.g., how social or political forces influence the growth and development of law). Some questions have a strong psychological component (e.g., why people obey the law, how people think about law). Others concentrate more on social justice (e.g., whether law can bring about social change). Some questions seem driven primarily by the concerns of lawyers (e.g., conviction of the innocent). Abstract issues animate others (e.g., the relevance of social theory). Missing is any overarching theory that would unite the work. Look at the typical syllabus or textbook in law and society and you will find a mere laundry list of topics: "The Nature of Law," "Legal Pluralism," "Law and Social Theory," "Law and Rights," "Law and Politics," "Law and Social Movements," "Law and Social Change," "Law and Culture," "Law and Globalization," "Law and Organizations," "The Legal Profession," and so on. As we shall see, it need not be so.

The Handling of Cases

The issue that interests us – how the social environment affects the handling of cases – has continued to occupy a small but persistent corner of the law and society universe. One influential paper by William Felstiner, Richard Abel, and Austin Sarat (1980–1981) addresses the natural history of disputes, making the important point that the number of cases that disputants could bring to court is much smaller than the number of cases they actually bring. They distinguish three crucial steps in the life of a dispute: the naming of an event as injurious, the blaming of another party for the injury, and the claiming of a remedy from that party. Cases drop out at each stage. Since formal litigation is therefore merely the proverbial tip of the iceberg, a full understanding of cases requires a move away from the study of courts to an investigation of the earlier stages of disputes. Why do cases move or fail to move from one stage to another? The authors emphasize the subjective nature of dispute transformation – how it depends on the disputants' "attitudes, feelings, objectives, and motives (as these change over time)" (1980–1981: 653). That subjective component depends, in turn, on many factors, including the number and identity of the parties, their statuses, the relationships between them, their tendency to attribute blame to others, their objectives, the people in whom they confide, the prevailing ideology that surrounds them, their reference groups, the lawyers with whom they come into contact, and the dispute institutions that process their case. However, the authors do not formulate any general principles that predict the transformation from one stage to the next.

A scientifically more important contribution to the study of cases comes from an even more widely cited paper: Marc Galanter's "Why the Haves Come out Ahead: Speculations on the Limits of Legal Change." Galanter's (1974) lengthy and discursive essay develops an explanation of who brings and who wins cases as part of a larger project that seeks to determine whether court cases can be a vehicle for mitigating inequality: "Our question, specifically, is, under what conditions can litigation be redistributive?" (95). He distinguishes four components of litigation: rules, courts, lawyers, and parties, arguing that each tends to reproduce the advantages of the rich and powerful. Perhaps the most celebrated aspect of the paper is his categorization of litigants into two types: "repeat players" and "one-shotters." Repeat players bring or defend cases frequently (e.g., the government, insurance companies) while one-shotters (e.g., ordinary citizens) have only occasional recourse to the courts. Repeat players who are wealthy and knowledgeable have access to a menu of strategies that allows them to further their long-term interests. In particular, because repeat players know they will be involved in more cases in the future, they will bring for adjudication the cases that should produce rules favorable to them and settle cases that might result in precedents that do not square with their abiding goals. One-shotters, by contrast, tend to be interested only in the outcome of their own case, an outcome that will inevitably be influenced by the past decisions of repeat players like their present adversary.[3] Galanter (1975: 347) later summarized the multiple advantages of repeat players as the:

> ability to structure the transaction; expertise, economics of scale, low start-up costs; informal relations with institutional incumbents; bargaining credibility; ability to adopt optimal strategies; ability to play for rules in both political forums and in litigation itself by litigation strategy and settlement policy; and ability to secure penetration of favorable rules.

A by-product of these advantages is that repeat players are more active and successful in litigation than one-shotters. Galanter (1975) subsequently found support for his argument in studies demonstrating that, compared to individuals, governmental and private organizations bring and win more cases as both plaintiffs and defendants, since organizations are an important species of repeat player.

Galanter's analysis advanced the field, but stopped short of being a general theory. Although Galanter insists that litigation success "may be closely related to being a repeat player in the narrow literal sense" (1975: 364), he acknowledges that repeat playing is neither sufficient nor necessary for litigation success. Some repeat players (e.g., "the alcoholic derelict") are not successful while some one-shotters (e.g., doctors) are (1974: 98). Second, while Galanter goes beyond the repeat player one-shotter continuum to include the wealth, organization, and social distance of the parties, he does not devote any sustained attention to several other variables that significantly predict legal behavior. These include how integrated people are into social life (e.g., married, employed), whether they belong to cultural minorities, and whether they have a morally compromised reputation.[4] Third, Galanter's theory provides a better explanation of who wins cases than who brings cases. His theory predicts that those who have brought cases previously are more likely to bring them again, but does not explain why they brought them in the first place (except with previous victories). Fourth, and most important of all, he limits his analysis to one aspect of the legal system – litigation – and does not address the numerically more important prior stages: police–civilian encounters, police or attorney investigation and screening of cases, the arrest process, or the filing of charges. For reasons such as these, we view Galanter's theory as a preliminary or proto-theory of the case that was to be superseded shortly afterward. Enter the geometrical theory of law.

Notes

1 For a lucid discussion of other stands of European social thought in early sociology of law, see Deflem (2008: chapter 4).
2 Durkheim proposed that as societies develop a division of labor, their dominant sanctions change from emphasizing punishment to compensation (1893: chapters 2–6); that punishment increases with societal evolution and with centralization of power (1899–1900: 32); and that punishment increasingly takes the form of imprisonment (1899–1900: 44).
3 Repeat players are particularly likely to litigate cases against one-shotters or more distant adversaries; in contrast, cases between socially close parties, between repeat players, or between one-shotters are more likely to be handed informally (e.g., negotiation, arbitration) (1974: 124–135).
4 There is some ambiguity in Galanter's key variable: at times, he treats the terms repeat players and one-shotters as referring simply to those who are, or are not, involved in more litigation (1975: 347); at other times, he treats them as referring to parties who are, or are not, more capable when playing the litigation game (1975: 363–364).

References

Abel, Richard L. 2010. "Law and Society: Project and Practice." *Annual Review of Law and Social Science* 6:1–23.

Abel, Richard L. and Philip S.C. Lewis, eds. 1988–1989. *Lawyers in Society,* Volume 1: *The Common Law World,* Volume 2: *The Civil Law World,* Volume 3: *Comparative Theories.* Berkeley: University of California Press.

Acker, James R., Robert M. Bohm, and Charles S. Lanier, eds. 2014. *America's Experiment with Capital Punishment: Reflections on the Past, Present, and Future of the Ultimate Penal Sanction.* Third edition. Durham: Carolina Academic Press.

Alexander, Michelle. 2010. *The New Jim Crow: Mass Incarceration in the Age of Colorblindness.* New York: New Press.

Baldus, David C., George Woodworth, and Charles A. Pulaski. 1990. *Equal Justice and the Death Penalty: A Legal and Empirical Analysis.* Boston: Northeastern University Press.

Banner, Stuart. 2002. *The Death Penalty: An American History.* Cambridge: Harvard University Press.

Baumgartner, Frank R., Suzanna L. De Boef, and Amber E. Boydstun. 2008. *The Decline of the Death Penalty and the Discovery of Innocence.* New York: Cambridge University Press.

Baumgartner, Frank R., Marty Davidson, Kaneesha R. Johnson, Arvind Krishnamurthy, and Colin P. Wilson. 2018. *Deadly Justice: A Statistical Portrait of the Death Penalty.* New York: Oxford University Press.

Bedau, Hugo Adam, ed. 1964. *The Death Penalty in America.* New York: Doubleday.

Berman, Paul Schiff. 2012. *Global Legal Pluralism: A Jurisprudence of Law Beyond Borders.* Cambridge: Cambridge University Press.

Bohannan, Paul, ed. 1967. *Law and Warfare: Studies in the Anthropology of Conflict.* Austin: University of Texas Press.

Bohm, Robert M. 2017. *Death Quest: An Introduction to the Theory and Practice of Capital Punishment in the United States.* New York: Routledge.

Boyle, Elizabeth Heger. 2002. *Female Genital Cutting: Cultural Conflict in the Global Community.* Baltimore: John Hopkins University Press.

Cabana, Donald A. 1996. *Death at Midnight: The Confession of an Executioner.* Boston: Northeastern University Press.

Chua, Lynette J. and David M. Engel. 2019. "Legal Consciousness Reconsidered." *Annual Review of Law and Social Science* 15:335–353.

Collier, Jane. 1973. *Law and Social Change in Zinacantan.* Stanford: Stanford University Press.

Comfort, Megan. 2007. *Doing Time Together: Love and Family in the Shadow of the Prison.* Chicago: University of Chicago Press.

Deflem, Mathieu. 2008. *Sociology of Law: Visions of a Scholarly Tradition.* Cambridge: Cambridge University Press.

Deflem, Mathieu, ed. 1996. *Habermas, Modernity and Law.* London: Sage.

Dezalay, Yves and Bryan G. Garth, eds. 2002. *Global Prescriptions: The Production, Exportation, and Importation of a New Legal Orthodoxy.* Ann Arbor: University of Michigan Press.

Dobbin, Frank. 2009. *Inventing Equal Opportunity.* Princeton: Princeton University Press.

Dow, David R. 2005. *Executed on a Technicality: Lethal Injustice on America's Death Row.* Boston: Beacon Press.

Durkheim, Emile. 1893. *The Division of Labor in Society.* New York: Free Press, 1964.

Durkheim, Emile. 1899–1900. "Two Laws of Penal Evolution." *University of Cincinnati Law Review* 38:32–60, 1969.

Edelman, Lauren B. 1992. "Legal Ambiguity and Symbolic Structures: Organizational Mediation of Civil Rights Law." *American Journal of Sociology* 97:1531–1576.

Edelman, Lauren B., Christopher Uggen, and Howard S. Erlanger. 1999. "The Endogeneity of Legal Regulation: Grievances Procedures as Rational Myth." *American Journal of Sociology* 105:406–454.

Ewick, Patricia and Susan S. Silbey. 1998. *The Common Place of Law: Stories from Everyday Life.* Chicago: University of Chicago Press.

Felstiner, William L. F., Richard L. Abel, and Austin Sarat. 1980–1981. "The Emergence and Transformation of Disputes: Naming, Blaming, Claiming…" *Law and Society Review* 15:631–654.

Frank, Jerome. 1949. *Courts on Trial: Myth and Reality in American Justice.* Princeton: Princeton University Press, 1973.

Frank, David John, Bayliss J. Camp, and Steven A. Boutcher. 2010. "Worldwide Trends in the Criminal Regulation of Sex, 1945 to 2005." *American Sociological Review* 75:867–893.

Galanter, Marc. 1974. "Why the 'Haves' Come Out Ahead: Speculation on the Limits of Legal Change." *Law and Society Review* 9:95–160.

Galanter, Marc. 1975. "Afterword: Explaining Litigation." *Law and Society Review* 9:346–368.

Galanter, Marc and Thomas Palay. 1991. *Tournament of Lawyers: The Transformation of the Big Law Firm.* Chicago: University of Chicago Press.

Garland, David. 2010. *Peculiar Institution: America's Death Penalty in an Age of Abolition.* Cambridge: Harvard University Press.

Garrett, Brandon L. 2011. *Convicting the Innocent: Where Criminal Prosecutions Go Wrong.* Cambridge: Harvard University Press.

Gluckman, Max. 1967. *The Judicial Process among the Barotse of Northern Rhodesia.* 2nd ed. Manchester: Manchester University Press.

Gross, Samuel. 2008. "Convicting the Innocent." *Annual Review of Law and Social Science* 4:173–192.

Halliday, Terrence C. and Bruce G. Carruthers. 2009. *Bankrupt: Global Lawmaking and Systemic Financial Crisis.* Stanford: Stanford University Press.

Heinz, John P., Robert L. Nelson, Rebecca L. Sandefur, and Edward O. Laumann. 2005. *Urban Lawyers: The New Social Structure of the Bar.* Chicago: University of Chicago Press.

Hood, Roger and Carolyn Hoyle. 2008. *The Death Penalty: A Worldwide Perspective.* New York: Oxford University Press.

Johnson, Robert. 1998. *Death Work: A Study of the Modern Execution Process.* Belmont, CA: West/Wadsworth.

Johnson, David T. and Franklin E. Zimring. 2009. *The Next Frontier: National Development, Political Change, and the Death Penalty in Asia.* Oxford: Oxford University Press.

Karstedt, Susanne, and Gary LaFree. 2006. "Democracy, Crime and Justice." *Annals of the American Academy of Political and Social Science* 605:6–25.

Keck, Thomas M. 2009. "Beyond Backlash: Assessing the Impact of Judicial Decisions on LGBT Rights." *Law and Society Review* 43:151–185.

Llewellyn, Karl N. 1931. "Some Realism about Realism – Responding to Dean Pound." *Harvard Law Review* 44:1222–1256.

Llewellyn, Karl N. and E. Adamson Hoebel. 1941. *The Cheyenne Way: Conflict and Case Law in Primitive Jurisprudence.* Oklahoma: University of Oklahoma Press.

Manza, Jeff and Christopher Uggen. 2006. *Locked Out: Disenfranchisement and American Democracy.* New York: Oxford University Press.

McCann, Michael. 1994. *Rights at Work: Pay Equity Reform and the Politics of Legal Mobilization.* Chicago: University of Chicago Press.

Merry, Sally Engel. 2006. *Human Rights and Gender Violence: Translating International Law into Local Justice.* Chicago University of Chicago Press.

Nader, Laura. 1990. *Harmony Ideology: Justice and Control in a Zapotec Mountain Village.* Stanford: Stanford University Press.

Nader, Laura and Harry F. Todd, eds. 1978. *The Disputing Process – Law in Ten Societies.* New York: Columbia University Press.

Nagin, Daniel S. and Cody W. Telep. 2017. "Procedural Justice and Legal Compliance." *Annual Review of Law and Social Science* 13:5–28.

Nielsen, Laura Beth. 2004. *License to Harass: Law, Hierarchy, and Offensive Public Speech.* Princeton: Princeton University Press.

Pager, Devah. 2007. *Marked: Race, Crime, and Finding Work in an Era of Mass Incarceration.* Chicago: University of Chicago Press.

Papachristos, Andrew V., Tracey L. Meares, and Jeffrey Fagan. 2012. "Why Do Criminals Obey the Law? The Influence of Legitimacy and Social Networks on Active Gun Offenders." *Journal of Criminal Law and Criminology* 102:397–440.

Paternoster, Raymond, Robert Brame, and Sarah Bacon. 2008. *The Death Penalty: America's Experience with Capital Punishment.* New York: Oxford University Press.

Prejean, Helen. 1993. *Dean Man Walking: An Eyewitness Account of the Death Penalty in the United States.* New York: Random House.

Radelet, Michael L., Hugo Adam Bedau, and Constance E. Putnam. 1992. *In Spite of Innocence: Erroneous Convictions in Capital Cases.* Boston: Northeastern University Press.

Rivkind, Nina, Steven F. Shatz, Sam Kamin, and Justin Marceau. 2016. *Cases and Materials on the Death Penalty.* 4th ed. St. Paul: West.

Rosenberg, Gerald. 1991. *The Hollow Hope: Can Courts Bring About Social Change?* Chicago: University of Chicago Press.

Rothstein, Richard. 2017. *The Color of Law: A Forgotten History of How Our Government Segregated America*. New York: W.W. Norton and Company.

Sarat, Austin. 2014. *Gruesome Spectacles: Botched Executions and America's Death Penalty*. Stanford: Stanford University Press.

Savelsberg, Joachim, and Suzy McElrath. 2014. "Crime, Law, and Regime Changes." *Annual Review of Law and Social Science* 10:259–279.

Steiker, Carol S. and Jordan M. Steiker. 2016. *Courting Death: The Supreme Court and Capital Punishment*. Cambridge: Harvard University Press.

Treviño, A. Javier, ed. 1996. *The Sociology of Law: Classical and Contemporary Perspectives*. New York: St. Martin's Press.

Treviño, A. Javier, ed. 2007. *Classic Writings in Law and Society: Contemporary Comments and Criticism*. New Brunswick: Transaction.

Tyler, Tom R. 1990. *Why People Obey the Law: Procedural Justice, Legitimacy, and Compliance*. New Haven: Yale University Press.

Valverde, Mariana. 2012. *Everyday Law on the Street: City Governance in an Age of Diversity*. Chicago: University of Chicago Press.

van den Haag, Ernest and John P. Conrad. 1983. *The Death Penalty: A Debate*. New York: Plenum Press.

van Krieken, Robert. 2019. "Law and Civilization: Norbert Elias as a Regulation Theorist." *Annual Review of Law and Social Science* 15:267–288.

Western, Bruce. 2006. *Punishment and Inequality in America*. New York: Russell Sage.

Zalman, Marvin and Julia Carrano, eds. 2014. *Wrongful Conviction and Criminal Justice Reform: Making Justice*. New York: Routledge.

1

THE GEOMETRICAL THEORY OF LAW

Anthony and Ben live in the same city. They grew up in different neighborhoods, move in different circles, and have never met. Due to an improbable coincidence their lives began to converge. A week apart, they committed identical murders – separately. Both men were addicted to drugs and, finding themselves broke and in desperate need of a fix, they decided to burglarize a dwelling. Armed with a pistol, they broke into a home and found some valuables. As they were leaving with the stolen property, they were confronted by a member of the household. Both men shot and killed the person who came upon them, and then fled. The authorities were notified, and a manhunt ensued. A few days after their crimes, they were each arrested. Unfortunately, for them, theirs is a death penalty state. The law of their state allows a defendant to be sentenced to death if convicted of capital murder – murder with one or more "aggravating factors," including murder during the commission of another felony, such as burglary. After reviewing their cases, the District Attorney charged both men with capital murder. Several months later, Anthony's case was tried before a judge and jury. Anthony was found guilty of capital murder. At the penalty phase of the trial, the jury voted not to impose the death penalty but, rather, to sentence Anthony to life imprisonment without parole. Not long afterward, Ben's case came to trial. He too was convicted of capital murder. However, his jury unanimously voted to sentence him to death.

These hypothetical scenarios raise an issue that frequently arises in capital murder cases: unpredictability. Judges, law professors, and legal commentators have spoken of the arbitrariness of the death penalty, sometimes likening the decision to impose it in one case but not in a similar case to a lightning strike (see Dieter 2011). If we wanted to probe the reason for the disparate decisions, we would naturally turn first to the written law – in particular, to statutes enacted by legislators and decisions rendered by judges. But nothing in the written law would allow us

DOI: 10.4324/9781003176633-2

to distinguish Anthony's case from Ben's. The burglary-murders were identical, yet only one case resulted in the defendant being dispatched to death row. Since the rules could not explain the divergent outcomes, what would? Press a lawyer for an answer and you will most likely be told "discretion." Anthony's jury exercised its discretion not to impose the death penalty; Ben's jury exercised its discretion in the opposite direction. That is clearly unsatisfactory. To explain the decision with "discretion" is not to explain the decision. Discretion is simply a fancy word for "we don't know" (see Baumgartner 1992).

But social scientists might not do much better. Ask why Ben was, and Anthony was not, dispatched to death row and the answer you will likely get is race. Ben must have been Black or must have killed a White person, or both. Anthony must have been White or killed a Black person, or both. Many social scientists know that a large body of research shows that race affects capital punishment. Some studies suggest that Black defendants are more likely to get the death penalty. Virtually all studies suggest that a defendant who kills a White victim is more likely to get the death penalty (for a review see Phillips and Marceau 2020). David Baldus and colleagues conducted the best-known study in Georgia in the 1970s. (We will have a lot more to say about this terrific source of data.) The Baldus study, which formed part of a constitutional argument against the death penalty in *McCleskey v. Kemp*, found a race-of-victim effect (Baldus, Woodworth, and Pulaski 1990).[1] Less well known is that the race effect was only one of many effects that Baldus found. Baldus and his team presented to the Supreme Court a statistical model that contained 41 variables. The model showed that a defendant's odds of receiving a death sentence were 4.3 times greater when the case included one or more White victims. But nine variables had an even stronger impact, including whether the victim was 12 years old or younger, whether there was a rape involved, and whether the victim had been physically tortured.[2] The lesson is clear: race matters, but it is not the only thing that matters. To obtain a fuller understanding of who gets sentenced to death we must include race while also looking beyond it. That is what the geometrical theory of law does.

The Theory

The geometrical theory of law was born in a police car, according to its father, Donald Black (2002: 109). As a graduate student at the University of Michigan, Black rode around with police officers as they patrolled the streets of Detroit. When his major professor, Albert Reiss, secured a large grant to conduct an observation study of police officers in three cities (Boston, Chicago, and Washington DC), Black worked on the study, writing his doctoral dissertation from the observations. He went on to publish several influential papers and, eventually, a book on police behavior (Black 1980). His gaze soon began to wander beyond the police to law more generally. After completing his Ph.D., Black moved to Yale University where he began to dream big. In a manifesto published in the *Yale Law Journal* ("The

Boundaries of Legal Sociology"), he argued that "the proper concern of legal sociology should be the development of a general theory of law" (1096). Four years later, Black delivered. In *The Behavior of Law* (1976), he proposed a theory designed to explain variation in law wherever and whenever it exists. The theory predicts and explains differences in the handling of cases, such as whether people call the police or contact a lawyer, whether the police arrest or a lawyer files suit, whether the case succeeds or fails, and, if it succeeds, the severity of the punishment imposed or the amount of compensation the defendant is required to pay. Black illustrated his theory by drawing on patterns of legal behavior not just in modern societies (e.g., modern America and Japan) but in earlier societies studied by historians (e.g., imperial China and colonial America) and structurally simpler societies studied by anthropologists in Africa, Asia, Australia, and the Americas. Ranging freely across time and place, this was indeed a general theory of law.

Black's theory comes at law from an unconventional angle. Departing from the traditional view of law as a system of rules, Black treats law as a quantitative variable, something that differs in amount from one case to the next according to who the parties are. More precisely, he argues that the quantity of law depends on where cases occur in social space – their "social structure" or "social geometry." His theory predicts, for example, that downward cases (brought by higher status actors against lower status actors) attract more law than upward cases (brought by lower status actors against higher status actors). And distant cases (e.g., between strangers) attract more law than close cases (between intimates). In this and the remaining chapters, we refer to this body of ideas as "Black's theory," "Blackian theory," and "geometrical theory" interchangeably. Let us examine the theory in some depth.

The Quantity of Law

"Law," Black (1976: 2) defines as "governmental social control." Law is a matter of degree, a quantitative phenomenon that can be measured by how far a case progresses in the legal system and the nature of its ultimate disposition. In a civil case over a broken contract or disputed will, for example, contacting a lawyer is more law than not contacting, filing a suit is more law than letting the matter drop, and a victory for the plaintiff is more law than a victory for the defendant. In a criminal case, more law similarly enters a case at each stage of the legal process: to call the police is more law than not to call, to arrest is more law than to let the suspect walk, to prosecute is more law than to drop the charges, and to convict is more law than to acquit. At sentencing, the amount of law increases with the size of the fine or the length of the prison sentence. The death penalty represents the greatest quantity of law in those systems that still allow it.

Law varies stylistically as well as quantitatively. Black distinguishes four styles of law: penal (oriented toward punishment), compensatory (oriented toward restitution), therapeutic (oriented toward restoring health), and conciliatory (oriented toward reconciliation). In this book, we are solely concerned with the penal style. Still, it is worth bearing in mind that while law sometimes takes the form of one party accusing another of wrongdoing that may result in punishment, many legal cases have a different character and Black's theory is designed to predict their outcomes too.[3]

Social Space

Lawyers explain case outcomes in terms of the rules and evidence governing the conduct of the parties. In a murder case, for instance, the central question is whether the admissible evidence proves beyond a reasonable doubt that the defendant intentionally killed the victim. The problem is that the parties' conduct can only provide a partial explanation, as our hypothetical cases involving Anthony and Ben illustrate. This is true across the legal system. Imagine some common scenarios: Morgan and Mallory each develop breast cancer despite receiving a clean bill of health from their doctors. Morgan sues for medical negligence; Mallory does not. When Juan and Jaime both fail to deliver goods on time to Carlos, Carlos brings a small claims action against Juan but not against Jaime. For the same bad check, the police arrest Jakeshia but let Jasmine go. A store presses shoplifting charges against Hideki but drops them against Hiroshi. The District Attorney charges Tom with rape but Tim with sexual battery for a similar incident. The court that sentenced DeShawn to ten years' imprisonment gave DeMarcus just five years for the same crime. Outcomes like these happen daily and yet traditional legal analysis cannot adequately explain them.

Blackian theory directs our attention away from the technical legal elements to the social characteristic of the parties, especially the victim and defendant in a criminal case and the plaintiff and defendant in a civil case. The theory proposes that for the same conduct, the amount of law a case attracts varies with its social geometry – the location, direction, and distance of the parties in a multidimensional social space.

"Social space" is that realm of reality humans create through interacting with one another. Social space has five principal dimensions:

* The *vertical* dimension (wealth)
* The *horizontal* dimension (relationships)
* The *symbolic* dimension (culture)
* The *normative* dimension (morality)
* The *corporate* dimension (organization)

Each dimension profoundly affects human behavior, and each has been the centerpiece of a major strand of social theory. To explain social life, Marx and Engels (1848) emphasized the distribution of wealth; Durkheim (1893) and network theorists (e.g., Granoveter 1973) stressed the centrality of social relationships;

TABLE 1.1 Black's Multidimensional Concept of Social Status

Dimensions				
Vertical Status:	*Radial Status:*	*Cultural Status:*	*Normative Status:*	*Organizational Status:*
Wealth	Integration in Social Life	Conventionality, Education	Respectability	Capacity for Collective Action

Parsons (1951) highlighted culture; Goffman (1956) drew attention to the normative or moral aspect of social life; and Weber (1922) underlined the importance of organizational capacity or power. Black's concept of social space brings these dimensions together into a single intellectual framework. He does not privilege one dimension over another – the variables are equal citizens, each helping to explain social reality (Black 2000a: 354–355).[4] The benefit of this synthesis is obvious: Black's system promises to generate more powerful theories than those of sociology's founding fathers.

Within each dimension, we all occupy positions or *locations* (e.g., high, medium, and low). Those locations are social statuses (see Table 1.1). A wealthy woman occupies a high vertical elevation (vertical status). A man who participates in social life by being married, employed, having children, or volunteering in the community occupies a high radial elevation (radial status, a part of the horizontal dimension). An individual who shares the culture of the majority of those around her occupies a high location in cultural space as does a person who is educated (cultural status). A youth with a sterling reputation for integrity occupies a high location within the normative dimension (normative status). A business corporation occupies a high organizational elevation, as do its employees (organizational status). People and groups with the opposite of these characteristics (e.g., poor, unemployed, less educated, criminal record, etc.) have low social status. Whether high or low, each status is a matter of degree. A billionaire has higher vertical status than a millionaire, for example, and a person with three felony convictions has lower normative status than someone with a single misdemeanor conviction.

When people interact, their interaction has a *direction* in social space. A request for spare change made by a homeless man of a passing businessperson travels upwardly in vertical space; the expulsion of a student from a university moves downwardly in organizational space; an assault by a student with a poor disciplinary record on a student with a good record flows upwardly in normative space, and so on.

Besides its location and direction, social interaction varies in its social *distance*. A conversation between spouses takes place over a small distance in relational space (a type of horizontal space) while a conversation between strangers at an airport spans a wide distance. Buying an item from a person of the same ethnicity bridges less cultural distance than buying the same item from a person of a different ethnicity.[5] All of this – the location, direction, and distance of a legal case in a multidimensional social space – constitutes its social structure or social geometry.

Core Propositions

The Behavior of Law consists of 137 pages of text.[6] However, the core of the theory is contained in just 29 general statements or propositions that link variation in the location, direction, and distance of cases in social space to variation in the quantity and style of law. Importantly, the propositions in one dimension of social space mirror those in all dimensions, giving the theory a highly symmetrical structure. Black states, for example, that the various statuses in his system "may be combined and compared so that one person or group may have, overall, more or less social status than another" (1979a: 161; see also 1989: 9–11). We therefore collapse the separate social statuses into a single overall status, greatly simplifying the theory. Indeed, following Black's lead in his 1989 book *Sociological Justice*, we can reduce the theory to three core geometrical propositions (9–11). The first two are:

- *Downward law is greater than upward law*: Predicting that a grievance brought by a higher status victim against a lower status defendant (a downward case) attracts a greater quantity of law than a grievance brought by a lower status victim against a higher status defendant (an upward case).[7] See Figure 1.1.
- *Law increases with social status*: Predicting that a grievance between higher status actors (a lateral high case) attracts a greater quantity of law than a grievance between lower status actors (a lateral low case).[8] See Figure 1.2.

Combining these two propositions gives us a fourfold pattern: downward cases should attract the most law, followed by lateral high cases, lateral

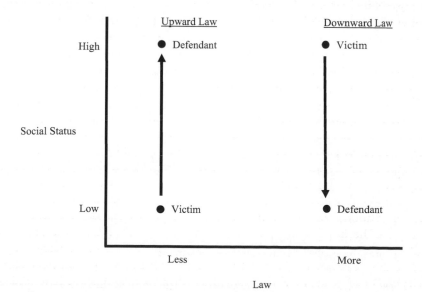

FIGURE 1.1 Downward Law Is Greater than Upward Law

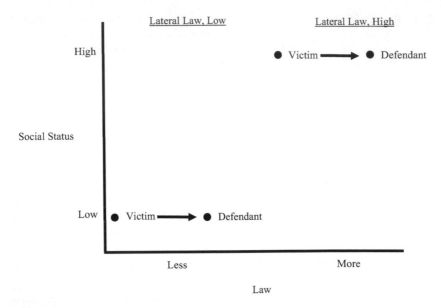

FIGURE 1.2 Law Increases with Social Status

low cases, and, finally, upward cases (Black 1976: 28; 1989: 11, figure 1). This pattern contains a surprising prediction: low-status defendants are not invariably treated with more severity. The status of the victim is a better predictor of case outcomes. Consequently, a higher status defendant who harms a higher status victim will be treated more severely than a lower status defendant who harms a lower status victim. Concretely: a wealthy lawyer who murders his wealthy physician spouse will be punished more severely than a poverty-stricken husband who kills his poverty-stricken wife.[9] But note that "status" here refers not just to economic status or wealth, but to status in all five dimensions of social space described in Table 1.1. It thus includes radial status or social integration (e.g., being married, employed), organizational status (e.g., being a state official), and normative status (a reputation for moral behavior). It also includes two types of cultural status – being literate or educated and being conventional. "Conventionality" refers simply to numerical representation and implies no value judgment.[10] In this sense, in American society, Whites are more conventional than Blacks, Christians than Hindus, English speakers than Mandarin speakers.[11]

- The third proposition is: *Law increases with social distance*[12] – predicting, for example, that the greater the relational distance between the parties, the greater the quantity of law a grievance attracts.[13]

"Relational distance" or intimacy, a central form of social distance, is the degree to which people participate in one another's lives. Spouses, for instance, are highly intimate; people who have never met are relationally distant; acquaintances of varying strength occupy the broad middle ground of intermediate distance.

All three propositions reference both principal parties to the case. They imply that we cannot predict outcomes by looking just at the social characteristics of the defendant or indeed the victim. And they require holding other factors constant, including the conduct of the parties (see, e.g., Black 1976: 24).

A Scientific Theory

In his 1972 manifesto, Black wrote, "a purely sociological approach to law should involve ... a scientific analysis of legal life as a system of behavior" (p. 1087; emphasis omitted). Not surprisingly, the theory Black went on to develop is self-consciously and unapologetically scientific. The Preface to *The Behavior of Law* states this succinctly: "This book contains a number of propositions about the variation of law across social space. The purpose of these propositions is to predict and explain this variation, and so to contribute to a scientific theory of law" (1976: ix).

To say the theory is scientific is not to claim that it is the final truth. Rather, like all scientific theories, natural and social, it has a central mission: to explain the most facts with the fewest testable ideas (Homans 1967; Black 1995). Because Black's theory is testable, we (or others) can do research to see, for example, whether wealthy and well-connected people are indeed more likely to bring and to win cases against each other than are poorer and more marginal people. If reality turns out to surprise us – as it often does – then we will have to reject the theory and try to find another. If we find that the evidence supports the theory, however, we can build on it, by, for example, seeking to discover the ways in which high status gets translated into legal advantages or whether the theory might apply to other, similar phenomena (such as non-legal social control). But without testability, we can never know whether we should accept or reject a theory: no matter what the research uncovers, the ideas can be said to be supported, rendering demonstrable intellectual progress impossible.

To be fully testable, a theory must consist entirely of factual statements and avoid value judgments. Blackian geometrical theory, therefore, has nothing to say about whether the facts it addresses are good or bad, moral or immoral. The theory describes how our system of justice actually operates but does not tell us how it ought to operate. That reticence might disappoint some readers, but such is the nature of science. For science is both very powerful and very weak. Powerful in that, unlike other forms of knowledge, it builds relentlessly. When ideas reference facts and only facts, other scholars can investigate a theoretical proposition and seek to replicate an empirical finding. We can then know more today than we did yesterday and will know more tomorrow than we do today. Weak in that it cannot answer many of life's most important questions: What is right and wrong? How should I live my life? What laws should a government enact? Is it just to punish people with criminal records more severely than those who have never been convicted of a crime? No research can ever settle these moral and political questions of value. And since value statements cannot be empirically tested they can never be shown to be wrong. Science can shed light on the likely outcome of a moral choice (Does execution deter murder?) or specify the means of attaining a goal somebody might morally desire (What types of jurors are more likely to vote for a life sentence?). But science cannot set the goal itself (Should the death penalty be abolished or retained?). On the other hand, by confining itself to the world of facts, science does something truly valuable: it grants us the most certain knowledge that humans can possess, even as it falls short of absolute certainty.

The claim that sociology can be value free is often misunderstood (see, e.g., Black 1972, 2013; Campbell 2014a). It is not to claim that sociology is objective – that it can adopt some lofty view of the world unaffected by moral or political bias. That is impossible. No idea is truly objective; all work is a product of its social environment, the time, place, and context in which it was created. Nor is it to claim that values have no influence on what sociologists study or how they analyze their data. Consciously or not, values influence scholarly inquiry. Rather, it is merely to claim that sociology is value free when it contains no statements about what any person or group ought to believe, say, or do. As Bradley Campbell (2014b: 7) succinctly puts it, "Value-free sociology is just sociology that is free of value judgments about its subject matter."

The most important value-free scientific ideas are a type of statement already mentioned: propositions. A proposition posits a specific relationship between certain facts (e.g., Homans 1967: 7–10). The relationship might be direct (as one thing increases, so does something else), inverse (as one thing increases, something else decreases), or more complex (e.g., subject to tipping points). By proposing a definite relationship, the proposition can be falsified if the evidence turns out to be inconsistent with it. The 29 propositions in *The Behavior of Law* are of this kind, as are the three propositions we presented earlier. For example, the proposition that "downward law is greater than upward law" goes beyond the vague claim that wealthy people enjoy legal advantages. It posits something more specific and nuanced: that the conflicts higher status people – including those who are wealthy, integrated, conventional, respectable, and so on – have against lower status adversaries are more likely to be brought to the legal system and to succeed than the same conflicts in the opposite direction – those pitting lower status people against higher status adversaries. Among propositions, the most important are highly general – they compress an enormous range of information into a single sentence or formula. "Downward law is greater than upward law" is a good example of a highly general proposition for it is not limited to America today or even to all modern legal systems but applies to law wherever and whenever it is found. For Black, "law everywhere obeys the shape of social space. Justice is geometrical" (2002: 128; 2011: xi).

Pure Sociology

The Behavior of Law was a scientific breakthrough, presenting an original, general, and testable theory of law. But the book did more. It introduced a new species of sociological theory, a novel theoretical paradigm. Like previous sociological paradigms – such as the rationalist, conflict, and functionalist approaches – Black's paradigm can be applied in principle to any form of behavior, including religion, science, medicine, art, commerce, and so much more. Pure sociology is the name Black (1979a) came to give this theoretical paradigm. Some might consider the name arrogant. Perhaps it is. But it is accurate: unlike other theories in the social sciences, pure sociology is sociology without three P's: psychology, purposes, or people (see Cooney 2009: 23–26). Pure sociologists seek to discover the distinctive laws of social life, laws that exist independently of those related to the human mind or body. For example, the proposition, "Downward law is greater than upward law" does not refer, explicitly or implicitly, to any biological characteristics (e.g., genes, hormones, brains). Similarly, it does not refer to any psychological states (e.g., motivations, desires, wants). Nor does it appeal to any preferences, goals, or interests that actors are said to be pursuing. And it says nothing about people as such. The principle refers to the behavior of law, not the behavior of individuals, groups, corporations, or states. It is a purely sociological principle (Black 1995, 2000a).

Pure sociology does not deny the validity of biological or psychological explanations of human behavior. It is not incompatible with laws of the body or mind. It simply addresses a separate level of reality – the social level (see, e.g., Horwitz 2002: 641). Still, if virtually every other social science theory explains the behavior of people in psychological and purposeful ways, why swim upstream? Why exclude the three P's? For scientific reasons, including the enhancement of testability. People's inner thoughts or purposes are subjective matters that are not directly observable (who can say with certainty what state of mind drove someone to do what they did?). If we cannot directly observe thoughts and purposes, then we cannot fully test statements about them. Moreover, statements about people's psychology or subjectivity may be limited to particular times and places: what goes on inside the mind of a New Yorker today may be quite different to what went on inside the mind of a subsistence farmer in rural seventeenth-century India. Removing subjectivity makes it easier to explain a broad range of facts – to realize the goal of generality. Moreover, since bypassing psychology, purposes, and people eliminates a host of variables, those facts can be explained in a simpler or more parsimonious manner – with fewer propositions. Finally, since no other theory explains social life in this manner, doing so realizes a highly desirable feature in any scientific theory – originality (Black 1995).

Pure sociology remains controversial (see, e.g., Frankford 1995; Black 1995). Not many theorists agree that it is possible or desirable to banish subjectivity from sociological explanation. Undaunted, Black (1995; 2000a; 2000b) has vigorously defended his position, emphasizing the scientific advantages of his style of theorizing. However, in this book, we are less concerned with the theoretical paradigm than the theory of law – meaning we are less concerned with *how* pure sociology explains law than *whether* the geometrical theory of law can explain the facts on the ground. That, too, is contentious.

Reactions to the Theory

On its publication in 1976, the distinguished legal anthropologist Laura Nader called *The Behavior of Law* "a major breakthrough." Arthur Stinchcombe (1977: 130), though unenthusiastic about Black's exclusion of people's intentions, allowed that as a theorist Black was "in the same class as Durkheim himself." Priscilla Michaels (1977) dismissed Black's theory as true by definition or circular. However, Lawrence Sherman's (1977: 11) review in the same journal was considerably more positive, noting, "this book has already been hailed as the most important contribution ever made to the sociology of law. It is that and more."

Early tests of the theory also pointed in different directions. In a study of the sentencing of female defendants, Candace Krutschnitt (1980–1981: 260) found that "the propositions of Black's theory of law are generally consonant with what actually happens in the courtroom; observable patterns in sentencing do correspond to a woman's location in social life." In contrast, Martha Myers's (1980: 851) analysis of the charges brought by prosecutors as well as the eventual outcome and sentences imposed in a sample of criminal cases found "neither consistent nor strong support for Black's specific hypotheses about the effects social direction and social location have on the behavior of law."

Perhaps it was the mixed response to the theory. Perhaps it was for other reasons. Regardless, over time, Black's theory gradually moved to the margins of legal sociology as well as the larger field of law and society (i.e., scholarship on the social dimensions of law by non-sociologists, such as anthropologists, political scientists, or lawyers). The theory continues to attract some attention – scholars published three quantitative tests in 2018. Indeed, *The Behavior of Law* is still cited over 100 times a year (according to Google Scholar). However, it no longer generates as much buzz. According to one study, the book was the seventh most cited publication in law and society in the period 1960s–1970s, only to disappear from the top 20 in the 1980–1990 and 1990–2000 eras (Morrill and Mayo 2015). But the marginalization goes beyond a comparative reduction in citations. A 2013 review paper titled "Is There a Canon of Law and Society?" surveyed the history of the field and cited 165 books and articles – but not *The Behavior of Law* or any of Black's other writings on law (Seron et al. 2013; see also Abel 2010). At least for some in the field, it is as if Black's theory never existed.

Yet law and society never found a replacement for Blackian theory. It never developed a general, testable theory of the case. Blackian theory, on the other hand, continued to develop and expand. Black and a co-author, M.P. Baumgartner (1983), extended the theory beyond the principal parties (victim or plaintiff and defendant) to include third parties such as witnesses, lawyers, judges, and jurors (discussed in Chapter 4). Black incorporated this additional component of case geometry into his 1989 book *Sociological Justice*. That book also has a number of strikingly innovative suggestions for how we could socially engineer legal cases to makes their outcomes more equal. In *The Social Structure of Right and Wrong*

(1993), Black tackled several additional legal issues, such as variation in pleading guilty, seeking compensation, and liability for wrongdoing. (However, most of the essays in the book expand his theories to non-legal forms of social control, such as toleration, avoidance, negotiation, and self-help.) In 2011, Black published an even more important extension. His book *Moral Time* presents a general theory of conflict, which, among many other things, explains why some conduct is illegal in the first place. We will discuss this theory at length in Chapter 3. For now, just note that this new theory promises to broaden the scope of pure sociology and to boost its ability to predict legal outcomes.

In sum, Black's general theory of law first published in 1976 and later extended presents a new geometrical way of thinking about and explaining social behavior. The theory consists of a series of propositions that are fully testable. It is elegant yet powerful. It has no real competitors and remains the only general sociological theory of legal conflicts. However, all of that ultimately amounts to naught if it cannot deliver the goods and explain the facts. Is the geometrical theory of law valid?

Testing the Theory

Validity is the truth of a theory. Validity is an easy question to pose but often a difficult one to answer. The relevant evidence may be slow to come in. The experts may disagree about whether and how strongly the evidence supports or undermines the theory. Black (1995: 845) observes that it may take many years for a theory to be accepted as valid. Einstein's general theory of relativity, for example, while supported observationally in 1919 three years after its publication, was not confirmed experimentally until 1959. Which brings us to our question: has Black's theory been confirmed?

Qualitative Studies

Writings by Black and others present a considerable amount of support for the theory:

- *The Behavior of Law* marshals a formidable body of modern, historical, and cross-cultural materials. This includes studies of Imperial Rome, the Mongolian empire, the ancient civilizations of Mesopotamia, Egypt, Hawaii, Peru, and Mexico, early modern England, colonial America, Renaissance Europe, the Soviet Union, Japan, Britain, and the modern United States, as well as the smaller scale indigenous societies of Africa, Asia, Australia, North and South America. Black presented additional evidence in his 1989 book, *Sociological Justice*.
- In a paper on the concept of discretion, M.P. Baumgartner (1992) brought together a wealth of evidence consistent with Black's theory from studies of

diverse offenses, including rape, theft, burglary, white-collar crime, environmental offenses, witchcraft allegations, and traffic law enforcement.

- Baumgartner (1998) compiled a book of scholarly articles that illustrates many of the applications of the theory, both in the United States today and at earlier times and places.[14]
- Jeffrey Mullis (1995) surveyed the literature on American medical malpractice cases. He argued that Blackian theory helps to explain a variety of patterns

> including the aggregate increase in claim rates over the past four decades; the persistence of toleration as the modal response to medical injury; why poorer patients are less suit-prone than higher income patients; why surgical specialties have higher claim rates than general practice and psychiatry; why hospitals are sued disproportionately less often than individual doctors; and the relatively high frequency of pro-defendant decisions when lawsuits are decided by a judge or jury
>
> *1995: 135*

- Mark Cooney (2009) analyzed the response to homicide in light of all the major strands of Blackian theory (as it then stood). Drawing on his own research (a cross-cultural study of pre-industrial societies and an interview study of men and women convicted of homicide in Virginia) and that of others – including work by anthropologists, historians, sociologists, criminologists, journalists, and lawyers – his book presents a comprehensive analysis of the handling of lethal violence in human societies. He found that, regardless of time or place, the severity of sanctions for killing another human being conform closely to the predictions of the theory.

These works employ a similar methodology. The author reads the empirical evidence to see whether it is consistent with the theory. The evidence includes ethnographies and surveys, archival investigations and experiments. It comes from studies that explicitly invoke Black's theory (e.g., Baumgartner 1978; Radelet 1989; Phillips 2009a) and from studies conducted without reference to it (e.g., Lundsgaarde 1977; Estrich 1987; Baldus and Woodworth 2003). Brought together, they represent a kind of qualitative test of the theory. Perhaps it was this evidence that Black (1995: 844) had primarily in mind when he wrote, "much of my theoretical work enjoys so much empirical support that its validity is nearly unquestionable." However, questioned it has been.

Quantitative Studies

Some writers contend that Blackian theory does not find much support from a different type of study: those that set out to test the theory using conventional quantitative methods. For these studies, the researcher assembles or acquires data from a source such as police or court records and then statistically analyzes the data to see whether the patterns match one or more of Black's propositions. Referring to quantitative tests, Kathleen Auherhan (2012: 113) contends that "with nearly all empirical tests of Black's theories, the results are mixed," leading Avakame, Fyfe, and McCoy (1999: 789) to state that "the available empirical research testing the theory, including ours, suggests that its claims may be too simple."

A weakness in the face of quantitative data would be an important limitation for geometrical theory. Many social scientists hold that quantitative studies are, on average, superior to qualitative studies, in large part because they are less subject to confirmation bias – researchers finding what they hoped to find (Michalski 2017: 156). Qualitative sociologists would likely disagree, pointing to the greater depth of qualitative research, its ability to probe beneath the surface of social life and extract what often remains hidden from quantitative methodologies. Black (1979b: 21, note 7) has questioned the ability of surveys (the data from which are invariably analyzed statistically) to elicit accurate information about past conflicts, adding that "data based upon direct and unobtrusive observation would therefore appear to be the most reliable way to test the theory of law or any theory of social control." However, even if quantitative studies are subject, on average, to less confirmation bias than qualitative studies, they are, importantly, still subject to some such bias. Quantitative researchers can certainly analyze and present their data in a variety of ways. They can put the best spin on a favored theory or the worst spin on a rival theory. They too can massage data to reach a desired result or minimize an undesired one. And quantitative studies may suffer from a variety of other imperfections as well, including nonrandom samples, imperfect measures of key variables, and missing cases. Quantity does not guarantee quality.

In light of this, we took a closer look at the published quantitative tests of Black's theory. To what extent do they conform to the general requirement that they use "proper evidence – not just what happens to be available – to test a theory's predictions" as Black (2010: 42) has urged? And do the better executed tests uphold or undermine the theory?[15]

How Good Are the Tests?

We began by compiling a list of studies published from 1976 to 2018 that explicitly assessed some of the propositions in Black's theory of law (though they did not have to use the word "test"). We included books and articles but not unpublished dissertations. We excluded studies that:

- State they are not a test of the theory (e.g., Phillips 2009a).
- Cite Black's work in passing without specifically testing the theory (see, e.g., Felson, Messner, and Hoskin 1999; Brown and Frank 2005).

- Analyze something other than case outcomes (e.g., which cities, states, or countries have higher clearance rates, more prosecutions, or more executions) (see, e.g., Borg and Parker 2001; Massey and Myers 1989; Wooditch 2012).
- Focus only on case outcomes that are not legal in nature (e.g., reporting wrongdoing to a Better Business Bureau) (e.g., Copes et al. 2001).
- Offer just a critique of the theory (e.g., Greenberg 1983).
- Provide only simple, bivariate analyses of the data (e.g., Baumgartner 1978). (A bivariate analysis examines the relationship between two variables, such as the effect of intimacy on arrest. A multivariate analysis considers the relationship between three or more variables at a time, such as the effect of intimacy on arrest adjusting or controlling for the degree of violence of the alleged crime.)

We were left with 38 multivariate tests. Of those, 33 analyzed the relationship between law and social status. We asked whether the test met three essential, though minimal, criteria:[16]

- Measured law correctly. While 29 studies did, four included additional non-legal actions, such as reaching out to a civilian for help.
- Examined the relative status of the principal parties. Only 14 did.
- Considered the seriousness of the conduct (by limiting the analysis to a particular offense or controlling for seriousness in a multivariate model). 27 studies did.

Ten studies had all three characteristics, and eight of those studies supported the theory, partially or fully.[17]

The most common fault was not considering the relative status of the parties. Recall Black's central argument: the location and direction of a case in social space dictates punishment. Does the case pit a high-status victim against a low-status defendant? Or a low-status victim against a high-status defendant? Perhaps the defendant and victim are both high status or both low status. Testing the relationship between relative status and punishment requires data on the defendant *and* the victim – by definition. Yet researchers often examined the status of the defendant *or* the victim.

Turning to relational distance, we found 18 tests. We looked at whether the test met two minimal criteria:

- Measured law correctly. While 15 studies did, three included additional non-legal actions.
- Held constant the conduct of the parties. All 18 did.

15 studies had both characteristics. Of those, eleven partially or fully supported the theory. Additionally, two of the four studies that did not provide support had important limitations. One study revealed that victims who knew the defendant were less likely to call the police as the theory would predict, but the finding was not statistically significant (probably because the researchers relied on a small sample with limited variation in relational distance; Zhang, Messner, and Liu 2007). A Canadian study of adolescents found that current intimate partners were more likely to be arrested than strangers, contradicting the theory (Rollwagen and Jacob 2018). But the research did not take account of the fact that intimates are more often at the scene when the police arrive, facilitating arrest.[18]

Quality matters. If we define a stronger test of the relationship between social status and law as one that measured relative status, held conduct constant, and measured law appropriately, then 80% of the stronger tests were partially or fully supportive of Black's theory, compared to 65% of the weaker tests. The better the test, then, the more it supports Blackian theory.[19] But what would happen if the theory was confronted with a truly first-class set of data? What would such a test involve?

A Better Test

Testing the theory rigorously requires holding constant the conduct of the parties. To do so, it helps to choose a narrow class of wrongful conduct and trace how the law responds to it. Murder is easily the single best type of wrongdoing to select, as the records are consistently better. Dead bodies are hard to conceal, enabling researchers to compile more complete samples of cases than they can for any other crime, many of which never reach the eyes or ears of the law. Once within the legal system, homicides tend to generate substantial paper trails. This is especially true of the ones with the highest stakes – capital murders, which virtually always produce a profusion of written records. Because their social geometry tends to be particularly well documented, capital cases allow us to gauge how well the theory stands up to good evidence. Moreover, because capital murder generates so much public scrutiny, it should hew closest to purely legal principles. As such, it provides a particularly stern test of Blackian theory.

There are other good reasons to study the death penalty. For one, the death penalty is humanly significant. People pay more attention to murder than any other crime. Think of the countless movies and television shows, books, magazine articles, and online postings that center around the taking of human life. Among murders, the most egregious capture the greatest share of interest, in part because they bring to the fore ethical questions about the state's right to kill those who kill.

And the death penalty is intellectually important. No criminal justice issue has attracted as much attention from scholars as capital punishment. Sociologists, criminologists, historians, political scientists, lawyers, and others have devoted entire careers to understanding the death penalty. One branch of that large body of scholarship addresses the handling of capital cases (see, e.g., Baumgartner et al. 2018: 69–116). Within that branch, most work focuses on the impact of race and gender on the decision to impose death. However, important as they are, geometrical theory prompts us to look wider, to go beyond differences in the racial and gender composition of cases. Is social status in general important? Does the degree of inequality between the parties matter? Are family murders as likely to result in a death sentence as stranger murders once everything else is considered? These are the questions we sought to address.

Our Test

We are fortunate to be able to draw on three superb death penalty data sets: Baldus and colleagues' Charging and Sentencing Study (CSS) in Georgia, Bowers's multistate Capital Jury Project (CJP), and Phillips's study of Houston cases (at the time the jurisdiction that, apart from the state of Texas, executed the most people in the country). Although these studies do not contain every item we may desire, their unusually detailed information should allow us to discover whether the death penalty behaves as Black's geometrical theory predicts. A word about each.

The Baldus Study

David Baldus and colleagues undertook a detailed analysis of a sample of Georgia murder cases from the 1970s with particular emphasis on the role race played in their legal outcomes. The background to their study is that in 1972, the United States Supreme Court ruled in *Furman v. Georgia* that the nation's existing death penalty laws were unconstitutional because they allowed capital punishment to be imposed arbitrarily (e.g., on racial grounds).[20] In response, the states rewrote their laws. In *Gregg v. Georgia* (1976) the Supreme Court upheld the constitutionality of a system adopted by several states: "guided discretion" laws.[21] Those laws contained a trio of new protections: (1) the death penalty could only be imposed when specific aggravating circumstances are present (e.g., the murder victim was tortured); (2) the trial was to be split into a guilt/innocence phase and, if guilty, a sentencing phase; and (3) all death sentences were to be automatically reviewed by an appellate court. The Supreme Court reasoned that this system of guided discretion would solve the problem of arbitrariness identified in *Furman*. The list of aggravating circumstances would force prosecutors and jurors to base their decision on the facts of the murder rather than the race of the parties. The bifurcation of the trial would allow the rules of evidence to be relaxed in the punishment phase and facilitate the introduction of more information regarding aggravation and mitigation. And automatic appellate review would root out any remaining arbitrariness. Problem solved.

Not so fast. Following the *Gregg* decision, researchers around the country began to focus attention on death penalty cases. They consistently found racial disparities. The research undertaken by Baldus and colleagues was the most rigorous and comprehensive of the studies (Baldus, Woodworth, and Pulaski 1990). They selected a stratified random sample of 1,066 cases from a universe of 2,483 individuals arrested and charged with homicide in Georgia between 1973 and 1979 who were later convicted of murder or voluntary manslaughter. Of those, 128 defendants were sentenced to death. The researchers found that a death sentence was imposed in 11% of cases with a White victim compared to just 1% of cases with a Black victim. Baldus and his team then controlled for additional factors in a statistical model that included the race of the victim, the race of the defendant, and 39 control variables. The model demonstrated that the adjusted odds of a death sentence were 4.3 times greater when the defendant killed one or more White victims. White lives mattered more.

The Baldus data formed a central part of a constitutional challenge to the death penalty. The 1987 case – *McCleskey v. Kemp* – eventually came before the Supreme Court. The Court ruled that the death penalty remained constitutional despite the racial disparities that Baldus documented. Specifically, the Court argued that statistical data about a sample of cases could not prove what McCleskey (or any other defendant) needed to prove in order to succeed – that legal actors purposely discriminated against him. (The Court was also concerned that ruling in McCleskey's favor would open the floodgates to endless litigation about the impact of social characteristics – from race to sex to facial features – on all aspects of the criminal justice system.)

Although the constitutional case failed, the scientific case remains compelling. With over two hundred variables about each case, the Baldus study provides the most complete data ever collected on the death penalty – or indeed any other aspect of criminal justice. A friend of the court (amicus) brief in *McCleskey* described it as "among the best empirical studies on criminal sentencing ever conducted" (cited in Gross 2012: 1916, note 61). Death penalty scholars Stephanie Hindson, Hillary Potter, and Michael Radelet (2006: 558) note: "By any measure, the most comprehensive research ever produced on sentencing disparities in US criminal courts is the work of David Baldus and his colleagues conducted in Georgia during the 1970s and 1980s." Marian Williams, Stephen Demuth, and Jefferson Holcomb (2007: 873, note 6) state that "... many contemporary data sources lack the kind of detail and richness provided by the Baldus, Woodworth, and Pulaski (1990) study."

Yet much more can be gleaned from the data. Williams and colleagues continue:

> Although the seminal importance of the Baldus, Woodworth, and Pulaski (1990) study as an investigation of the influence of race on death penalty outcomes and its legal implications is certain, it is also clear that much can be learned by revisiting the data.

However, the comprehensiveness of coverage of each case that makes the data set so impressive also makes it difficult to master. Indeed, only two sets of scholars – Williams and colleagues and Phillips and Marceau – have published from the publicly available but under-utilized data.

We mine the Baldus data set more deeply. Although the Baldus murder cases are several decades old (from 1973 to 1979), scientifically that is irrelevant: data are data. Indeed, the age of the cases is something of an advantage. With their extremely high stakes, death penalty cases are long drawn-out affairs with the ultimate fate of the defendant often being decided only many years after the trial ends. The significant amount of time that has elapsed since the imposition of the sentence enabled Scott Phillips and Justin Marceau (2020) to update the data to include who was executed. As a result, the Baldus data now combine the most rigorous case information ever gathered with the fullest picture of the entire criminal process from indictment to execution. Incidentally, Phillips and Marceau found that those who killed a White victim were also more likely to be executed: 22% of the defendants sentenced to death for killing a White victim were executed, compared to 10% of the defendants sentenced to death for killing a Black victim (a conservative estimate, as the disparity increases if a small number of errors in the original data are corrected). Combining Baldus's findings with those of Phillips and Marceau reveals that the overall execution rate is 17 times greater in White victim cases (2.26% of the defendants who killed White victim were executed, compared to just 0.13% of the defendants who killed a Black victim).

The Capital Jury Project

The Baldus project did not address the race of the jurors. That fell to the CJP, a study funded by the National Science Foundation. Over a period of several years beginning in 1990, project staff interviewed 1,198 capital jurors. The jurors had served in 353 trials completed since 1988 across 14 states (Alabama, California, Florida, Georgia, Indiana, Kentucky, Louisiana, Missouri, North Carolina, Pennsylvania, South Carolina, Tennessee, Texas, and Virginia) (Anon. 2019). These states had adopted somewhat different guided discretion statutes post-*Furman*. The researchers selected 20 to 30 capital trials in each state, all of which had a guilty verdict and a penalty trial. They chose an equal number of cases ending in life sentences and death sentences. For each case, they randomly selected four jurors (Bowers 1995: 1081). If the four randomly sampled jurors did not produce four interviews (e.g., could not be located, refused, etc.), they randomly sampled more jurors until four interviews were conducted.

Interviews took place in the home of the respondent and were tape-recorded with the respondent's permission. The interviews were conducted by "advanced law and/or social science students who were supervised by faculty" (Bowers 1995: 1077). The interviews included closed-ended and open-ended questions and lasted 3 to 4 hours (Anon. 2019). Each interview "yielded data on over 750 variables" (Blume, Eisenberg, and Garvey2003).

CJP data have been drawn upon in about 100 articles, book chapters, doctoral dissertations, and master's theses (Anon. 2019). Those publications have addressed various aspects of jury behavior, including when jurors decide to impose a life or death sentence, whether jurors are confused by the legal instructions they receive, and the effect of the racial composition of the jury on the life–death decision. We draw on the CJP data to assess whether the social status of jurors affects their decision to impose or withhold the death penalty.

The Houston Study

Scott Phillips (2008) tracked the legal fate of all 504 adult defendants who were indicted for capital murder in Harris County (Houston), Texas from 1992 to 1999. By combining information from up to eight sources, including case files maintained by the Medical Examiner and the District Attorney, he was able to compile a detailed dossier on each case. In addition, he had student research assistants collect every article published in the *Houston Chronicle* about each case – more than 3,400 newspaper articles. Of the 504 death-eligible cases, the District Attorney sought the death penalty in 129 cases and the jury returned a death sentence in 98 cases (Phillips 2008).

Key variables included in the study are: the social characteristics of the defendant and victim (race, age, gender, social status), the defendant's form of legal counsel (hired, appointed, both), the type of capital murder (statutory aggravator), and the heinousness of the crime. We do not quantitatively analyze the Houston data here (see Phillips 2008; 2009a; 2009b; Phillips, Potter, and Coverdill 2012). Instead, particularly at the opening of the following chapters, we use qualitative case studies from the Houston research to illustrate the empirical patterns that we uncover with the other two data sets. The cases we highlight are all aggravated murders. Some have multiple victims, some have victims who were tortured and beaten to death, and some have victims who were robbed or raped. These kinds of murders are typical of modern death penalty cases which, as is often remarked, arise out of "the worst of the worst" crimes.

Conclusion

The death penalty is the most severe punishment the law levies – and the most controversial. Among the debates it generates are whether it deters crime and whether it can be administered without ever executing innocent people. But there is a still more basic question to be answered: why one person, like Ben in our hypothetical case earlier, receives the death sentence and another, like Anthony, does not. But then, for all the brainpower devoted to them, legal outcomes in general remain somewhat enigmatic. The written law is a poor guide to how the law operates in individual cases. It is much easier to explain what the formal law of contract, copyright, theft, or assault states than to predict how that law will be applied in particular cases. Why does this person sue and that person not even consult a lawyer for the same injury? Why is one defendant sent to prison and another not even arrested for the same crime? Faced with such questions, legal scholarship has often fallen back on the concept of "discretion" – the idiosyncratic choices that civilians, police offices, prosecutors, judges, and jurors make in individual cases. But discretion does not explain anything; it simply puts a word on that which cannot be explained (Baumgartner 1992). Surely, we can do better.

Sociology is uniquely suited to fill the gap between legal rules and legal outcomes. Alas, it has largely failed in that mission. Legal sociology, and the broader field of law and society, have veered off in multiple directions with no clear destination in sight. Even after more than a half-century, the field has failed to come up with a testable theory of legal conflicts. The only exception is Donald Black's geometrical theory. More than 40 years after its publication, Black's is still the only general sociological theory of the case. In the intervening years, his theory has continued to evolve. In later chapters, we consider some significant ways the theory has been extended. But even the original core of the theory – as laid out in *The Behavior of Law* – has been clarified and specified in important ways. For one thing, it has become apparent that the theory does not directly explain aggregate level facts – such as rates of arrest, conviction, sentencing, or suing in civil court. Instead, it explains cases and only cases – when they are brought and when they succeed.[22] In addition, the theory has come to be formulated more holistically – as a single unit rather than a collection of similar yet discrete parts. In practical terms, there has been a shift from treating it as consisting of an array of single-variable propositions to treating it as consisting of a small number of multidimensional propositions.

Geometrical theory is highly original, extremely general, admirably simple, and fully testable. Evidence supporting the theory comes from premodern and modern societies alike. It includes studies of police officers, detectives, prosecutors, lawyers, witnesses, judges, and juries. It applies to all types of cases, criminal, civil, and regulatory. It extends to the entire life span of legal conflicts, from initial complaint to final disposition. Still, some have argued that the theory has an Achilles heel: quantitative tests. Looking closely at those tests, we find that many are not well conceived and executed. Many do not consider the relative status of the parties, have weak measures of key variables, or do not focus exclusively on legal outcomes. We find that, in general, the better the test, the more support it provides for the theory. But even the better tests may have flaws (e.g., poor measures of key variables). To help answer the question of validity, we propose to pit the theory against the best data available to sociologists of law. Those data relate, moreover, to the most heavily scrutinized and consequential decision the law ever makes: whether to condemn a defendant to death and, ultimately, to execute the person. If the theory can survive our test, its validity will be all the better established; if it fails, hard questions as to its continued viability will have to be addressed. The stakes are high: Can we better understand legal cases, or are they forever to remain an enigma?

In answering such a question, Baldus's study and the Capital Jury Project have an additional advantage we have not yet mentioned – the data were not assembled to test Black's theory. The CJP was initiated to understand the range of factors that influence jurors in capital cases. The Baldus study was undertaken with litigation in mind: it was conducted at the request of the NAACP's Legal Defense and Education Fund in order to challenge the constitutionality of the Georgia death penalty. Black (1995: 843) calls evidence gathered without reference to a theory "naïve evidence." He regards naïve evidence as providing a particularly persuasive basis for a test because the data are unlikely to be biased either for or against the theory.[23] To that evidence we now turn.

Appendix 1

In the main text, we have briefly described our key quantitative findings. We use the appendix to provide technical details for the interested reader, including the information needed to replicate our statistical models.[24]

Testing Black's theory is not a simple or straightforward matter. Data on both defendants and victims are not always easily available. The researcher must often contend with limited information and imperfect indicators. More significantly, the core nature of geometrical theory took some time to emerge. Studies now clearly inappropriate might have been fine earlier. Although Black has always illustrated his theory primarily with case-level data, *The Behavior of Law* contains propositions designed to explain the quantity of law across larger units, such as neighborhoods and countries. Only later did Black (1989) focus exclusively on the handling of cases and clarify that the unit of analysis in his theory is the conflict case (1995: 853–855). We, therefore, do not wish to be too hard on scholars who have gone to the trouble of testing the theory. We sympathize with Kathleen Auerhahn who laments "the sometimes frustrating theoretical project of the empirical validation of Donald Black's theories" (2012: 114). Still, many tests fail to meet minimal standards. In Chapter 1, we reviewed 38 existing multivariate tests of Black's theory of law. Full citations for the studies are included below.

Table 1.2 reports our coding decisions for the studies that addressed the relationship between social status and law. We determined whether the authors: collected original data or relied on secondary data, examined the relative status of the parties, measured law appropriately, and held conduct constant.

We also assessed the degree of support for Black's theory. If the findings from a study generally conformed to Black's theoretical predictions, then the study was

TABLE 1.2 Review of Multivariate Studies that Explicitly Test Black's Theory of Law: The Proposed Relationship Between Social Status and Law[1]

Citation	Original Data v Secondary Data	Relative Status of the Parties	Law Measured Appropriately	Control Conduct	Support Theory
Akers and Kaukinen 2009	S	Victim Only	Yes	Yes	No
Ariel and Tankebe 2018	O	**Yes**	**Yes**	**Yes**	**Partial**
Auerhahn 2012	O	**Yes**	**Yes**	**Yes**	**No**
Avakame et al. 1999	S	Partial	Yes	No	Partial
Chappell and Maggard 2007	O	Yes	Yes	No	Partial
Clay-Warner and McMahon-Howard 2009	S	Partial	Yes	Yes	No
Dawson and Welsh 2005	O	DVS	Partial	Yes	Partial
Doyle and Luckenbill 1991	S	Victim Only	Yes	No	No
Felson and Ackerman 2001	S	DVS	Yes	Yes	Yes
Felson and Pare 2005	S	Yes	Partial	Yes	No
Fielding 1999	O	DVS	Yes	Yes	Partial
Geiger-Oneto and Phillips 2003	O	**Yes**	**Yes**	**Yes**	**Yes**
Graham et al. 2013	S	Victim Only	Yes	No	Yes
Holtfreter 2008	S	DVS	Yes	Yes	Partial
Kaukinen 2002	S	Victim Only	Partial	Yes	Partial
Kruttschnitt 1980–1981	O	**Yes**	**Yes**	**Yes**	**Yes**
Kruttschnitt 1982	O	**Yes**	**Yes**	**Yes**	**Yes**
Kruttschnitt 1985	O	**Yes**	**Yes**	**Yes**	**Partial**
Kuo et al. 2011	S	Victim Only	Yes	Yes	Partial
Lee 2005	O	Victim Only	Yes	Yes	Partial
Light 2014	S	Defendant Only	Yes	Yes	Yes
Litwin 2004	S	Victim Only	Yes	No	No
Mastrofski et al. 2000	O	Yes	Partial	Yes	No
McCamman and Mowen 2018	S	**Yes**	**Yes**	**Yes**	**Yes**
Myers 1980	O	**Yes**	**Yes**	**Yes**	**No**
Petersen 2017	O	Victim Only	Yes	Yes	Partial
Rojek et al. 2012	O	Yes	Yes	No	Yes
Silberman 1985	O	Victim Only	Yes	Yes	Partial
Smith 1987	O	**Yes**	**Yes**	**Yes**	**Yes**

TABLE 1.2 Cont.

Citation	Original Data v Secondary Data	Relative Status of the Parties	Law Measured Appropriately	Control Conduct	Support Theory
Staples 1987	O	Defendant Only	Yes	Yes	Yes
Xie and Lauritsen 2012	**S**	**Yes**	**Yes**	**Yes**	**Partial**
Zavala 2010	S	Victim Only	Yes	Yes	No
Zhang et al. 2007	O	Victim Only	Yes	Yes	No

Note:
Studies in bold meet the criteria for a stronger test of the theory.

coded as supportive. If not, then the study was coded as not supportive. Partial support means the findings were mixed.

Of the 33 studies in question:

• Relative status: 14 considered the relative status of the parties;[25] 11 only considered the status of the victim; 2 only considered the status of the defendant; 4 considered the status of the defendant and victim separately (abbreviated as DVS); and 2 examined relative status in some models, but not others (partial).
• Law: 29 measured law appropriately.[26]
• Conduct: 27 held conduct constant.[27]
• In total, 10 studies met the above criteria for a stronger test of the relationship between social status and law (see bolded studies).
• Of the 10 studies in question, 8 were partially or fully supportive of Black's theory.

We suspect that the failure to consider relative status stems from the relentless pressure on professors to publish. The siren song of available data tempts researchers into turning out quick publications. But a unique theory, like Black's, will typically require unique data that cannot be pulled off the shelf. Data sets focused on victims do not usually contain detailed information about the defendant, and data sets focused on defendants do not usually contain detailed information about the victim. Appropriate tests of Blackian theory often require the slow and arduous collection of original data.

Table 1.3 reports our coding decisions for the studies that addressed the relationship between relational distance and law.[28] We determined whether the authors: collected original data or relied on secondary data; measured law appropriately; and held conduct constant. Again, we assessed the degree of support for Black's theory.[29]

TABLE 1.3 Review of Multivariate Studies that Explicitly Test Black's Theory of Law: The Proposed Relationship Between Relational Distance and Law[1]

Citation	Original Data v Secondary Data	Law Measured Appropriately	Control Conduct	Support Theory
Akers and Kaukinen 2009	S	Yes	Yes	Yes
Auerhahn 2012	O	Yes	Yes	Yes
Avakame et al. 1999	S	Yes	Yes	Yes
Clay-Warner and McMahon-Howard 2009	S	Yes	Yes	Yes
Felson and Ackerman 2001	S	Yes	Yes	**Partial**
Felson and Pare 2005	S	Partial	Yes	Partial
Felson and Pare 2007	S	Yes	Yes	**Partial**
Felson and Lantz 2016	S	Yes	Yes	**Partial**
Gartner and Macmillan 1995	S	Yes	Yes	**Yes**
Kaukinen 2002	S	Partial	Yes	No
Kruttschnitt 1985	O	Yes	Yes	**Yes**
Mastrofski et al. 2000	O	Partial	Yes	Yes
Myers 1980	O	Yes	Yes	**Partial**
Rollwagen and Jacob 2018	S	Yes	Yes	**No**
Silberman 1985	O	Yes	Yes	**Yes**
Smith 1987	O	Yes	Yes	**No**
Spohn and Holleran 2001	O	Yes	Yes	**No**
Zhang et al. 2007	O	Yes	Yes	**No**

Note:
Studies in bold meet the criteria for a stronger test of the theory.

Of the 18 studies in question:

- Law: 15 measured law appropriately.[30]
- Conduct: 18 held conduct constant.
- In total, 15 studies met the above criteria for a stronger test of the relationship between relational distance and law (see bolded studies).
- Of the 15 studies in question, 11 were partially or fully supportive of Black's theory.

Our findings suggest that most of the stronger tests supported Black's theory. But very few strong tests have been conducted. The limited number of strong tests led us to speculate that: (1) authors often had not read Black's work closely, and (2) a superficial reading would be more common among authors who relied on secondary data. To test our hypotheses, we analyzed citation patterns. Specifically, we examined whether an author cited Black's books. Authors were given a three-year window to begin citing a book. For example, *The Behavior of Law* was published in 1976, so an author would be expected to cite the book from 1979 forward.

TABLE 1.4 Citations to Black's Books by Type of Data

Type of Data	The Behavior of Law[1]		The Manners and Customs of the Police[2]		Sociological Justice[3]		Social Structure of Right and Wrong[4]	
	Number	Percent	Number	Percent	Number	Percent	Number	Percent
Original	19 / 19	100%	7 / 16	44%	5 / 12	42%	3 / 12	25%
Secondary	19 / 19	100%	2 / 19	11%	1 / 18	6%	1 / 17	6%

Notes:
1 Published in 1976; citation expected by 1979.
2 Published in 1980; citation expected by 1983.
3 Published in 1989, citation expected by 1992.
4 Published in 1993; citation expected by 1996.

Detailed in Table 1.4, our findings provide strong support for both predictions. It is true that all the authors cited *The Behavior of Law*. But most authors did not cite Black's other books, and the authors who relied on secondary data were even less likely to do so:

- 44% of the authors who collected original data cited *The Manners and Customs of the Police*, compared to 11% of the authors who relied on secondary data;
- 42% of the authors who collected original data cited *Sociological Justice*, compared to 6% of the authors who relied on secondary data;
- 25% of the authors who collected original data cited *The Social Structure of Right and Wrong*, compared to 6% of the authors who relied on secondary data.

To be clear, we are not suggesting that an author who tests Black's theory must cite every book he has written – a particular book might not be relevant for a particular test. Instead, we are highlighting a more general concern. Some of the authors who tested Black's theories do not appear to be deeply immersed in the literature and may not fully understand the key ideas (although it is conceivable that an author read a book without citing it).

Unfortunately, the problem does not end with citations. Authors who relied on secondary data were also less likely to conduct a stronger test of the relationship between social status and law: 13% of the studies based on secondary data met the criteria for a stronger test, compared to 44% of the studies based on original data. Not surprisingly, then, studies based on secondary data were also less supportive of Black's predictions regarding social status and law: 60% of the studies based on secondary data were partially or fully supportive, compared to 78% of the studies based on original data.[31]

Secondary data are not necessarily inferior. Indeed, data collected for a different purpose are often superior – the evidence is not biased for or against a theory.

Nonetheless, secondary data must be deployed appropriately (such as examining the relative status of the parties).

The 38 Studies Included in Our Review of Prior Tests

Akers, Caroline and Catherine Kaukinen. 2009. "The Police Reporting Behavior of Intimate Partner Violence Victims." *Journal of Family Violence* 24:159–171.

Ariel, Barak and Justice Tankebe. 2018. "Racial Stratification and Multiple Outcomes in Police Stops and Searches." *Policing and Society* 28:507–525.

Auerhahn, Kathleen. 2012. "'Social Control of the Self' and Pleading Guilty in Criminal Court." *International Review of Sociology* 22:95–122.

Avakame, Edem F., James J. Fyfe, and Candace McCoy. 1999. "Did You Call the Police? What Did They Do? An Empirical Assessment of Black's Theory of Mobilization of Law." *Justice Quarterly* 16:765–792.

Chappell, Allison T. and Scott R. Maggard. 2007. "Applying Black's Theory of Law to Crack and Cocaine Dispositions." *International Journal of Defendant Therapy and Comparative Criminology* 51:264–278.

Clay-Warner, Jody and Jennifer McMahon-Howard. 2009. "Rape Reporting: 'Classic Rape' and the Behavior of Law." *Violence and Victims* 24:723–743.

Dawson, Myrna and Sandy Welsh. 2005. "Predicting the Quantity of Law: Single versus Multiple Remedies in Sexual Harassment Case." *The Sociological Quarterly* 46:699–718.

Doyle, Daniel P. and David F. Luckenbill. 1991. "Mobilizing Law in Response to Collective Problems: A Test of Black's Theory of Law." *Law and Society Review* 25:103–116.

Felson, Richard B. and Jeff Ackerman. 2001. "Arrest for Domestic and Other Assaults." *Criminology* 39:655–675.

Felson, Richard B. and Paul-Philippe Pare. 2005. "The Reporting of Domestic Violence and Sexual Assault by Nonstrangers to the Police." *Journal of Marriage and Family* 67:597–610.

Felson, Richard B. and Paul-Philippe Pare. 2007. "Does the Criminal Justice System Treat Domestic Violence and Sexual Assault Defendants Leniently?" *Justice Quarterly* 24:435–459.

Felson, Richard B. and Brendan Lantz. 2016. "When are Victims Unlikely to Cooperate with the Police?" *Aggressive Behavior* 42:97–108.

Fielding, Stephen L. 1999. "Going to Court: The Plight of New York State's Female Physicians in Medical Malpractice Claims, 1986–1992." *Journal of Applied Sociology* 16:89–111.

Gartner, Rosemary and Ross Macmillan. 1995. "The Effect of Victim-Defendant Relationship on Reporting Crimes of Violence against Women." *Canadian Journal of Criminology* 37:393–429.

Geiger-Oneto, Stephanie and Scott Phillips. 2003. "Driving while Black: The Role of Race, Sex, and Social Status." *Journal of Ethnicity in Criminal Justice* 1:1–25.

Graham, Kristin Tennyson, Marian J. Borg, and Bryan Lee Miller. 2013. "Mobilizing Law in Latin America: An Evaluation of Black's Theory in Brazil." *Law and Social Inquiry* 38:322–341.

Holtfreter, Kristy. 2008. "The Effects of Legal and Extra-Legal Characteristics on Organizational Victim Decision-Making." *Crime Law and Social Change* 50:307–330.

Kaukinen, Catherine. 2002. "The Help-Seeking Decisions of Violent Crime Victims: An Examination of the Direct and Conditional Effects of Gender and the Victim-Defendant Relationship." *Journal of Interpersonal Violence* 17:432–456.

Kruttschnitt, Candace. 1980–1981. "Social Status and Sentences of Female Defendants." *Law and Society Review* 15:247–265.

Kruttschnitt, Candace. 1982. "Respectable Women and the Law." *The Sociological Quarterly* 23:221–234.

Kruttschnitt, Candace. 1985. "Are Businesses Treated Differently? A Comparison of the Individual Victim and the Corporate Victim in the Criminal Courtroom." *Sociological Inquiry* 55:225–238.

Kuo, Shih-Ya, Steven J. Cuvelier, Chuem-Jim Sheu, and Kuang-Ming Chang. 2011. "Crime Reporting Behavior and Black's Behavior of Law." *International Sociology* 27:51–71.

Lee, Catherine. 2005. "The Value of Life in Death: Multiple Regression and Event History Analyses of Homicide Clearance in Los Angeles County." *Journal of Criminal Justice* 33:527–534.

Light, Michael T. 2014. "The New Face of Legal Inequality: Noncitizens and the Long-Term Trends in Sentencing Disparities across US District Courts, 1992–2009." *Law and Society Review* 48:447–478.

Litwin, Kenneth J. 2004. "A Multilevel Multivariate Analysis of Factors Affecting Homicide Clearances." *Journal of Research in Crime and Delinquency* 41:327–351.

Mastrofski, Stephen D., Jeffrey B. Snipes, Roger B. Parks, and Christopher D. Maxwell. 2000. "The Helping Hand of the Law: Police Control of Citizens on Request." *Criminology* 38:307–342.

McCamman, Michael and Thomas Mowen. 2018. "Does Residency Matter? Local Residency as a Predictor of Arrest." *Criminal Justice Studies* 31:128–142.

Myers, Martha A. 1980. "Predicting the Behavior of Law: A Test of Two Models." *Law and Society Review* 14:835–857.

Petersen, Nick. 2017. "Neighborhood Context and Unsolved Murders: The Social Ecology of Homicide Investigations." *Policing and Society* 27:372–392.

Rojek, Jeff, Richard Rosenfeld, and Scott Decker. 2012. "Policing Race: The Racial Stratification of Searches in Police Traffic Stops." *Criminology* 50:993–1024.

Rollwagen, Heather and Joanna C. Jacob. 2018. "The Victim-Defendant Relationship and Police Charging Decisions for Juvenile Delinquents: How does Social Distance Moderate the Impact of Legal and Extralegal Factors?" *Youth Violence and Juvenile Justice* 16:378–394.

Silberman, Matthew. 1985. *The Civil Justice Process: A Sequential Model of the Mobilization of Law*. Orlando: Academic Press.

Smith, Douglas A. 1987. "Police Response to Interpersonal Violence: Defining the Parameters of Legal Control." *Social Forces* 65:767–782.

Spohn, Cassia and David Holleran. 2001. "Prosecuting Sexual Assault: A Comparison of Charging Decisions in Sexual Assault Cases Involving Strangers, Acquaintances, and Intimate Partners." *Justice Quarterly* 18:651–688.

Staples, William G. 1987. "Law and Social Control in Juvenile Justice Dispositions." *Journal of Research in Crime and Delinquency* 24:7–22.

Xie, Min and Janet L. Lauritsen. 2012. "Racial Context and Crime Reporting: A Test of Black's Stratification Hypothesis." *Journal of Quantitative Criminology* 28:265–293.

Zavala, Egbert. 2010. "Deviant Lifestyles and the Reporting of Physical Victimization to the Police." *Journal of Family Violence* 25:23–31.

Zhang, Lening, Steven F. Messner, Jianhong Liu. 2007. "An Exploration of the Determinants of Reporting Crime to the Police in the City of Tianjin, China." *Criminology* 45:959–984.

Notes

1 *McCleskey v. Kemp*, 481 US 279 (1987).
2 A variable had a stronger impact if it was statistically significant with a larger odds ratio (all the variables in the model were dichotomous except the number of prior prison terms, a nonsignificant variable). Dichotomous variables with an odds ratio less than 1 were reverse coded for comparison. Model available upon request.
3 Black later addressed two additional forms of legal variation: liability (accountability for an event) (Black 1987) and third-party partisanship and settlement (Black and Baumgartner 1983; Black 1993: chapters 7, 8). We discuss third parties in Chapter 4.
4 However, one dimension might prove to be more powerful in explaining a given set of data.
5 Social distance also includes the degree of difference between actors' locations or statuses (see note 8 below).
6 Unusually, the book contains not a single footnote.
7 Downward law is triggered by an upward offense, and upward law is triggered by a downward offense.
8 The offenses may be actual or merely alleged.
9 Two additional propositions elaborate "Downward law is greater than upward law." First, "Downward law varies directly with vertical distance" (the greater the status disparity of the parties, the more law downward cases attract). Second, "Upward law varies inversely with vertical distance" (the greater the status disparity of the parties, the less law upward cases attract). Black's original discussion can be found in *The Behavior of Law*, pp. 24–28, 50–53, 65–67, 70–73, 93–97, 116–117. We return to the first of these propositions later in the chapter.

10 What is conventional can vary across groups. Eating meat is conventional among most Americans, but unconventional among vegans. For purposes of the theory of law, the conventionality that matters is that of the decision-makers.

11 Race and ethnicity are often correlated with other sociological variables, such as wealth and education. However, not all Whites are wealthy and highly educated and not all Blacks and Latinos are poor and less educated. Moreover, Asians, on average, have more wealth and education than Whites. But in America, all Blacks, Latinos, and Asians are part of a numerical minority and hence we treat race and ethnicity as an indicator of cultural frequency or "conventionality."

12 Social distance also includes cultural distance – the degree to which people share a similar or distinct culture, as evident in their language, religion, beliefs, and ethnicity. Cultural distance is narrow when two people possess the same nationality, speak the same language, or belong to the same ethnicity, and broad when they do not. The only measure of cultural distance in the Baldus data is the race (Black/White) of the defendant and victim. However, since we are treating race as an indicator of conventionality, we do not examine cultural distance. For a similar discussion about gender, see Chapter 3, note 10.

13 The relationship between relational distance and law is direct within a society, but curvilinear across societies (Black 1976: 40–48; 1989: 12).

14 Baumgartner's compilation is the second edition of a book originally edited by Black and Mileski (1973).

15 Michalski (2008, 2017) has conducted two quantitative surveys of research that has been conducted to test Blackian theory. Although Michalski does not provide many methodological details, the results are supportive. Michalski (2008) analyzed 72 empirical tests of Blackian theory in journal articles, conference proceedings, and dissertation, 1966–2006, finding that more than 80% had highly consistent evidence. 45 of the publications addressed the theory of law: in those, "more than 70 percent of the research has yielded strongly supportive, confirmatory evidence for various aspects of the theory" (2008: 260–261). Michalski (2017) analyzed 191 peer-reviewed articles published 1976–2015 that empirically developed, refined, or tested aspects of Blackian theory. He again found that "more than 80 percent of the published research produced positive results for pure sociology ideas, while 7 in 10 articles yielded strongly positive results (75 percent or more positive results)" (2017: 162). However, this latter paper does not report the results of articles that addressed the theory of law (as distinct from other subjects of Blackian theory, such as violence or conflict management).

16 These criteria are minimal in that they do not include other factors that might affect the results (e.g., the data are not derived from random samples, the study does not control for all the dimensions of social space or only analyzes a limited number of stages of the legal process).

17 A list of the studies and how we coded them can be found in Appendix 1, Table 1.2.

18 A list of the studies and how we coded them can be found in Appendix 1, Table 1.3.

19 Calculated from Table 1.2 in Appendix 1.

20 *Furman v. Georgia*, 408 US 238 (1972).

21 *Gregg v. Georgia*, 428 US 153 (1976).

22 Blackian theory would explain aggregate outcomes with case level characteristics (e.g., an increase in the average relational distance of cases should lead to more cases – higher rates of cases being filed).

23 More details about the Baldus study can be found in Appendix 2.

24 Our data are available upon request.

25 In some studies, the authors examined the relative status of the parties despite only having data on one party. Doing so was possible because the status of the police officer was a constant (Geiger-Oneto and Phillips 2003; Ariel and Tankebe 2018; McCamman and Mowen 2018), the status of the victim was a constant (Kruttschnitt 1980–1981; Kruttschnitt 1982), or the offense was a "victimless crime" (Chappell and Maggard 2007; Kruttschnitt 1980–1981; Kruttschnitt 1982a).

26 Black defines law as government social control. For four studies, we concluded that the measure of law was partially appropriate. Dawson and Welsh (2005) examined sexual harassment cases handled by the Canadian Human Rights Commission (CHRC). But the authors included an unknown number of cases where the complainant and respondent reached an agreement before the CHRC completed its investigation and determined the outcome (meaning before government social control occurred). Felson and Pare (2005) examined whether the victim or a third party called the police, a distinction that is not relevant to the quantity of law. Kaukinen (2002) examined whether the victim contacted police or reached out to someone else for help. Mastrofski et al. (2000) examined whether the police did what the citizen requested. In this study, doing what the citizen requested always involved more law. Nonetheless, whether the police accommodate a citizen's request is not a reliable measure of law, as accommodation might mean more law (arrest) or less law (do not arrest).

27 An author could hold conduct constant by limiting the analysis to one crime or controlling for conduct in a multivariate model. We coded whether the author attempted to hold conduct constant, not whether the attempt was adequate (a subjective assessment).

28 Table 1.3 does not include a study by Dannefer (1984) because we concluded that the author's measure of intimacy was questionable. Dannefer coded parents and children as intimates, a decision that would ordinarily be correct. However, Dannefer noted that the parents and children were "estranged" (250), clearly indicating a degree of distance in the relationship.

29 Partial support for the theory came in two forms: intimates attracted less law than non-intimates if the offense was minor, but the pattern did not hold for serious offenses (Felson and Ackerman 2001; Felson and Pare 2007; Felson and Lantz 2016); non-strangers attracted less law than strangers, but subcategories of non-strangers did not conform to the theoretical prediction (Felson and Pare 2005).

30 In three studies, we concluded that the measure of law was partially appropriate: Felson and Pare (2005), Kaukinen (2002), and Mastrofski et al. (2000). See note 26 for details.

31 Calculated from Table 1.2.

References

Abel, Richard L. 2010. "Law and Society: Project and Practice." *Annual Review of Law and Social Science* 6:1–23.

Anonymous. 2019. "What Is the Capital Jury Project?" www.albany.edu/scj/13189.php. Retrieved 8/26/2019.

Auerhahn, Kathleen. 2012. "'Social Control of the Self' and Pleading Guilty in Criminal Court." *International Review of Sociology* 22:95–122.

Avakame, Edem F., James J. Fyfe, and Candace McCoy. 1999. "Did You Call the Police? What Did They Do? An Empirical Assessment of Black's Theory of Mobilization of Law." *Justice Quarterly* 16:765–792.

Baldus, David C. and George Woodworth. 2003. "Race Discrimination in the Administration of the Death Penalty: An Overview of the Empirical Evidence with Special Emphasis on the Post-1990 Research." *Criminal Law Bulletin* 39:194–226.

Baldus, David C., George Woodworth, and Charles A. Pulaski. 1990. *Equal Justice and the Death Penalty: A Legal and Empirical Analysis*. Boston: Northeastern University Press.

Baumgartner, Frank P., Marty Davidson, Kaneesha R. Johnson, Arvind Krishnamurthy, and Colin P. Wilson. 2018. *Deadly Justice: A Statistical Portrait of the Death Penalty*. New York: Oxford University Press.

Baumgartner, M.P. 1978. "Law and Social Status in Colonial New Haven, 1639–1665." Pp. 153–174 in *Research in Law and Sociology: An Annual Compilation of Research*, Volume 1, edited by Rita J. Simon. Greenwich: JAI Press.

Baumgartner, M.P. 1992. "The Myth of Discretion." Pp. 129–162 in *The Uses of Discretion*, edited by Keith Hawkins. Oxford: Clarendon Press.

Baumgartner, M.P., ed. 1998. *The Social Organization of Law*. San Diego: Academic Press (second edition; first edition edited by Donald Black and Maureen Mileski, 1973).

Black, Donald. 1972. "The Boundaries of Legal Sociology." *Yale Law Journal* 81:1086–1100.

Black, Donald. 1976. *The Behavior of Law*. New York: Academic Press.

Black, Donald. 1979a. "A Strategy of Pure Sociology." Pp. 149–168 in *Theoretical Perspectives in Sociology*, edited by Scott G. McNall. New York: St. Martin's Press (reprinted as an appendix in Black 1993).

Black, Donald. 1979b. "Common Sense in the Sociology of Law." *American Sociological Review* 44:18–27.

Black, Donald. 1980. *The Manners and Customs of the Police*. New York: Academic Press.

Black, Donald. 1987. "Compensation and the Social Structure of Misfortune." *Law and Society Review* 21:563–584.

Black, Donald. 1989. *Sociological Justice*. New York: Oxford University Press.

Black, Donald. 1993. *The Social Structure of Right and Wrong*. San Diego: Academic Press.

Black, Donald. 1995. "The Epistemology of Pure Sociology." *Law and Social Inquiry* 20:829–870.

Black, Donald. 2000a. "Dreams of Pure Sociology." *Sociological Theory* 18:343–367.

Black, Donald. 2000b. "The Purification of Sociology." *Contemporary Sociology* 29:704–709.

Black, Donald. 2002. "The Geometry of Law: An Interview with Donald Black." *International Journal of the Sociology of Law* 30:101–129.

Black, Donald. 2010. "How Law Behaves: An Interview with Donald Black." *International Journal of Law, Crime and Justice* 38:37–47.

Black, Donald. 2011. *Moral Time*. New York: Oxford University Press.

Black, Donald. 2013. "On the Almost Inconceivable Misunderstandings Concerning the Subject of Value-Free Sociology." *British Journal of Sociology* 64:763–780.

Black, Donald and M.P. Baumgartner. 1983. "Toward a Theory of the Third Party." Pp. 84–114 in *Empirical Theories about Courts*, edited by Keith O. Boyum and Lynn Mather. New York: Longman.

Black, Donald and Maureen Mileski, eds. 1973. *The Social Organization of Law*. New York: Seminar Press.

Blume, John H., Theodore Eisenberg, and Stephen P. Garvey. 2003. "Lessons from the Capital Jury Project" Pp. 144–177 in *Beyond Repair? America's Death Penalty*, edited by Stephen P. Garvey. Durham: Duke University Press. 144–177.

Borg, Marian J. and Karen F. Parker. 2001. "Mobilizing Law in Urban Areas: The Social Structure of Homicide Clearance Rates." *Law and Society Review* 35:435–466.

Bowers, William J. 1995. "The Capital Jury Project: Rationale, Design, and Preview of Early Findings." *Indiana Law Journal* 70:1043–1102.

Brown, Robert A. and James Frank. 2005. "Police-Citizen Encounters and Field Citations: Do Encounter Characteristics Influence Ticketing?" *Policing: An International Journal* 28:435–454.

Campbell, Bradley. 2014a. "Anti-Minotaur: The Myth of a Sociological Morality." *Society* 51:443–451.

Campbell, Bradley. 2014b. "Sociology, Morality, and Social Solidarity: On Christian Smith's *Sacred Project of American Sociology*." *Altruism, Morality, and Social Solidarity Forum: Newsletter of the AMSS Section of the American Sociological Association* 5:4–8.

Cooney, Mark. 2009. *Is Killing Wrong? A Study in Pure Sociology*. Charlottesville: University of Virginia Press.

Copes, Heith, Kent R. Kerley, Karen A. Mason, and Judy Van Wyk. 2001. "Reporting Behavior of Fraud Victims and Black's Theory of Law: An Empirical Assessment." *Justice Quarterly* 18:343–363.

Dannefer, Dale. 1984. "Who Signs the Complaint? Relational Distance and the Juvenile Justice Process." *Law and Society Review* 18:249–271.

Dieter, Richard C. 2011. *Struck by Lightning: The Continuing Arbitrariness of the Death Penalty 35 Years After Its Reinstatement in 1976*. Washington D.C.: Death Penalty Information Center.

Durkheim, Emile. 1893. *The Division of Labor in Society*. New York: Free Press, 1964.

Estrich, Susan. 1987. *Real Rape*. Cambridge: Harvard University Press.

Felson, Richard B., Steven F. Messner, and Anthony Hoskin. 1999. "The Victim-Defendant Relationship and Calling the Police in Assaults." *Criminology* 37:931–947.

Frankford, David M. 1995. *Social Structure of Right and Wrong*: Normativity without Agents." *Law and Social Inquiry* 20:787–803.

Geiger-Oneto, Stephanie and Scott Phillips. 2003. "Driving while Black: The Role of Race, Sex, and Social Status." *Journal of Ethnicity in Criminal Justice* 1:1–25.

Goffman, Erving. 1956. "The Nature of Deference and Demeanor." *American Anthropologist* 58:473–502.

Granovetter, Mark. 1973. "The Strength of Weak Ties." *American Journal of Sociology* 78:1360–1380.

Greenberg, David F. 1983. "Donald Black's Sociology of Law: A Critique." *Law and Society Review* 17:337–368.

Gross, Samuel R. 2012. "David Baldus and the Legacy of *McCleskey v. Kemp*." *Iowa Law Review* 97:1906–1924.

Hindson, Stephanie, Hillary Potter, and Michael L. Radelet. 2006. "Race, Gender, Region, and Death Sentencing in Colorado, 1980–1999." *Colorado Law Review* 77:549–574.

Horwitz, Allan V. 2002. "Toward A New Science of Social Life: A Retrospective Examination of *The Behavior of Law*." *Contemporary Sociology* 31:641–644.

Homans, George. 1967. *The Nature of Social Science*. New York: Harcourt, Brace, and World.

Krutschnitt, Candace. 1980–1981. "Social Status and Sentences of Female Defendants." *Law and Society Review* 15:247–266.

Lundsgaarde, Henry P. 1977. *Murder in Space City: A Cultural Analysis of Houston Homicide Patterns*. New York: Oxford University Press.

McCamman, Michael and Thomas Mowen. 2018. "Does Residency Matter? Local Residency as a Predictor of Arrest." *Criminal Justice Studies* 31:128–142.

Marx, Karl and Friedrich Engels. 1848. *The Communist Manifesto*. Oxford: Oxford University Press, 1992.

Massey, James and Martha A. Myers. 1989. "Patterns of Repressive Social Control in Post-Reconstruction Georgia, 1882–1935." *Social Forces* 68:458–488.

Michaels, Priscilla. 1977. "Review of *The Behavior of Law*." *Contemporary Sociology* 7:10–11.

Michalski, Joseph. 2008. "The Social Life of Pure Sociology." *Sociological Quarterly* 49:253–274.

Michalski, Joseph. 2017. "Scientific Partisanship: The Social Geometry of Intellectual Support." *Canadian Review of Sociology* 54:147–173.

Morrill, Calvin and Kelsey Mayo. 2015. "Charting the 'Classics' in Law and Society: The Development of the Field over the Past Half-Century." Pp. 18–36 in *The Handbook of Law and Society*, edited by Austin Sarat and Patricia Ewick. New York: John Wiley and Sons.

Mullis, Jeffrey. 1995. "Medical Malpractice, Social Structure, and Social Control." *Sociological Forum* 10:135–163.

Myers, Martha A. 1980. "Predicting the Behavior of Law: A Test of Two Models." *Law and Society Review* 14:835–857.

Parsons, Talcott. 1951. *The Social System*. New York: Free Press.

Phillips, Scott. 2008. "Racial Disparities in the Capital of Capital Punishment." *Houston Law Review* 45:807–840.

Phillips, Scott. 2009a. "Status Disparities in the Capital of Capital Punishment." *Law and Society Review* 43:807–837.

Phillips, Scott. 2009b. "Legal Disparities in the Capital of Capital Punishment." *Journal of Criminal Law and Criminology* 99:717–756.

Phillips, Scott, Laura Potter, and James E. Coverdill. 2012. "Disentangling Victim Gender and Capital Punishment: The Role of Media." *Feminist Criminology* 7:130–145.

Phillips, Scott and Justin Marceau. 2020. "Whom the State Kills." *Harvard Civil Rights-Civil Liberties Law Review* 55:585–656.

Radelet, Michael L. 1989. "Executions of Whites for Crimes against Blacks: Exceptions to the Rule?" *Sociological Quarterly* 30:529–544.

Rollwagen, Heather and Joanna C. Jacob. 2018. "The Victim-Defendant Relationship and Police Charging Decisions for Juvenile Delinquents: How Does Social Distance Moderate the Impact of Legal and Extralegal Factors?" *Youth Violence and Juvenile Justice* 16:378–394.

Seron, Carroll, Susan Bibler Coutin, and Pauline White Meeusen. 2013. "Is There a Canon of Law and Society?" *Annual Review of Law and Social Science* 9:287–306

Sherman, Lawrence W. 1977. Review of *The Behavior of Law*. *Contemporary Sociology* 7:11–15.

Stinchcombe, Arthur L. 1977. Review of Lawrence M. Friedman's *The Legal System* and Donald Black's *The Behavior of Law*. *Law and Society Review* 12:129–131.

Weber, Max. 1922. "Bureaucracy." Pp. 196–244 in *From Max Weber: Essays in Sociology*, edited by Hans Gerth and C. Wright Mills. New York: Oxford University Press, 1958.

Williams, Marian R., Stephen Demuth, and Jefferson E. Holcomb. 2007. "Understanding the Influence of Victim Gender in Death Penalty Cases: The Importance of Victim Race, Sex-Related Victimization, and Jury Decision Making." *Criminology* 45:865–891.

Wooditch, Alese. 2012. "Human Trafficking: Law and Social Structures." *International Journal of Defendant Therapy and Comparative Criminology* 56:673–690.

Zhang, Lening, Steven F. Messner, and Jianhong Liu. 2007. "An Exploration of the Determinants of Reporting Crime to the Police in the City of Tianjin, China." *Criminology* 45:959–983.

2

SOCIAL SPACE

Houston, Texas: June 4, 1995

Three Jacinto City gang members – 17-year-old Rodolfo "Rudy" Flores, 18-year-old Enrique Alejandro Cruz, and 22-year-old Adrian Raymond Montoya – met 25-year-old Robin Owers at a McDonald's on Federal Road at 1 am. The young men were drunk and flirted with Robin. She agreed to leave with the men and "party." Initially, the men took Robin back to her house. From there she went with them to one of the gang member's homes. After she resisted sexual advances, the men took a golf club and beat her over the head. All three men raped her. They drove Robin to an area off Old Beaumont Highway, dumped her body in a ditch, and Flores shot her in the neck with a high-powered rifle. Flores had shot at people before, but he had never hit anyone. According to Sheriff's department Lieutenant Bert Diaz, Flores said "it would be cool to shoot someone." Robin was reported missing by her mother. Her body was found a week later, on June 11. The police arrested Montoya and Cruz at home in Jacinto City on June 22, 1995. Flores left town but was arrested in the Rio Grande Valley on June 24, 1995. The District Attorney charged each defendant with capital murder.

Houston, Texas: July 29, 1997

Nancy Adleman left her home at 7:30 pm for her usual 3.5-mile jog around the bayou. Arthur Burton, riding a bike, saw Nancy jogging. Burton rode up behind Nancy, jumped off his bike, and dragged her screaming into the woods. Throwing her down, he choked her until she was unconscious. He removed her shorts and underwear and tried to rape her; she regained consciousness and started screaming

DOI: 10.4324/9781003176633-3

and talking to him; he once again choked her into unconsciousness, dragged her further from the trail, and strangled her with a shoelace. Nancy's jog typically took 30 minutes. When she was not back after an hour, her husband called the police. The police mounted a search that included officers on bicycle, foot, and horseback plus the use of helicopters and dogs. The search lasted most of the night and continued at daybreak. The following day around 3 pm an officer on horseback found some of Nancy's clothing. Tracking hounds then located her partially clothed body (nude from the waist down) in a heavily wooded, bushy, and isolated area near the bayou. After a witness described a man on a bicycle to the police, they released a composite sketch. Brought in for questioning, Burton failed a polygraph and confessed. Since the victim had been kidnapped by being abducted from the trail, the District Attorney charged Burton with capital murder. Burton denied the rape and claimed that police had coerced his confession.

These two cases occurred in the same city, within two years of each other. Both were murders coupled with a sexual assault (a triple rape in one case and, it appears, an attempted rape in the other). The same District Attorney brought capital murder charges in both cases. However, in one of the cases, the District Attorney went ahead and pursued the death penalty; in the other, he did not. (All four defendants were death-eligible. Even though Flores was only 17 at the time of the Owers murder, it was not until 2005 that the Supreme Court held that the death penalty could not be imposed on a person under 18 years of age.) In the case in which the prosecutor sought the death penalty, the jury convicted and, at the penalty phase, deliberated for just 30 minutes before sentencing the defendant to death.

Which crime resulted in a death sentence? Looking at the cases through the prism of the written law, one would probably pick the Owers murder. The criminal law provides harsher penalties depending on how the crime is committed, such as the amount of preplanning and victim suffering it entails. Robin had to endure being beaten and raped by three different men before being killed in a particularly callous manner.

In fact, it was the Adleman murder that resulted in a sentence of death for Arthur Burton. In the Owers murder, Flores pled guilty to aggravated kidnapping and testified against Montoya in exchange for a 30-year sentence. Enrique Cruz and Adrian Montoya were convicted of capital murder and given a life term.[1]

The contrasting outcomes are a testament to the power of Black's idea of social geometry. Concretely, social geometry refers to the social structure or composition of the case — who the parties are. The two Houston cases had similar racial compositions: both victims were White females, all four defendants were minority males (Flores, Cruz, and Montoya were Latino; Burton was Black). However, as we shall later see, in other respects their geometrical structures differed significantly. Social geometry promises to provide a more complete explanation of the handling of legal cases. Does it deliver on that promise?

The Geometry of Death

We saw in Chapter 1 that *The Behavior of Law* contains a series of propositions linking variation in social geometry to variation in the quantity and style of law. Since all our cases are criminal cases in which the death penalty is in play, we are analyzing only the penal style of law. Our focus is therefore the quantity of law, as measured by the severity of punishment. We test Black's theory by asking: Are death penalty decisions consistent with the predictions of geometrical theory?

Testing a theory involves a number of steps. The researcher must find or generate data that are appropriate for testing the theory, specify which aspects of the theory are being tested, devise measures or indicators of the theory's key concepts, and then analyze the data to see to what extent the findings match the theory's predictions.

The usual way of testing Black's theory is to try to develop measures of wealth, intimacy, integration, conventionality, organization, and respectability and see whether each variable affects the quantity of law in the way predicted by the theory. The problem is that there are often no good measures of each variable. Victim characteristics are particularly likely to be poorly documented. To make up for the missing information, researchers have to resort to weak, indirect measures of the theory's concepts. Fortunately, the comprehensiveness of Baldus's Charging and Sentencing Study (CSS) allows us to largely avoid that problem.

Recall that Black's theory can be reduced to three principal propositions:

1. Downward law is greater than upward law
2. Law varies directly with social status
3. Law increases with social distance

Consistent with this three-proposition summary, we combine the various indicators of social status and social distance to create overall or holistic variables (Phillips 2009). This strategy has the virtue of being consistent with Black's treatment of social status and social distance in his writings subsequent to *The Behavior of Law* (see, e.g., Black 1989; 2000; 2004; 2018). It is also more faithful to legal reality. Legal officials do not respond to the vertical, radial, cultural, normative, and organizational statuses of the parties individually but holistically: they judge the entire person, not discrete characteristics. Hence, we adopt this second tack.[2]

Social Status, Social Distance

How we went about testing Black's theory is a long and somewhat technical story. To avoid overwhelming the reader with a plethora of detail, we provide here a broad overview of how we selected and measured our variables, how we analyzed the data, and, most crucially, what we found. For those interested, Appendix 2 provides a complete description of our methods. To discover the relative status of the parties, we searched the Baldus data set for indicators that provided a clear measure of status in each of the five dimensions of social space. We chose

TABLE 2.1 Measuring Social Status

Dimensions of Social Status				
Vertical	*Radial*	*Cultural*	*Normative*	*Organizational*
Definition				
Wealth	Integration in Social Life	Conventionality	Respectability	Capacity for Collective Action
Measurement of Defendant and Victim Social Status Using Data from the CSS				
Professional Job	Parent Supporting Child	White	Clean Record	State Official

information that was documented for both the defendant and the victim, as we needed a consistent measuring rod. As Table 2.1 shows, we consider the status of defendants and victims to be higher if they were professionals (e.g., doctor, accountant), a parent supporting a child, White, had a clean criminal record, or were state officials (e.g., police officer, corrections officer, or active duty military personnel).[3] We gave each of these five characteristics a score of 1 and added them up for an overall status score. For example, a White defendant on active duty in the military with a child and a clean criminal record would receive a status score of 4. A Black defendant with a criminal record working as a cashier to support a newborn would receive a status score of 1. Defendants who were above the average status score for all defendants we treat as higher status, and those below the average as lower status. Similarly, we treat higher-than-average victims as higher status and lower-than-average victims as lower status.

Ours is a measure of relative, not absolute, social status. Most parties to homicide today, whether defendants or victims, tend to be low status in one or more ways: poor, unemployed, single, less educated, members of cultural minorities, or possessing criminal records (e.g., Cooney 1998: 22–31).[4] The Georgia defendants and victims are no exception. Few of the parties in the Baldus data would clearly qualify as being high status in the society at large. However, some are clearly less disadvantaged than others. Our categories of higher and lower status reflect salient differences in the social standing of the defendants and victims.

With the social status of both parties in hand, we could determine the location and direction of the case in social space:

- Downward law: higher status victim killed by lower status defendant
- Lateral law, high: higher status victim killed by higher status defendant
- Lateral law, low: lower status victim killed by lower status defendant
- Upward law: lower status victim killed by higher status defendant

For our social distance variable, we divided the relationships between defendant and victim into those who were strangers and non-strangers. This dichotomy is not an ideal measure of the continuum of relational distance as it precludes exploration of differences in the legal response to, say, homicides between family members and between friends, or between closer and more distant acquaintances. However, it is the measure available to us in the Baldus data set. Even the best data sets have limitations.

Finally, we measured the quantity of law by whether the defendant received a sentence of death or life imprisonment, and, among those sentenced to death, whether the defendant was executed.[5]

Findings

Does the social geometry of the case help to predict who receives a sentence of death? The results presented in Figure 2.1 indicate that it does: among cases eligible for the death penalty under Georgia law, the relative status of the parties is clearly related to the imposition of the penalty. Where downward cases result in a death sentence 11% of the time, upward cases only wind up with a death sentence 1% of the time. When the parties are of approximately equal status, higher status defendants who killed higher status victims stand a greater risk of being sentenced to death than lower status defendants who killed lower status victims: 7% versus 1%.[6]

Recall that the Baldus study was launched to provide the foundation for a possible constitutional challenge to the death penalty on grounds of racial discrimination. When Baldus and his colleagues analyzed the data, they therefore concentrated heavily on the role of race. They found that the probability of a death sentence was greater in White victim cases.

Since we include race in our measure of status (White higher, Black lower), we checked whether race drives our results. To do so, we removed race from our measure of status. As Figure 2.2 shows, the results do not change appreciably – the underlying pattern is the same. For example, the difference between downward and upward cases in both Figures 2.1 and 2.2 is 10 percentage points. In short,

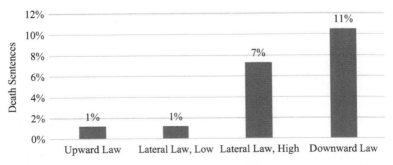

FIGURE 2.1 Death Sentences by Location and Direction in Social Space (with race) ($n = 2,483$)

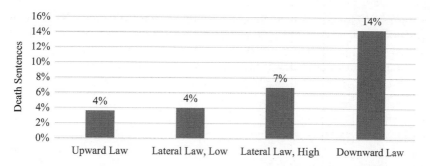

FIGURE 2.2 Death Sentences by Location and Direction in Social Space (without race) (*n* = 2,483)

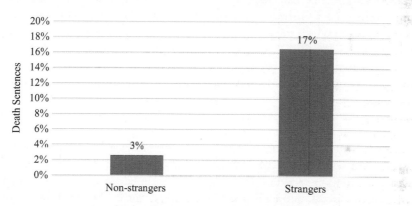

FIGURE 2.3 Death Sentences by Relational Distance (*n* = 2,483)

whether we include or exclude race, the social status of the parties helps to predict who gets sentenced to death.

The effect of relational distance is even stronger. Figure 2.3 reveals that defendants indicted for killing a stranger were considerably more likely to wind up with a death sentence than those who killed a non-stranger (17% versus 3%). As with Figures 2.1 and 2.2, the results are statistically significant beyond the 0.001 level (meaning that the probability of finding such a relationship in the random sample if it did not actually exist in the population is less than 1 in 1,000).[7] Thus, we can be highly confident that the location, direction, and distance of the case in social space influences the likelihood of a death sentence. In short, in capital cases, much depends on who kills whom.

Does the theory continue to hold up once we introduce other variables? Perhaps the reason certain cases result in a death sentence is because the defendant killed in a calculating, deliberate manner rather than acting spontaneously. Or maybe there was more evidence against the defendant. We considered the effect of these factors in additional analyses (for details, see Appendix 2) and found that our key findings remained the same. Specifically, we found that the odds of a death sentence were:

- 7.5 times greater in downward cases than upward cases
- 4.8 times greater in lateral high cases than lateral low cases
- 4.7 times greater in stranger cases than non-stranger cases[8]

In short, even when we control for key aspects of the legal dimensions of the case, the social geometry of the case predicts the imposition of a death sentence.

Downward Distance

Parties to a legal case may differ not just in whether they are unequal but in how unequal they are. In geometrical terms, this is vertical distance. Upward distance is the degree to which the victim is lower in status than the defendant; downward distance is the degree to which the victim is higher in status than the defendant. In the Baldus data, upward cases almost never resulted in a death sentence, as geometrical theory would predict (just two death sentences in 172 upward cases). As a result, we cannot look more deeply at upward cases. But we can push our examination of downward law further because 78 of 734 such cases resulted in a death sentence. As an example of how the status gap might vary in downward cases, consider two hypothetical murders. In both, the defendant is a working-class Black civilian with a criminal record. In Case A, the victim is a Black civilian professor with no criminal record. In Case B, the victim again has no criminal record but is a White professor employed by the United States Military Academy (West Point) with an officer's rank. Both are downward cases but, with its wider status gap, Case B is more distantly downward than Case A. Figure 2.4 illustrates the theoretical relationship between downward distance and law: the left side corresponds to Case A; the right side corresponds to Case B. Since Black's (1976: 24, 50, 65–66, 70, 93, 117) theory predicts that downward law increases with vertical distance, Case B should attract greater severity. Does it?

To find out, we measured downward distance by subtracting the defendant's status score from the victim's status score. In downward cases, the defendant's total status score was 0 or 1 and the victim's total status score was 2, 3, or 4. The degree of downward distance could therefore range from a minimum of one unit (2 minus 1) to a maximum of four units (4 minus 0). As the status gap increases in downward cases so too should the chance of a death sentence.

Figure 2.5 displays the probability of a death sentence when the status gap in downward cases is one, two, and three or more units, respectively.

Among cases where the victim was just one step above the defendant on the ladder of status, relatively few defendants were sentenced to death. But when victims were two steps higher the chance of a death sentence quadrupled from 4% to 16%. Remarkably, for victims three or more status steps above the defendant

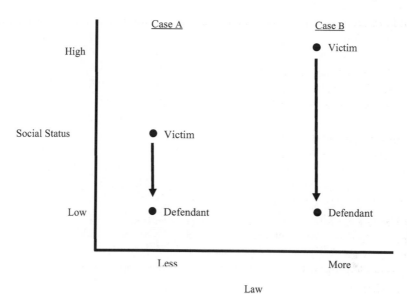

FIGURE 2.4 Downward Distance

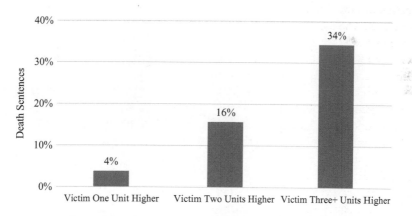

FIGURE 2.5 Death Sentences by Vertical Distance (among downward cases) ($n = 734$)

the percentage doubles again to 34%. Or, to put the point differently, comparing the most distant cases to the least distant cases reveals a 30-percentage point gap.[9] Moreover, the effect of downward distance remains strong when we control for several factors that might explain the results: the number and types of evidence against the defendant, whether the defendant deliberated before killing, and whether the defendant was not the actual killer. We found that for each unit increase in downward distance the odds of a death sentence more than doubles.[10] In short, downward capital cases attract more severity than upward cases, and the more distantly downward they are, the greater the severity they attract.

Executions

Who gets sentenced to death depends, then, on who kills whom. What about who gets executed? Most people sent to death row avoid execution. Out of the 128 defendants Georgia sentenced to death during the period Baldus studied (1973–1979), the state has executed 24 (19%). The courts (or the governor in rare cases) granted relief to 96 defendants. Eight defendants were neither granted relief nor executed: five died of natural causes on death row, one was executed by the state of Virginia for a different murder, one escaped and was beaten to death in a bar fight, and one remains on death row. We excluded these eight defendants from our execution analysis, leaving 120 cases. Given the small number of executions, we do not include control variables in the analysis.

Figure 2.6 addresses whether the relative status of the parties predicts execution.[11] The same pattern emerges. Indeed, downward cases and lateral high cases were the only cases to end in an actual execution.

Figure 2.7 presents the relationship between relational distance and execution.[12] Cases with stranger victims were almost twice as likely to result in an

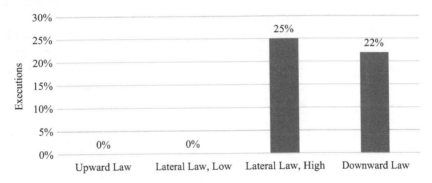

FIGURE 2.6 Executions by Location and Direction in Social Space (*n* = 120)

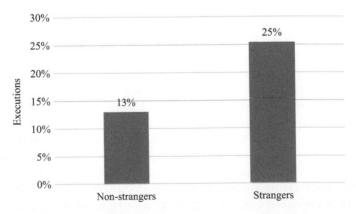

FIGURE 2.7 Executions by Relational Distance (*n* = 120)

execution as cases with non-stranger victims. As with the sentence of death, whom the state kills depends in part on who killed whom. Social geometry continues to matter at the execution stage.

Conclusion

We set out to conduct as strong a quantitative test of Black's geometrical theory of law as we possibly could. In this chapter, we relied on the superb data assembled by David Baldus and colleagues on the Georgia death penalty. The Baldus data set offers the kind of "naïve evidence" (i.e., collected without reference to the theory) that, according to Black (1995: 843), provides a particularly persuasive basis for a test because the data are unlikely to be biased either for or against the theory.[13] It is all the more striking, then, that we find strong support for the core predictions of Black's theory: downward law is greater than upward law (downward cases were more likely than upward cases to produce a death sentence and an execution); law varies directly with social status (lateral high cases were more likely than lateral low cases to produce a death sentence and an execution); and law increases with relational distance (defendants who killed a stranger were more likely to be sentenced to death and executed).

To visualize how these patterns operate in real life, recall the two cases with which we began the chapter: Flores, Cruz, and Montoya raping and killing Robin Owers; Arthur Burton killing Nancy Adleman after having attempted to rape her. Both cases took place in Houston, both cases involved minority males killing and sexually assaulting White females, and all the defendants were eligible for death (indicted for capital murder). Yet while Burton was dispatched to death row, Flores and his two companions were spared. Race is only one aspect of social status, however. The crucial difference between the cases lies in the overall social elevation of the parties.

The Burton case was clearly an instance of downward law. As Head of Marketing for a company, Nancy Adleman enjoyed vertical and organizational status. Her cultural and normative statuses were high as well: she held a Master's degree in Fine Arts and had no criminal record. Her radial status (or social integration) was particularly high: she had been married to her husband for 18 years and had three children; she and her husband participated in several runs every year for charity; she was an active member of the Methodist church, and had even declined her husband's offer to join her on her run that fateful night because she was writing a play about the role of women in the bible and wanted to think about the ending. Such was the esteem in which Nancy was held that after her death two local businesses offered rewards for information leading to the arrest of her killer and a restaurant donated $1 for each meal it served over a weekend to a trust established for her children's education. In addition, residents of her neighborhood wanted to erect a small white cross near the location where she died. This caused a church-state controversy with the city that led eventually to a compromise: they installed a bench at the site instead and her family and friends held a memorial event there.

Nancy's killer, by contrast, was of considerably lower status. Although Burton was employed by his father as a concrete finisher and had a wife and four children, his respectability or normative status was seriously compromised. He had sold drugs. During the punishment phase, the Police Chief from an Arkansas town in which Burton had lived testified that Burton was linked to 22 burglaries in 1988; 43 pieces of evidence from those burglaries were found at Burton's mother's house. Burton confessed to the burglaries. And Burton admitted to detectives that during the attack Nancy said she forgave him, but he killed her anyway.

The Flores case was more of a lateral low case. Robin Owers worked as a bartender and lived off Federal road. The median household income in her neighborhood was $34,000 (compared to $60,000 in Nancy Adelman's neighborhood). She had three children but was divorced. Robin's respectability was compromised by her conduct on the night she was murdered: not only did she agree to accompany three drunken men who flirted with her at a McDonalds at 1 am, but she later left her home to party with them rather than staying behind with her young children.[14] All these factors combined to bring her status closer to that of the men responsible for her murder.

Perhaps it is worth reiterating that scientific theories can only tell us what is, not what should be. Geometrical theory therefore does not propose that Nancy's life matters more than Robin's, that her murder ought to have resulted in a death sentence while Robin's ought to have resulted in a life sentence. The theory simply says that is likely to happen – and the data support the theoretical prediction.

The two Houston cases, then, concretely illustrate just how important the social geometry of a case can be. Even relatively small changes in the status of the parties can make the difference between life or death. Our analysis of the Baldus data confirms that in a large sample of murder cases, the legal outcomes vary with the social status and distance of the parties, as predicted by the theory. Still, no one test of a theory is ever conclusive, and ours is no exception. One limitation is that we only controlled for a limited number of variables. We have not included gender in our analysis, for example. Nor have we paid attention to the nature of the murder – its heinousness. Consistent with Black's theory, we have held the murder constant (all the defendants committed a murder that was eligible for death in Georgia). But Black's newer theory of moral time promises to overthrow that restriction, to explain why some murders are even worse than others. Chapter 3 takes up these issues.

Sources for the Robin Owers Case

Staff. 1995. "Autopsy blames gunshot," *Houston Chronicle*, June 17, p. 32.

Bardwell, S.K. 1995. "Border towns searched for third murder suspect," *Houston Chronicle*, June 24, p. 32.

Urban, Jerry. 1995. "Third person arrested in rape–murder case," *Houston Chronicle*, June 26, p. 14.

Staff. 1996. "Suspected gang member on trial for murder," *Houston Chronicle*, September 17, p. 19.

Zuniga, Jo Ann. 1996. "Gang member gets life term in rape-slaying," *Houston Chronicle*, September 24, p. 18.

Sources for the Nancy Adleman Case

Teachey, Lisa. 1997. "Lawmen find jogger's body/Nightly run along bayou ends in assault, death," *Houston Chronicle*, July 31, p. 29.

Staff. 1997. "Jogger strangled, medical report says," *Houston Chronicle*, August 1, p. 31.

Staff. 1997. "Reward offered in murder," *Houston Chronicle*, August 2, p. 37.

Staff. 1997. "Widower, detectives seek slaying witness," *Houston Chronicle*, August 7, p. 26.

Hanson, Eric. 1997. "Suspect, 27, is charged in jogger's death," *Houston Chronicle*, August 10, p. 37.

Teachey, Lisa. 1997. "Suspect's kin claims police abuse/Confession coerced by deputies, family says," *Houston Chronicle*, August 12, p. 13.

Sternberg, Susan. 1997. "Tragedy on trails saps spirit," *Houston Chronicle*, September 4, p. 11.

Stinebaker, Joe. 1997. "County weighs desire to bear victim's cross/Residents want to mark homicide scene," *Houston Chronicle*, September 9, p. 13.

Stinebaker, Joe. 1997. "Park bench wins OK as jogger's memorial," *Houston Chronicle*, September 10, p. 17.

Brewer, Steve. 1998. "Judge refuses to suppress confession in slaying," *Houston Chronicle*, June 9, p. 17.

Brewer, Steve. 1998. "Witnesses recall scene before jogger's slaying: Testimony places defendant on same trail the victim used just prior to her abduction," *Houston Chronicle*, June 16, p. 15.

Brewer, Steve. 1998. "Ex-cellmate testifies in rape-murder trial," *Houston Chronicle*, June 17, p. 27.

Brewer, Steve. 1998. "Confession tells victim's last words /'She was asking me did I know God'," *Houston Chronicle*, June 18, p. 37.

Brewer, Steve. 1998. "Murder suspect testifies he didn't kill jogger: Burton takes stand before defense rests, jury begins deliberation," *Houston Chronicle*, June 19, p. 38.

Brewer, Steve. 1998. "Man who strangled jogger convicted of capital murder," *Houston Chronicle*, June 20, p. 1.

Brewer, Steve. 1998. "Prosecutors to ask for death penalty in woman's slaying," *Houston Chronicle*, June 23, p. 17.

Brewer, Steve. 1998. "Man receives death sentence in jogger's abduction, slaying," *Houston Chronicle*, June 24, p. 21.

Brewer, Steve. 1998. "Judge denies retrial for man convicted in murder of jogger," *Houston Chronicle*, September 5, p. 41.

Muck, Patti. 1998. "Running to cope: Sport helped man deal with murder of wife," *Houston Chronicle*, October 22, p. 13.

Glenn, Mike. 2000. "Killer gets new punishment hearing," *Houston Chronicle*, October 26, p. 27.

Villafranca, Armando. 2000. "Photo causes new sentencing for murderer," *Houston Chronicle*, December 7, p. 1.

Teachey, Lisa. 2002. "Jury sends man back to death row for slaying," *Houston Chronicle*, September 7, p. 35.

Turner, Allan. 2014. "Courts Justices reject Houston killer's appeal," *Houston Chronicle* (TX), June 10, p. 1.

Appendix 2

We used the Baldus data to test three core geometrical propositions:

- Downward law is greater than upward law
- Law varies directly with social status
- Law increases with social distance

   Here, we provide methodological details for the interested reader (including the information needed to replicate our statistical models). Consider the data, measures, and findings.

   The Baldus data are a hybrid – part random sample, part population. Specifically, the CSS includes a stratified random sample of 1,066 defendants selected from the population of 2,483 defendants who were convicted of murder or voluntary manslaughter in Georgia between 1973 and 1979 (Baldus, Woodworth, and Pulaski 1990: 2–3, 45–46, 67–68, footnote 10). Given the stratified random sample, the researchers used inverse probability sampling weights (each case "counts" as the reciprocal of its probability of being included in the sample; if, for example, a defendant had a 1 in 3 chance of being included in the sample, then the defendant counts as three cases). Once the sampling weights are applied, the number of cases in the sample equals the number of cases in the population (allowing the estimation of population parameters) (Woodworth 1983; Baldus, Woodworth, and Pulaski 1990: 67–68, footnote 10).

   Importantly, the CSS includes the population of defendants who were sentenced to death – *the complete census of 128 condemned defendants.*[15] Baldus modified the "strict probability" research design to "...ensure full coverage of death-sentence cases" (Baldus, Woodworth, and Pulaski 1990: 429).

   The hybrid nature of the data necessitates a brief discussion of statistical significance. Statistical significance does not signify whether a relationship is "big" or "important" (Wasserstein and Lazar 2016). Instead, tests of statistical significance indicate the probability (p-value) of observing a relationship in a random sample if no relationship exists in the population (Morrison and Henkel 1970).[16] To illustrate the meaning of statistical significance, consider Baldus's original findings regarding race. Baldus found a strong relationship between victim race and sentencing in the random sample: 11% of the defendants convicted of killing a White victim were sentenced to death, compared to just 1% of the defendants convicted of killing a Black victim. The *p*-value for the model was less than 0.001. Thus, the chance of finding such a substantial difference in the random sample if no difference existed in the population is less than 0.1%. Based on such a miniscule *p*-value, Baldus rejected the null hypothesis. Put simply, Baldus rejected the notion that victim race and the imposition of a death sentence are unrelated in the population. Nonetheless, a Type I error – rejecting a null hypothesis that is true – remains possible. The chance that Baldus drew a misleading random sample from a population in which no difference exists is close to zero, but not zero (a *p*-value cannot be zero because sampling error is always possible) (Fox 1995).

Indeed, a researcher can only be *certain* that observed differences are real if one has data on the entire population (Fox 1995). Here, we have data on the population of defendants who were sentenced to death in the place and period in question. Because our execution models examine the fate of *all* the condemned defendants, we can be certain that any observed patterns are real (as opposed to the product of sampling error) (Cowger 1985; Anderson 2019).

The above discussion leads to the following conclusion: if an analysis examines a random sample of cases, then reporting tests of statistical significance is appropriate; if an analysis examines an entire population of cases, then reporting tests of statistical significance is inappropriate (Cowger 1984; Fox 1995; Engman 2013).[17] Accordingly, we report statistical significance for models based on Baldus's sample data (the stratified random sample of 1,066 cases weighted to 2,483 cases). But we do not report statistical significance for models based on Baldus's population data (the census of 128 condemned defendants). In the models based on population data – the execution models – we simply focus on the strength of the empirical patterns (Bollen 1995).

Having described the hybrid nature of the data and the implication for tests of statistical significance, we turn to how we operationalized the theoretical concepts. To measure the location and direction of a case in social space, we identified parallel indicators of the defendant's social status and the victim's social status (the indicators in the CSS are dichotomous; a code of 1 denotes higher status). Using parallel indicators provides a common scale of status for the defendant and victim – a consistent yardstick. Table 2.2 describes our measurement strategy in detail (Baldus's variable names are listed in CAPS with recoding instructions in parentheses). The highest status defendants and victims: had a professional job (wealth) or worked as a state official including firefighters, police officers, corrections officers, and active duty military personnel (capacity for collective action); were parents supporting children (integration in social life); were White (conventionality);[18] and had a clean criminal record (respectability).

TABLE 2.2 Indicators of Social Status[1]

Dimensions of Social Status

Vertical	*Radial*	*Cultural*	*Normative*	*Organizational*
Definition				
Wealth	Integration in Social Life	Conventionality	Respectability	Capacity for Collective Action

Measurement: Defendant Social Status with Baldus's Indicators in CAPS (recode instructions)

Vertical	*Radial*	*Cultural*	*Normative*	*Organizational*
Professional Job	Parent Supporting Child	White	Clean Record	State Official
LDF61	LDF49	DOC33	LDF80	LDF61
(1 – 4 = 1, 8 – 10 = 1, else = 0)	(1 – 2 = 1, else = 0)	(1 = 1, else = 0)	(3 – 4 = 1, else = 0)	(5 – 7 = 1, else = 0)
EJDP, pp. 517–518	EJDP, p. 517	EJDP, p. 512	EJDP, p. 519	EJDP, pp. 517–518

Measurement: Victim Social Status with Baldus's Indicators in CAPS (recode instructions)[2]

Vertical	*Radial*	*Cultural*	*Normative*	*Organizational*
Professional Job	Parent Supporting Child	White	Clean Record	State Official
LDF112	LDF169	WHVICRC[3]	LDF296	LDF112
(1 – 4 = 1, 8 – 10 = 1, else = 0)	(1 – 2 = 1, else = 0)	(no recode)	(1 – 2 = 0, else = 1)	(5 – 7 = 1, else = 0)
EJDP, p. 522	EJDP, p. 527	EJDP, p. 522	EJDP, pp. 534–535	EJDP, p. 522

Notes:

1 EJDP refers to Baldus, Woodworth, and Pulaski's (1990) book: *Equal Justice and the Death Penalty*.

2 In a case with multiple victims, indicators were coded as 1 if any victim had the characteristic in question (see Codebook page 53A for information on multiple victim cases).

3 In the CSS, the race of the victim is missing in a small number of cases. To address the problem, Baldus assumed the crimes were intra-racial (EJDP, page 456; codebook page 90). We used Baldus's recoded variable for victim race (the variable used in Baldus's core model in *McCleskey v. Kemp*) (EJDP, page 320).

The social status of the defendant is defined as the sum of the defendant's status indicators. Defendant status ranged from 0 to 4 with a mean of 1.0032. Thus, defendants who scored 0 or 1 were coded as lower status (below the mean) and defendants who scored 2, 3, or 4 were coded as higher status (above the mean).

Using the same approach, the social status of the victim is defined as the sum of the victim's status indicators. Victim status ranged from 0 to 4 with a mean of 1.6259. Thus, victims who scored 0 or 1 were coded as lower status (below the mean) and victims who scored 2, 3, or 4 were coded as higher status (above the mean).

Next, we determined the location and direction of each case in social space:

* Downward law: higher status victim, lower status defendant
* Lateral law, high: higher status victim, higher status defendant
* Lateral law, low: lower status victim, lower status defendant
* Upward law: lower status victim, higher status defendant

Table 2.3, Panel A, examines whether the location and direction of a case in social space influences death sentences. The pattern supports Black's theoretical prediction: downward cases are more likely than upward cases to end in a death sentence; lateral high cases are more likely than lateral low cases to end in a death sentence. Specifically:

TABLE 2.3 Death Sentences by Social Geometry ($n = 2,483$)

	Death Sentences	
	Number	Percent
Panel A: Location and Direction in Social Space[1]		
Downward Law	78/734	10.6%
Lateral Law, High	35/482	7.3%
Lateral Law, Low	13/1,095	1.2%
Upward Law	2/172	1.2%
Panel B: Relational Distance[2][3]		
Strangers	74/448	16.5%
Non-Strangers	54/2,034	2.7%

Notes:
1 $p < 0.001$; chi-square = 63.747 with 3 DF (percentages are based on the weighted data, but chi-square is based on the unweighted data because it assumes independent observations).
2 $p < 0.001$; chi-square = 107.395 with 1 DF (percentages are based on the weighted data, but chi-square is based on the unweighted data because it assumes independent observations).
3 The number of cases sums to 2,482 because the sampling weights produce rounding error.

- 11% (78/734) of downward cases resulted in a death sentence, compared to 1% (2/172) of upward cases
- 7% (35/482) of lateral high cases resulted in a death sentence, compared to 1% (13/1,095) of lateral low cases ($p < 0.001$)[19,20]

Table 2.3, Panel B, examines whether relational distance influences death sentences.[21] Again, the pattern supports geometrical theory:

- 17% (74/448) of cases between strangers ended in a death sentence, compared to 3% (54/2,034) of cases between non-strangers ($p < 0.001$)[22]

Does support for Black's theory of law remain after controlling for confounding variables regarding the defendant's culpability, the evidence in the case, and the year of the conviction (to account for unmeasured temporal patterns)?[23] Odds ratios from the weighted logistic regression of death sentences on social geometry are presented in Table 2.4. Model 1 shows that the odds of a death sentence were

TABLE 2.4 Odds Ratios from the Weighted Logistic Regression of Death Sentences on Social Geometry ($n = 2,483$)

	Model 1: Odds Ratio	Model 2: Odds Ratio
Location and Direction in Social Space		
Downward Law	7.5*	5.7***
Lateral Law, High	6.3*	4.8***
Lateral Law, Low	1.3	Comparison Group
Upward Law	Comparison Group	0.76
Relational Distance		
Strangers	4.7***	4.7***
Controls (Baldus variable name)		
Defendant deliberated (DTHINK)	5.9***	5.9***
Defendant did not kill (NOKILL)	0.46	0.46
# types of evidence against defendant (EVINDX2)	4.4***	4.4***
Sentenced 1974 (LDF4B)	4.7	4.7
Sentenced 1975 (LDF4B)	4.1	4.1
Sentenced 1976 (LDF4B)	6.2*	6.2*
Sentenced 1977 (LDF4B)	5.6	5.6
Sentenced 1978 (LDF4B)	4.7	4.7
Sentenced 1979 (LDF4B)	5.2	5.2
Sentenced 1980 (LDF4B)	4.3	4.3

Note:
The reference category for year is 1973.
*$p < 0.05$; **$p < 0.01$; ***$p < 0.001$

7.5 times greater in downward cases than upward cases ($p < 0.05$). Model 2 shows that the odds of a death sentence were 4.8 times greater in lateral high cases than lateral low cases ($p < 0.001$).[24] Turning to relational distance, the odds of a death sentence were 4.7 times greater if the defendant and victim were strangers ($p < 0.001$).

In Table 2.5, we focus exclusively on downward cases ($n = 734$). In all the downward cases, the victim's status is higher than the defendant's status. But the gap – vertical distance – can be smaller or larger. As vertical distance expands, so too should the chance of a death sentence. Black notes: "Downward law varies directly with vertical distance" (1976: 24). We measured vertical distance as follows: victim status minus defendant status. If the victim's status was just one unit greater than the defendant's status, then 4% (17/422) of the cases resulted in a death sentence. But if the victim's status was two units greater, then 16% (39/248) of the defendants were condemned. And if the victim's status was three (or more) units greater, 34% (22/64) of the defendants were sent to death row ($p < 0.001$).[25]

Continuing the focus on downward cases, Table 2.6 examines whether the effect of vertical distance on death sentences remains after controlling for confounding variables. The weighted logistic regression model indicates that each unit-increase in downward distance more than doubles the odds of a death sentence ($p < 0.01$).

We now turn from death sentences to executions.[26] Narrowing our gaze to the subset of condemned defendants, did social geometry influence who was executed? Table 2.7, Panel A, considers the location and direction of a case in social space. Supporting Black's theoretical prediction, downward cases were more apt to produce an execution than upward cases: 22% (16/73) versus 0% (0/2). Also, lateral high cases were more apt to produce an execution than lateral low cases: 25% (8/32) versus 0% (0/13). Panel B shows that defendants who killed a stranger were about twice as likely as those who killed a non-stranger to be executed: 25% (17/67) versus 13% (7/53).

TABLE 2.5 Death Sentences by Downward Distance ($n = 734$)

	Death Sentences	
	Number	*Percent*
Vertical Distance[1]		
Victim Higher in Social Status by One Unit	17/422	4.0%
Victim Higher in Social Status by Two Units	39/248	15.7%
Victim Higher in Social Status by Three (or more) Units[2]	22/64	34.4%

Notes:

1 $p < 0.001$; chi-square = 40.281 with 2 DF (percentages are based on the weighted data, but chi-square is based on the unweighted data because it assumes independent observations).

2 In three cases, the victim was higher in social status by four units. A death sentence was imposed in two of the three cases.

TABLE 2.6 Odds Ratios from the Weighted Logistic Regression of Death Sentences on Downward Distance ($n = 734$)

	Odds Ratio
Vertical Distance and Relational Distance	
Downward Distance	2.3**
Strangers	6.0***
Controls (Baldus variable name)	
Defendant deliberated (DTHINK)	9.5***
Defendant did not kill (NOKILL)	0.11*
Number of types of evidence against defendant (EVINDX2)	5.2***
Sentenced 1974 (LDF4B)	12.4*
Sentenced 1975 (LDF4B)	5.1
Sentenced 1976 (LDF4B)	14.0*
Sentenced 1977 (LDF4B)	14.1*
Sentenced 1978 (LDF4B)	13.3*
Sentenced 1979 (LDF4B)	12.9*
Sentenced 1980 (LDF4B)	12.7*

Note:
The reference category for year is 1973.
*$p < 0.05$; **$p < 0.01$; ***$p < 0.001$

TABLE 2.7 Executions by Social Geometry ($n = 120$)

	Executions	
	Number	Percent
Panel A: Location and Direction in Social Space		
Downward Law	16/73	21.9%
Lateral Law, High	8/32	25.0%
Lateral Law, Low	0/13	0.0%
Upward Law	0/ 2	0.0%
Panel B: Relational Distance		
Strangers	17/67	25.4%
Non-Strangers	7/53	13.2%

Note:
We do not present tests of statistical significance because the calculation is based on population data.

Notes

1 Information about the Robin Owers and Nancy Adleman cases comes from newspaper articles in the Houston Chronicle (see the sections Sources for the Robin Owers Case and Sources for the Nancy Adleman Case).

2 It is also appropriate to analyze the dimensions of social status separately provided the data allow the researcher to disentangle the dimensions. But such data are likely to be rare: people who are high status on one dimension tend to be high status on all the

dimensions, and those who are low status on one dimension tend to be low status on all the dimensions. In the Baldus data, of the 159 victims who had a professional job, 154 had a clean criminal record. Consequently, the victim's vertical status and normative status cannot be separated. Analyzing the dimensions of social status separately is appropriate from a theoretical perspective but often challenging from a practical perspective.

3 Table 2.2 (Appendix 2) provides additional details about the indicators we used to measure victim and defendant status.

4 In the past, homicide was found more often at all status levels (see Cooney 1997).

5 Black (1979) proposes that the quantity of law can be measured by the degree to which people will take steps to avoid it. Although an occasional defendant might choose death over life imprisonment, the vast majority choose life and will go to great lengths to avoid death. Of the 1,505 defendants put to death in the United States from 1977 to the present, only 149 dropped all their appeals and volunteered to be executed (https://deathpenaltyinfo.org/; last updated November 7, 2019).

6 Note that the comparison between upward cases and lateral low cases is inconsistent with the four-fold status pattern, as both have the same chance of a death sentence at 1%.

7 See Appendix 2 for additional details.

8 See Table 2.4 in Appendix 2 for additional details.

9 See further Appendix 2, Table 2.5.

10 See further Appendix 2, Table 2.6.

11 See further Appendix 2, Table 2.7.

12 See further Appendix 2, Table 2.7.

13 More details about the Baldus study can be found in Appendix 2.

14 Information about the social characteristics of the parties is derived from Phillips's Houston study and the Library Edition of Ancestry.com.

15 Baldus's original weighted data include 2,484 defendants of whom 128 were sentenced to death (Baldus, Woodworth, and Pulaski 1990: 314–315, table 50). However, closer inspection of the data revealed that 127 defendants were sentenced to death (Baldus, Woodworth, and Pulaski 1990: 45). The slight discrepancy occurred because 122 of the condemned defendants were weighted as one case and five of the condemned defendants were weighted as 1.2 cases: (122*1) + (5*1.2) = 128. Because the Baldus data include the population of defendants who were sentenced to death, weights are unnecessary for the condemned defendants. Thus, we weighted each condemned defendant as one case (meaning the condemned defendants are not weighted). After adjusting the weight from 1.2 to 1.0 for the five cases in question (515, 516, 593, Z24, Z26), the data include 2,483 defendants of whom 127 were sentenced to death (Baldus's original weighting variable is CASEWGT; our adjusted weighting variable is CASE_WEIGHT_ADJUSTED). We also discovered that the Baldus team miscoded death sentence (DSENTALL) in one case: Edward Ward (case 250). The Baldus team coded Ward as a life sentence. But Ward was ultimately sentenced to death for the murders of Edward Surgalski and Sharon Denise. The coding error is understandable, as the case took several twists and turns. In the initial trial, Ward received a life sentence. After the conviction was overturned, the second trial ended in a hung jury and the third trial ended in a death sentence. In Ward's case, we changed the code for DSENTALL from 0 to 1. Thus, the total number of death sentences climbs back to 128. For details on Edward Ward's case, see: Stewart, Jim. April 17, 1976. "Convicted Killer Ward Is Sentenced to Die." *The Atlanta Journal Constitution*, page 2A.

16 In technical language, tests of statistical significance indicate the probability of producing a sample statistic as extreme as (or more extreme than) the observed sample statistic if the null hypothesis (no relationship in the population) is true.

17 Some have suggested that reporting tests of statistical significance is appropriate for population data, as the population can be conceptualized as "a random sample from a hypothetically infinite universe of possibilities" (Blalock 1970: 270). Morrison and Henkel (1970: 190) disagree: "Are some or all of the specific benefits of probability sampling available regardless of whether the sample is a probability sample? We doubt it." Setting the theoretical debate aside, we are not interested in a hypothetically infinite universe of possibilities. Rather, we are interested in what actually happened to the defendants who were sentenced to death in the place and period in question. We do not attempt to generalize beyond the defendants in question.

18 During our research, we discovered that the Baldus team miscoded the race of the victim (WHVICRC) in the case of William Hance (defendant D51). Thus, we changed the code for WHVICRC from 0 to 1 in the Hance case. For a detailed discussion, see Phillips and Marceau 2020.

19 The crosstabulation in Table 2.3, Panel A, is 4x2 (four categories describing the location and direction of a case in social space, predicting whether the case ended in a life sentence or a death sentence). Because chi-square provides an omnibus test of statistical significance, the p value indicates the probability of committing a Type I error if one rejects the null hypothesis of equal treatment across groups (Franke et al. 2012). The p value does not indicate whether specific differences are significant. But the logistic regression model in Table 2.4 does provide p values for specific comparisons (Model 1 compares downward cases to upward cases, and Model 2 compares lateral high cases to lateral low cases).

20 If we remove race from the measure of social geometry, the pattern is the same: 14.3% (28/196) of downward cases resulted in a death sentence, compared to 6.7% (27/404) of lateral high cases, 4.1% (40/969) of lateral low cases, and 3.6% of upward cases (33/915). The p value is < 0.001.

21 To measure relational distance, we used Baldus's variable STRANGER (1 = victim is a stranger, 0 = not).

22 The omnibus nature of the chi-square test of statistical significance does not pose a concern in Table 2.3, Panel B. Here, only two groups are being compared: strangers and non-strangers.

23 In the Baldus data, the variable for date of sentencing is LDF4B. The date of sentencing was missing in two cases: defendant 773 and defendant E15. But the date of the offense was included for both cases: July 1, 1977 and September 20, 1979, respectively. Among the defendants who committed an offense on/after July 1 of a given year, the majority were sentenced the following year. Thus, we assumed that defendant 773 was sentenced in 1978 and defendant E15 was sentenced in 1980.

24 If we remove race from the measure of social geometry, the odds ratios attenuate but remain substantial and significant. Specifically: the odds of a death sentence were 3.3 times greater in downward cases than upward cases (p < 0.01); the odds of a death sentence were 1.8 times greater in lateral high cases than lateral low cases (p < 0.10).

25 See note 19 for a discussion of chi-square as an omnibus test of statistical significance. Table 2.6 examines the effect of a one-unit change in downward distance on death sentences, a statistically significant relationship.

26 In our data, the variable for execution is EXECUTION.

References

Anderson, Andrew A. 2019. "Assessing Statistical Results: Magnitude, Precision, and Model Uncertainty." *The American Statistician* 73:118–121.

Baldus, David C., George Woodworth, and Charles A. Pulaski. 1990. *Equal Justice and the Death Penalty: A Legal and Empirical Analysis.* Boston: Northeastern University Press.

Black, Donald. 1976. *The Behavior of Law.* New York: Academic Press.

Black, Donald. 1979. "A Note on the Measurement of Law." *Informationsbrief für Rechtssoziologie Sonderheft* 2:92–106.

Black, Donald. 1989. *Sociological Justice.* New York: Oxford University Press.

Black, Donald. 1995. "The Epistemology of Pure Sociology." *Law and Social Inquiry* 20:829–870.

Black, Donald. 2000. "Dreams of Pure Sociology." *Sociological Theory* 18:343–367.

Black, Donald. 2004. "The Geometry of Terrorism." *Sociological Theory* 22:14–25.

Black, Donald. 2018. "Domestic Violence and Social Time." *DILEMAS: Revista de Estudos de Conflito e Controle Social* 11:1–27.

Blalock, Hubert M. 1970. *Social Statistics.* New York: McGraw-Hill.

Bollen, Kenneth A. 1995. "Apparent and Nonapparent Significance Tests." *Sociological Methodology* 25:459–468.

Cooney, Mark. 1997. "The Decline of Elite Homicide." *Criminology* 35:381–407.

Cooney, Mark. 1998. *Warriors and Peacemakers: How Third Parties Shape Violence.* New York: New York University Press.

Cowger, Charles D. 1984. "Statistical Significance Tests: Scientific Ritualism or Scientific Method?" *Social Service Review* 58:358–372.

Cowger, Charles D. 1985. "Author's Reply." *Social Service Review* 59:520–522.

Engman, Athena. 2013. "Is There Life After P < 0.05? Statistical Significance and Quantitative Sociology." *Quality and Quantity* 47:257–270.

Fox, William. 1995. *Social Statistics: An Introduction Using Microcase.* Bellevue, Washington: MicroCase Corporation.

Franke, Todd Michael, Timothy Ho, and Christina A. Christie. 2012. "The Chi-Square Test: Often Used and More Often Misinterpreted." *American Journal of Evaluation* 33:448–458.

Morrison, Denton E. and Ramon E. Henkel. 1970. "Significance Tests Reconsidered." Pp. 182–198 in *The Significance Test Controversy: A Reader,* edited by Denton E. Morrison and Ramon E. Henkel. Chicago: Aldine Publishing Company.

Phillips, Scott. 2009. "Status Disparities in the Capital of Capital Punishment." *Law and Society Review* 43:807–837.

Phillips, Scott and Justin Marceau. 2020. "Whom the State Kills." *Harvard Civil Rights – Civil Liberties Law Review* 55:585–656.

Wasserstein, Ronald L. and Nicole A. Lazar. 2016. "The ASA's Statement on *p*-Values: Context, Process, and Purpose." *The American Statistician* 70:129–133.

Woodworth, George G. 1983. "Analysis of a Y Stratified Sample: The Georgia Charging and Sentencing Study." Pp. 18–22 in *Proceedings of the Second Workshop on Law and Justice Statistics.* US Department of Justice, Bureau of Justice Statistics.

3

SOCIAL TIME

Houston, Texas: August 26, 1998

A morning jogger found a dead body in Galena Park. The deceased was 59-year-old Louis "Buddy" Musso. Musso, who was said to have the mind of a 7- or 8-year-old child, had moved to Texas from New Jersey, having been promised by 48-year-old Susan Basso, an ex-security guard, that she would marry him. Once Musso arrived in Houston, Basso shut Musso off from contact with his relatives and friends. She took control of his financial assets, having him sign blank checks and trying to have his social security checks made out to her. She made him sleep on a mattress in the living room of her house and she regularly forced him to kneel naked on a floor mat for long periods, denying him food and water. The abuse escalated. On various occasions, Basso, who weighed over 350 pounds, jumped up and down on Musso as he lay on a mat, used a baseball bat in each hand to beat him on the back and groin, beat him with her hands, a belt, and a vacuum cleaner attachment, and encouraged her adult son to kick him while wearing heavy combat boots. Several times, she had her son bathe Musso in a bath filled with bleach, cleaning fluids, and alcohol and then scrub him with a wire brush. Musso had a $15,000 life insurance policy with a clause that provided for an additional payout of $50,000 if he died of violence. Twelve days before he died, Musso signed a will leaving his property to Basso.

Basso and her son were close friends with four other people. The group would regularly beat Musso for various infractions, such as moving too slowly or not finishing his chores. When they went to a restaurant, they would handcuff Musso and leave him in the car. A neighbor reported seeing Musso with a black eye and blood on his shirt, but he had said, "don't call nobody because they'll beat me up again."[1] A few days before Musso died, Basso and her son were at the apartment

DOI: 10.4324/9781003176633-4

of the four friends when Musso accidentally broke a Mickey Mouse ornament. All six people started beating Musso with bats, belts, and fists, all over his body. This continued on and off for several days. By the time they were finished, Musso had, according to the autopsy report, a fractured skull, two dislocated vertebrae, eight right and six left broken ribs, at least 28 cuts and cigarette burns on his back, at least 17 cuts on his head, and multiple bruises on his testicles, anus, chest, and abdomen as well as on his arms and hands and legs and toes. After they dumped the body in a ditch in Galena Park, Basso reported Musso missing and gave the police his photograph. When the police discovered the body, they were unable to identify the victim because of the profusion of cuts and bruises. The District Attorney charged all six defendants with capital murder but sought the death penalty only against one of them – Basso, judged to have been the principal culprit.

Houston, Texas: September 8, 1998

Michael and Tina McCann had been married for 14 years and had four children together. After Michael had been repeatedly violent toward Tina, she left him, taking the children with her. Despite a restraining order against Michael forbidding him from contacting Tina, he regularly harassed her. On the fateful day, he went to her place of residence and waited for her to return. When she arrived, he blocked her car in the parking lot. Michael brandished a gun and ordered Tina into his car. As Tina attempted to run away, Michael shot her in the back. When a neighbor saw Michael holding Tina by the hair, he tried to intervene but was deterred when Michael pointed the gun at him. Tina managed to make it to the apartment of a friend, Suzanne Smith. Michael shot the lock off the apartment door, nearly hitting Suzanne, and entered. He allowed Suzanne to leave and then held his wife hostage. Suzanne heard Michael tell his wife, "If I can't see my children, you will not either." Bystanders heard another gunshot from inside the apartment. A SWAT team arrived at around 3:15 pm and sought to provide medical assistance to Tina. Michael refused to allow it. The SWAT team then entered the next-door apartment (which was Tina's apartment) and tried to peek through a hole in the wall to see what was happening. Michael shot several times at the wall. The SWAT team eventually stormed the apartment at around 2:15 am the following morning and shot Michael in the leg. They discovered that Tina had been shot in the back and abdomen and had bled to death. The District Attorney charged Michael with capital murder, arguing that he had intentionally committed murder in the course of a burglary, kidnapping, and retaliation.

One of these cases resulted in a death sentence, and one did not. Which one? Looking purely at their social geometry, the answer is not immediately clear. Neither case travels downward in social space, and the defendant and victim are not relationally distant – the geometrical configurations that attract capital punishment. In fact, the Basso case produced the death sentence. That is not surprising, as the killing appears more vicious. While both murders involved acts of considerable violence, the sheer amount of pain and suffering inflicted on Buddy Musso was greater than the pain and suffering inflicted on Tina McCann.[2]

Here we bump up against a limitation of traditional Blackian theory. In *The Behavior of Law* (1976) and some later publications, the conduct of the parties is not part of the explanation. Instead, the theory holds conduct constant – for the same murder, the outcome will vary with the case geometry. But murders are rarely the same and some attract more law than others. The killing of a family of four, for example, will be punished more severely than the killing of a single individual, and a murder accompanied by rape and robbery will be punished more severely than a murder alone. So why does the theory of law not include the obvious variable of the seriousness of criminal conduct? This issue arose in the first major test of Black's theory.

Three years after the appearance of *The Behavior of Law*, a pair of well-known criminologists, Michael Gottfredson and Michael Hindelang (1979a), published a test of the theory in the premier sociology journal, *The American Sociological Review*. For data, they relied on the National Crime Survey (NCS).[3] The NCS samples some 60,000 households. Members of the households who are 12 years or older are interviewed twice a year for three years. The survey asks the respondents about themselves (age, sex, race, marital status, etc.), whether they have been a victim in the last six months of any of a list of crimes, and, if so, whether they notified the police. Using data from 1974 to 1976, the authors reported that their measures of social geometrical variables had only a weak impact on whether crimes were reported to the police. For example, stranger victimizations were only slightly more likely to be reported to the police than nonstranger victimizations (48% versus 42%) (1979a: 8). Gottfredson and Hindelang found instead that crimes were more likely to be reported to the police when they were more serious. They went on to argue that "an adequate theory of the behavior of criminal law must incorporate a proposition stating that the quantity of criminal law varies directly with the seriousness of the infraction" (1979a: 16).

Seriousness and Science

Black (1979) responded to the paper, saying that it had two major flaws (see also Black 2010: 40–42). The first was the limitation of testing the theory with data from a single stage of the legal process, such as the decision to call the police. This is an important scholarly issue, but it takes us away from the issue of seriousness.[4]

Black's second point was that Gottfredson and Hindelang's criticism – that the seriousness of the offense is a better predictor of the behavior of law – makes no scientific sense. Whether conduct is "serious" depends on the subjective opinion of the person evaluating it. As such, seriousness is a value judgment, not a fact, and hence beyond the reach of science. Gottfredson and Hindelang apparently accepted the common-sense notion that some acts simply *are* more serious than others. They used a measure of crime seriousness created by two highly respected criminologists, Thorsten Sellin and Marvin Wolfgang (1964). The measure was based on a survey of middle-class people: juvenile court judges, police officers, juvenile bureau officers, and university students. Sellin and Wolfgang (1964: 381–386) asked the survey respondents to rate the seriousness of a list of behaviors (e.g., "The defendant stabs a person to death." "The defendant robs a victim of $1,000 at gunpoint." "The defendant wounds a person with a blunt instrument. The victim requires no medical treatment." "The defendant possesses heroin."). Those ratings proved highly consistent: people generally rated killing to be more serious than minor injury, for instance. The authors then created an index of event seriousness ranked from zero (e.g., no injury) to 26 (victim killed) (1964: 298).

The flaw, Black points out, is that the seriousness scale inevitably incorporated the subjective moral opinion of the respondents. Indeed, that was baked into the instructions given to the respondents before filling out the questionnaire: "Your task is to show how serious *you* think each violation is" (1964: 254; emphasis in original). However consistent the ratings are from person to person or even from country to country, they rest on nothing more solid than the opinions of the respondents.[5] As Black (1979: 24) succinctly puts it, the survey "objectively portrays the subjectivity of their respondents."

Other possible ways of defining seriousness run into the same problem of subjectivity. To gauge seriousness by the punishment attached to particular crimes, for example, is simply to rely on the subjective moral values of the people who assigned those punishments. When virtually all legislators were men, relatively lenient punishments attached to crimes committed predominately by men against women, such as domestic violence, sexual assault, and sexual harassment. As more women have become lawmakers, those same acts now carry more severe punishments. Similarly, to declare that some conduct is more serious because it is more harmful to people or society does not eliminate the problem either. Many, perhaps most, people in Western countries once held that adultery, homosexuality, and interracial marriage were morally dangerous to those who engaged in them and to their society. Nowadays increasingly few do. Conversely, some conduct once considered unexceptional, even desirable, such as spanking children, is increasingly treated as harmful ("child abuse"). "Harmfulness," "dangerousness," and related concepts are not objective properties of conduct. They are labels applied to conduct that often differ considerably from one time or place to another. Harmfulness is, to a significant degree, in the eye of the beholder (see also Warr 1989: 812–817).

Seriousness, then, turns out to be a serious problem: some acts consistently attract more law than others, yet we cannot explain why without invoking subjective values. We know that a homicide committed in the course of a robbery is treated as more serious than a homicide committed in the course of a fight. But why is it more serious, apart from people thinking it so? In his response to Gottfredson and Hindelang, Black (1979: 25) acknowledged that "more work is needed on the problem of conduct itself … [T]he fact remains that, under given conditions, some conduct is handled as more 'serious' than other conduct." However, "the question is how this is to be understood in a theoretical framework" (1979: 24, note 12). Black granted that it might be possible to create a purely fact-based concept of seriousness, though he did not downplay the challenge involved in doing so. Indeed, coming up with a scientific conception of conduct seriousness probably requires, he argued, a revolution in how we understand human behavior:

> Simply to designate conduct … as more "serious" does not explain any-thing, however, but only begs the question of why it is handled as more "serious." Before this problem can be solved, it is likely that conduct itself will have to be understood in an entirely different way.
>
> *Black 1979: 25*

After this exchange, scholarly life went ahead pretty much as before. Most legal sociologists who worked on the handling of cases adopted a pragmatic position, including both legal variables (e.g., what the parties did) and extra-legal variables (e.g., who the parties were) in their analyses (see e.g., Myers and Hagan 1979; Nagel 1982–1983). Doing so, they typically found that each set of variables helped to predict the outcome of cases. That was fine from a purely practical point of view. But it was not satisfying theoretically. Like oil and water, the legal variables and extra-legal variables did not mix. Still elusive was that new way of thinking about conduct that Black mentioned. Seriousness remained a substantial gap in the theory of law.

Until 2011. That year, some three decades later, Black published *Moral Time*, a book that claimed to provide a solution, a novel way of thinking about seriousness that was purely factual, a breakthrough that transformed seriousness from a moral justification to an empirical explanation of legal penalties. The solution is based upon a new conception of human behavior in general, the key to which is the idea of "social time."

Social Time

Social time is the dynamic aspect of social geometry. Just as physical time can be understood as a change in physical space (e.g., the orbit of the earth around the sun), so social time is a change in social space. Social time moves whenever social space fluctuates – when people marry or divorce, make money or go bankrupt, get hired or fired, become ill or recover, join or leave a religion, adopt or criticize an idea, and so forth. Social time never stands still – people's circumstances are constantly altering, however slightly. The movement of social time is unceasing yet variable. Most movements of social time are small and barely noticeable, but some are large and historic (e.g., revolutions). Large or small, movements of social time matter because they underlie a central feature of human existence: conflict.

A conflict is a clash of right and wrong (Black 2011: 3). It occurs whenever someone defines someone else's behavior as impolite, inappropriate, immoral, or even illegal – in short, as wrong.[6] Black's previous work addresses the response to conflict – whether someone takes no action, gossips, files a lawsuit, ostracizes or fights the wrongdoer, and so on. It does not explain the cause of conflict. Nor could it. The original idea of social geometry is static – a snapshot of the location and direction of the parties in social space. As such, it cannot account for a dynamic event like the emergence of conflict. It takes a change to explain a change. The new concept of social time allowed Black to address the central issue of why conflict occurs in the first place: "the fundamental cause of conflict is the movement of social time" (2011: 4).

Movements of Social Time

Social time has three primary dimensions: vertical, relational, and cultural. *Vertical time* is any behavior or event that alters inequality in any dimension of social space, such as an increase or decrease in wealth, health, organizational standing, reputation, or position of authority. Slandering a peer, for example, increases inequality (as the peer's reputation falls, equality is replaced by inequality); disrespecting a boss decreases inequality (as the boss's reputation falls, a prior status gap shrinks). Both cause conflict.

Relational time is any change in relational space or intimacy, such as an increase or decrease in friendship, attention, or privacy. Departing from the common, psychological conception of intimacy as warmth and affection, Black defines intimacy sociologically, as involvement in the life of another. Thus, trespassing onto a stranger's property, for example, increases intimacy (more involvement); abandoning one's family decreases intimacy (less involvement). Both cause conflict.

Cultural time is any change in cultural space or diversity such as an increase or decrease in the number of languages, religions, or ethnicities. Immigration, for example, increases diversity; deporting immigrants decreases diversity. Both cause conflict.

Each of these movements of social time is a matter of degree – a quantitative variable. The larger and faster the movement of social time, the more conflict it causes. Small and slow movements of social time tend to be mild transgressions, while large and fast movements are more serious offenses. Consider relational time. Staring, touching, stalking, and sexual assault all increase physical intimacy. Yet although they belong to the same family of wrongdoing, they represent different amounts of relational time and trigger different amounts of conflict. While staring is usually just a mild form of invasive rudeness, touching somebody is a greater intrusion and technically a crime, though rarely prosecuted. Stalking is a still greater incursion into someone's life and more likely to be reported to the police, investigated, and charged. Sexual assault, an even larger violation of bodily integrity, is a grave crime that can lead to lengthy prison sentences.[7]

Just as changes in social space cause conflict, so conflict causes changes in social space. Conflict may reduce a person's wealth (e.g., paying fines or damages), intimacy (e.g., losing friendships), and diversity (e.g., being fired from a job in a diverse workplace).

Importantly, movements of social time depend not just on what is done, but who does it to whom. The same action is a greater movement of social time among some parties than others. Since a law-abiding citizen has more reputation to lose than a criminal, to be accused of a crime is a greater loss of status (a larger movement of vertical time) for a person with a clean record than one with a criminal record. Since a stranger is less intimate than a spouse, touching a stranger crosses more relational distance (a larger movement of relational time) than touching a spouse. And since people in foreign lands are generally more culturally distant than people in one's own land, relocating to a different continent introduces more diversity (a larger movement of cultural time) than relocating to a different part of the same country.

The theory of moral time, then, incorporates social geometry – the status and relationship of the parties. This means that the new theory can explain some of the patterns predicted by the original geometrical theory. Why does law increase with relational distance? The older theory has no answer: that is just how law behaves. By contrast, the theory of moral time provides an explanation for at least some of the facts predicted by the earlier theory. For example, the original theory correctly predicts that rape by a stranger will be punished more severely than rape by an intimate (see, e.g., Estrich 1987; Tasca et al. 2012). The newer theory goes further and explains why: since the rape of a stranger crosses more relational distance than does the rape of an intimate, it is a larger movement of relational time and hence a more serious offense (Black 2015: 388).[8]

To support his new theory, Black cited a vast body of secondary research. *Moral Time* discusses murder, adultery, witchcraft, incest, heresy, lynching, robbery, nudity, trespass, genocide, rioting, theft, homosexuality, rudeness, mental illness, racism, terrorism, masturbation, lying, rape, secrecy, desertion, resistance to innovation, war, and much more. He draws on data from the distant past and the immediate present, from the simplest to the most complex societies, and from every corner of the globe. His theory applies to the conflicts of individuals, groups, corporations, countries, and civilizations. For Black, the movement of social time explains moral time or, more simply, conflict.

Applying the Theory

Black's theory of moral time has inspired a number of scholars to develop theories of particular types of conflict. Bradley Campbell (2013) argues that genocide (mass ethnic killing) is typically preceded by the clash of cultural groups (cultural time) and a decline, actual or threatened, in the superiority of a high-status ethnic group (vertical time). Jason Manning (2015) proposes that most suicides are triggered by the loss of a close relationship (relational time) or by the loss of status (vertical time). A movement of vertical time – a challenge to the authority of the patriarchal, collective, and gerontocratic family – is the precipitator of family honor violence, according to Mark Cooney (2014). Extending his theory to domestic violence,

Black (2018) argues that the most common causes of physical force between individuals who live together as a couple are movements of relational time (e.g., adultery) and vertical time (e.g., putting a partner down through insults).

Black's theory of moral time can illuminate divisive social issues that drive the daily news cycle. For pro-life activists, abortion is a movement of vertical and relational time – a murderous rejection of the unborn (abortion stops a beating heart). For pro-choice activists, criminalizing abortion is a movement of vertical and relational time – a degrading restriction of freedom (my body, my choice). Advocating socialism in a capitalist country is promoting a movement of vertical time (the redistribution of wealth) and a movement of cultural time (a different political ideology). But advocating socialism is a response to stark economic inequality, itself a movement of vertical time. Affirmative action is a movement of vertical time (one person's chance of being admitted to a school or hired for a job increases, another person's chance decreases). However, affirmative action is also a response to centuries of discrimination, itself a massive movement of vertical time. People who oppose the teaching of evolution in schools are objecting to a perspective that undermines the traditional religious understanding of the universe; teaching evolution is the rejection of old culture, and therefore a movement of cultural time. Those in favor of teaching evolution are angered by what they see as narrow-minded provincialism; insisting that God created the universe in six days and rested on the seventh is the rejection of new culture, and therefore a movement of cultural time. The theory of moral time has nothing to say about whether abortion, socialism, affirmative action, or evolutionary theory are right or wrong, good or bad, desirable or undesirable. Again, science tells us what is, not what should be. Instead, Black's theory explains why each side is so fervent: extreme movements of social time cause extreme conflicts. Read the newspaper – or Facebook, Twitter, or other social media platforms – and you will find that people who have never heard of social time are nonetheless obsessed with it.

In sum, Black's theory of moral time is audaciously general: social time explains why conflict occurs and how intense it will be. Several sociologists have applied and extended the theory to illuminate the causes of particular types of conflict. But the theory offers more. Social time, Black proposes, explains why deviance is deviant, and why some deviant acts are more deviant than others. Social time explains what morality forbids and which acts are illegal. And, most important for our purposes, social time explains why some criminal conduct attracts more law than other criminal conduct. The greater the movement of social time an act entails the more serious it is. Take, for example, murder.

The Seriousness of Murder

Murder is not a single movement of social time, but several movements. To kill is to deprive a person of their most precious asset – life – and is, as such, a movement of vertical time. Black (2011: 76–78) posits that the human body is a form of wealth, and the most fundamental means of production … Injury and sickness belong to the same family as other fluctuations of wealth. A loss of health is a form of downward mobility, and the greatest decline is death.

If person A is murdered, then A's social standing drops precipitously, drastically increasing inequality between A and other people. But, as we shall see in more detail later, some killings involve even greater slices of vertical time. Anything that magnifies the loss of status increases the movement of vertical time. Killing (or injuring) several victims, for example. Similarly, killing a high-status victim is a greater movement of vertical time because the victim has further to fall and because the killing usually has negative repercussions for a wider range of people: killing a doctor hurts patients; killing a teacher hurts students; killing a lawyer hurts clients; killing a Chief Executive Officer hurts employees; and killing a priest hurts parishioners.

Murder and other forms of violence are, in addition, a movement of relational time. Interpersonal violence (physical force) involves contact with the body of another and thereby increases physical intimacy. As Black states (2011: 23): "Because all physical contact is a form of involvement, it is always a form of intimacy as well. Even violence is a form of intimacy, and all the more when it inflicts pain." Murder, therefore, is a large movement of relational time. Even so, some murders are larger movements of relational time – when they involve additional forms of violent physical contact, such as torturing the victim before death or mutilating the corpse after death. The murder of a stranger is also a greater movement of relational time: a killing crosses more relational distance when the parties have no prior relationship.

And some murders are movements of cultural time. When the killer and the victim belong to different religions, speak different languages, or belong to different nationalities, the murder may be a rejection of the victim's culture.[9]

What about law? Law is a response to conflict, and so it too varies with the movement of social time (Black 2011: 13). The more movements of vertical, relational, and cultural time an act entails, the more law it should attract.

To summarize, *Moral Time* makes big claims. If Black is correct, the abstract concept of social time yields the long-awaited factual concept of seriousness. Seriousness in this view consists of larger and faster movements of social time. The movement of social time is known by the actions of the parties, the relative status of the parties, and the social ties between them. So conceived, assessments of seriousness do not rest on any value judgments. As such, they can be part of a scientific theory of law.

A conceptual breakthrough is one thing; a more powerful theory that works is another. While Black has come up with a novel way of thinking about seriousness – no small intellectual feat – it would be all the more impressive if it strengthens our ability to explain the behavior of law. Does social time do that – does it boost our explanatory power? For an answer, we turn to the data.

The Death Penalty

We first measured the movement of social time in each case. Since we include race as a measure of status, and have no other measures of cultural time, we restrict our analysis to movements of vertical and relational time. Figure 3.1 provides the full list of variables in the Baldus data that indicate changes in vertical space, and the categories in which we have grouped them.

Each of these indicators represents an increase in inequality between the parties occasioned by the murder. Killing multiple victims and injuring additional people are clearly greater movements of vertical time than killing or injuring a single individual. Killing a high-status victim is similarly a greater movement of vertical time – the victim has further to fall and the harm ripples outward. Beyond *devastation*, the defendant might also *dominate* the victim as tends to happen in predatory murders. In contrast to moralistic murders committed in response to an

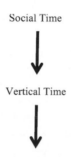

Social Time

Vertical Time

Increase in Inequality between Defendant and Victim

Indicators

Devastation
- Defendant killed multiple victims
- Defendant caused bodily harm to someone besides the murder victim
- Defendant killed high status victim

Domination
- Defendant committed a predatory murder (exploitation in the absence of conflict)
- Defendant subjugated the victim (bound, gagged, killed execution style)

Denigration
- Defendant expressed pleasure regarding the killing

Abuse of Physical Power
- Defendant killed a victim who was vulnerable/defenseless (pregnant, intellectually or physically disabled, bedridden, weak or frail, especially young or old, small or outnumbered, female)

FIGURE 3.1 The Movement of Vertical Time in a Capital Murder

argument or dispute (e.g., intimate partners, gangs), predatory murders are a form of exploitation. Predatory murders are committed for gain or intrinsic satisfaction and entail a greater degree of supremacy over the victim. Examples include murders committed during a robbery or rape, killings to eliminate a witness, and serial killings. A victim who has been bound, gagged, or killed execution style also suffers the indignity of subjugation. A defendant who expresses pleasure at the killing belittles and *denigrates* the victim. Killing a victim who is vulnerable or defenseless is an *abuse of physical power* and thus a greater movement of vertical time (such as killing a victim who is pregnant, intellectually or physically disabled, bedridden, frail, or outnumbered). It also includes female victims.

Research shows that the killing of women elicits more severe punishment than the killing of men (at least in modern Western countries) (see. e.g., Baumer et al. 2000; Cooney 2009: 100–101; Dawson 2016). The Baldus data are consistent: a death sentence was imposed in 7% of cases with female victims compared to just 3% of cases with male victims. But explaining this pattern geometrically was a challenge, as Black explains:

> I once found it difficult to explain why modern American violence by men against women attracts more social control (such as punishment) than violence by women against men, men against men, or women against women. But the theory [of moral time] has allowed me to see that it is because of the greater physical power of men: Because violence by a man against a woman is typically against a physically weaker party, it is an abuse of male power – oversuperiority, a form of overstratification (too much inequality). It belongs to the same sociological family as violence against other physically weaker parties, such as the beating of a child ("child abuse"), an elderly person ("elder abuse"), a smaller peer ("bullying"), or anyone else who is relatively weak and vulnerable (including an injured or disabled person). Also similar is the use of violence against defenseless parties by police officers ("police brutality") or soldiers ("atrocities" or "war crimes").
>
> *2015: 390; citations omitted* [10]

Does vertical time matter in capital cases? Figure 3.2 provides a clear answer: the more movements of vertical time a murder entails, the more likely it is to attract a sentence of death. Among murders that did not involve any additional movement of vertical time – beyond the killing itself – no defendant was sentenced to death. Add additional movements and the probability of a death sentence increases in a step-wise, linear fashion. For murders with five or more total movements of vertical time, the probability of a death sentence jumps to over 40%.

What about relational time? Figure 3.3 displays the variables in the Baldus data that measure additional violations of intimacy, and the categories we use to group them.

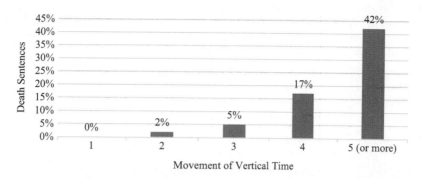

FIGURE 3.2 Death Sentences by the Movement of Vertical Time ($n = 2,483$)

Each indicator of relational time constitutes an additional trespass or invasion. Several are large *violations of bodily integrity* – the victim was raped, sexually defiled, tortured, brutalized, or mutilated. Leaving the victim's body nude is an *invasion of privacy*. Some cases involve *obstructions of movement*, as when the victim is seized, ambushed, or their body is disposed of or hidden. What unites these variables is that they are all further intrusions into the life of the person killed. The intrusion is even more extreme if the victim is a stranger – *a collapse of relational space*.

Figure 3.4 demonstrates the impact these additional movements of relational time have on the probability of a death sentence. The relationship is linear and extremely strong. Among murders that did not involve any additional movement of relational time – beyond the killing itself – less than 1% of defendants were sentenced to death. At the other end, when the murder involves 6 or more total movements of relational time, the chance of a death sentence is better than even.

Clearly, movements of vertical and relational time powerfully influence the outcome of capital cases. But in the real world, cases are not divided up in this way. Police officers, prosecutors, judges, and juries respond instead to the entire case in all its dimensions. Figure 3.5 reveals what happens when we combine relational and vertical time into a single overall movement of social time (by summing the movements).

The results in Figure 3.5 are exceptionally strong. They reveal that when the murder involves no movements of relational or vertical time other than the killing itself, a death sentence is never imposed. As the number of additional movements of social time increases, so does the chance of a death sentence (apart from a slight departure from linearity for seven total movements). At the top end, the most serious murders – those involving ten or more total movements – wind up with a death sentence in 7 out of 10 cases. Social time has the acceleration of a sports car – from 0 to 70 in 10 movements.

Still, it is possible – though unlikely, given their strength – that something else might explain these findings. Perhaps the evidence against the defendant is simply

Social Time

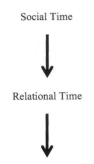

Relational Time

Increase in Intimacy between Defendant and Victim

Indicators

Violation of Bodily Integrity
- Victim raped
- Victim defiled (sexual perversion other than rape)
- Victim tortured (mentally or physically)
- Vitim brutalized (brutal beating, throat slashed, strangled, stabbed multiple times)
- Victim mutilated (body mutilated before or after death)

Invasion of Privacy
- Victim found nude

Obstruction of Movement
- Victim seized (kidnapped or held hostage)
- Victim ambushed (ambushed, defendant lurking)
- Victim body concealed (disposed or hidden)

Collapse of Relational Space
- Victim stranger

FIGURE 3.3 The Movement of Relational Time in a Capital Murder

stronger where the movement of social time is greater. We, therefore, took into account additional potential predictors of the death penalty. Controlling for the number and types of evidence against the defendant, whether the defendant was not the actual killer, whether the defendant deliberated before killing, and the year the sentence was imposed, we found that the odds of a death sentence roughly double with each unit-increase in vertical time, relational time, and the overall movement of social time (see Appendix 3).

Recall that most defendants sentenced to death are not actually executed. Does the movement of social time predict execution? Because the number of executions is too small for an elaborate statistical analysis, and given that execution is likely to be reserved for the most egregious murders, we split the 120 cases into just the least and most extreme. With 11 to 14 movements of social time, the most extreme murders were at least one standard deviation above the mean; see

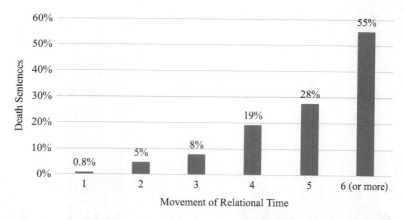

FIGURE 3.4 Death Sentences by the Movement of Relational Time (n = 2,483)

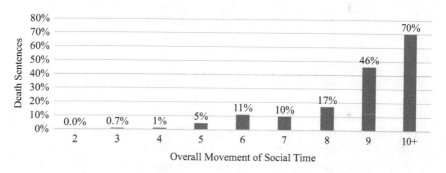

FIGURE 3.5 Death Sentences by the Overall Movement of Social Time (n = 2,483)

Appendix 3. Figure 3.6 reveals a stark difference in outcome with the defendant's risk of being put to death leaping from 1 in 8 of the least extreme cases to 1 in 2 of the most extreme cases.

Online Hostility

To be executed is to experience the most severe punishment our legal system can inflict. But among those who are executed, some may suffer additional sanctions of a non-legal nature. While some murderers are quietly forgotten, others become the object of widespread public criticism and contempt. The leveling of harsh criticism and public scorn against prisoners is facilitated by the Internet, which enables people in faraway places to participate in verbal attacks on death row prisoners. One example is the website Prodeathpenalty.com, an online community composed of supporters of the death penalty. At one time, the website provided a forum for members to post anonymous opinions about executions, upcoming or completed. Other people could then comment on the posts, creating

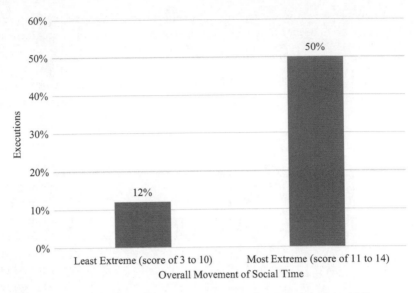

FIGURE 3.6 Executions by the Overall Movement of Social Time ($n = 120$)

a thread. Most threads displayed a high degree of hostility toward the condemned person. They commonly referred to the prisoners as a "turd" or "POS" (piece of shit) and they celebrated imminent executions (e.g., "I have a bottle of really good wine I have been saving for a special occasion. Tonight's the night").[11] Since the prisoners did not have access to the Internet, those barbs and insults were a type of gossip taking place behind their back. But unlike traditional gossip, this electronic gossip was, in principle, both permanent and broadcast to the world at large.

Your present authors, Scott Phillips and Mark Cooney (2015), analyzed the threads relating to 149 Texas executions. We chose Texas primarily because it leads the nation in executions. We included all executions from May 2005, when every case began to generate at least one thread, to November 2012, the final date for which information was available when we did the research. We counted the number of hostile posts, regardless of length, that each execution generated, finding 3,770 in total. For the 149 executions, the number of hostile posts ranged from 2 to 124 with an average of 25. The question we sought to answer was: why do some murders generate so much more hostility among supporters of the death penalty? Is it due to random chance or is there some kind of logic at work?

To find an answer, we turned to the theory of moral time. Analyzing the movements of social time entailed by each murder, we found a clear and convincing pattern: the more movements of social time a murder entailed, the more hostile posts it attracted even after adjusting for the year of the execution and the amount of time that had lapsed since the last execution.[12] In short, the more serious the murder, the more the executions of the defendants were celebrated, and the more hostility was directed toward them.

Many people would surely find the comments posted on Prodeathpealty.com deeply offensive and even immoral. Others clearly see them as expressions of righteous anger at despicable deeds. Regardless of one's view, the data further bolster the theory of moral time. Among this group of death penalty supporters, the scale of condemnation of people who were scheduled to be, or had been, executed was not arbitrary. The largest movements of social time attracted the largest amount of hostility.

Conclusion

The Behavior of Law and other Blackian work had addressed the *response* to conflict, but it did not explain the *cause* of conflict – why it occurs at all. The concept of social time fills that large hole. In doing so, it solves the previously intractable problem of offense seriousness. The movement of social time is a fact-based measure of the seriousness of conduct. It does not rest, explicitly or implicitly, on the values of politicians, priests, professors, or the public. Solving the riddle of seriousness permits conduct to be incorporated into Black's theory. And because social time includes both conduct and the social status and distance of the parties, it greatly increases our ability to explain the handling of legal cases. The larger the movement of social time, the more likely a murder is to result in a death sentence and an execution. To the theoretical propositions we listed in Chapter 2, we now add the following: law increases with social time.[13]

The theory of moral time operates at a high level of generality. Yet it has the ability to explain the difference in concrete cases. To see the theory in action, let us return to the Basso and McCann cases we described at the beginning of the chapter. Although neither case was downward or relationally distant, the level of wanton cruelty in the Musso murder puts it in a different category. While Michael McCann beat, kidnapped, and shot his estranged wife and watched her bleed to death, Susan Basso regularly beat and humiliated Buddy Musso and presided over his torturous killing. The sheer amount of pain and suffering inflicted on the two victims surely helps to explain the contrasting case outcomes. Analyzed in terms of the categories we used for the Baldus data, the McCann killing involved the ambush and seizure of a vulnerable victim. The Basso killing involved domination, denigration, vulnerability, torture, brutality, seizure, and concealment. The Basso killing was a greater disturbance of social space – a larger movement of social time. Not surprisingly, it was Michael McCann who was sentenced to life imprisonment while Susan Basso was sentenced to death – and subsequently executed.

Source for the Louis "Buddy" Musso Case

Rendon, Ruth. 1998. "6 charged in death of mentally impaired man/Police say broken ornament led to fatal beating," *Houston Chronicle*, August 28, p. 29.

Crocker, Ronnie and Kevin Moran. 1998. "Inquiry grows as beating-death case takes odd twist/Suspect was featured in bogus wedding ad," *Houston Chronicle*, August 29, p. 1.

Rendon, Ruth. 1998. "Slaying possibly tied to insurance/Victim's policy paid off extra if he died from violent crime," *Houston Chronicle*, September 17, p. 25.

Brewer, Steve. 1999. "6 suspects in retarded man's slaying to be tried separately," *Houston Chronicle*, February 24, p. 23.

Brewer, Steve. 1999. "Defendant tries to blame mother for his role in man's death," *Houston Chronicle*, April 20, p. 15.

Brewer, Steve. 1999. "O'Malley is convicted in kidnapping, fatal beating/First of six defendants is sentenced to life in prison," *Houston Chronicle*, April 22, p. 29.

Brewer, Steve. 1999. "Mother, son sentenced for murder/Jury delivers long terms in torture-slaying case," *Houston Chronicle*, May 11, p. 13.

Brewer, Steve. 1999. "Man gets life for role in torture-slaying case/Jury finds Singleton guilty of capital murder," *Houston Chronicle*, May 20, p. 27.

Brewer, Steve. 1999. "Basso admitted role in beatings, jury told," *Houston Chronicle*, August 20, p. 31.

Brewer, Steve. 1999. "Witness says Basso used bats in beating," *Houston Chronicle*, August 26, p. 33.

Brewer, Steve. 1999. "Basso weeps at hearing death sentence/Daughter cries tears of joy over punishment in mother's plot to kill," *Houston Chronicle*, September 2, p. 1.

Zuniga, Jo Ann. 1999. "Woman pleads guilty, gets 20 years in Musso murder," *Houston Chronicle*, October 29, p. 31.

Sources for the Tina McCann Case

Bardwell, S.K. 1998. "Man is charged in wife's slaying after standoff with SWAT officers," *Houston Chronicle*, September 10, p. 21.

Staff. 1999. "Jury told of wife's last minutes as capital murder trial begins," *Houston Chronicle*, June 2, p. 28.

Brewer, Steve. 1999. "Man given life sentence in killing of abused wife/Defendant avoids getting death penalty," *Houston Chronicle*, June 9, p. 29.

Trial Transcript. Reporters Record, Vol 25 of 32, Trial Court Cause No. 811730.

Appendix 3

Chapter 3 investigates the relationship between social time and law. Specifically, we used the Baldus data to consider whether the movement of social time predicted death sentences and executions (for a detailed discussion of Baldus's Charging and Sentencing Study, see Appendix 2).

Table 3.1 describes how we measured the movement of vertical time in a capital murder. All murders are momentous movements of vertical time, but some are

TABLE 3.1 Measuring the Movement of Vertical Time in a Capital Murder

	Baldus's Variable(s)	Code
Devastation		
Defendant killed multiple victims	TWOVIC	1 if yes
Defendant caused bodily harm to someone besides the murder victim	HARMOTH	1 if yes
Defendant killed high status victim (victim status above average)	See Chapter 2 for a description of victim social status	1 if yes
Domination		
Defendant committed a predatory murder (exploitation in the absence of conflict)	AVENGE; BDBLOOD; BLVICMOD; DISFIGHT; EMOTION; FAMDIS; HATE; JEALOUS; MITMOTIVE; MONDIS; PROVPASS; RACEMOT; RAGE; REVENGE; SMPROVOK; SPOUSESK; VABUSEAR; VICVERB; VINJDEAR	1 if no on all indicators of conflict
Defendant subjugated the victim (bound, gagged, killed execution style)	BDGAG; EXECUT	1 if yes on either
Denigration		
Defendant expressed pleasure regarding the killing	DPLEAS	1 if yes
Abuse of Physical Power		
Defendant killed a victim who was vulnerable/defenseless (pregnant, intellectually or physically disabled, bedridden, weak or frail, especially young or old, small or outnumbered, female)	VPREG; VDEFNSLS; VDEFECT; VBED; VWEAK; VDEFENLS; VDEFOLD; VDEFENS; VSMALL; FEMVIC	1 if yes on any

even worse than others – some involve added elements of devastation, domination, denigration, and the abuse of physical power.

The murder is an especially large movement of vertical time if it includes:

- Devastation
  - the defendant killed multiple victims
  - the defendant caused bodily harm to someone besides the murder victim
  - the defendant killed a high-status victim

- Domination
  - the defendant committed a predatory murder (exploitation in the absence of conflict)
  - the defendant subjugated the victim (bound, gagged, killed execution style)
- Denigration
  - the defendant expressed pleasure regarding the killing
- Abuse of Physical Power
  - the defendant killed a victim who was vulnerable/defenseless (pregnant, intellectually or physically disabled, bedridden, weak or frail, especially young or old, small or outnumbered, or female)

To measure the movement of vertical time in each case, we assigned a baseline score of 1. After all, the murder was a substantial movement of vertical time even if none of the above circumstances occurred. For each additional circumstance, we added a point. The movement of vertical time ranged from a minimum score of 1 (none of the above circumstances occurred) to a maximum score of 7 (6 of the above circumstances occurred).

Table 3.2 describes how we measured the movement of relational time in a capital murder. All murders are catastrophic movements of relational time, but some are even worse than others – some involve gruesome violations of bodily integrity, invasions of privacy, the obstruction of movement, and the collapse of relational space.

The murder is an especially large movement of relational time if it includes:

- Violation of Bodily Integrity
  - the defendant raped the victim
  - the defendant defiled the victim (sexual perversion other than rape)
  - the defendant tortured the victim (mentally or physically)
  - the defendant brutalized the victim (brutal beating, throat slashed, strangled, stabbed multiple times)
  - the defendant mutilated the victim's body (before or after death)
- Invasion of Privacy
  - the victim was found nude
- Obstruction of Movement
  - the victim was seized (kidnapped or held hostage)
  - the victim was ambushed
  - the victim's body was concealed (disposed or hidden)
- Collapse of Relational Space
  - the victim was a stranger

To measure the movement of relational time in each case, we followed the same approach: we assigned a baseline score of 1 and then added a point for each additional circumstance. The movement of relational time ranged from 1 to 10.

TABLE 3.2 Measuring the Movement of Relational Time in a Capital Murder

	Baldus's Variable(s)	Code
Violation of Bodily Integrity		
Victim raped	RAPE	1 if yes
Victim defiled (sexual perversion other than rape)	PERVER	1 if yes
Victim tortured (mentally or physically)	MENTORT; TORTURE; LDFB7E	1 if yes on any
Victim brutalized (brutal beating, throat slashed, strangled, stabbed multiple times)	BEAT, THROAT, STRANGLE, MULSTAB	1 if yes on any
Victim mutilated (body mutilated before or after death)	MUTILATE; LDFB7A	1 if yes on either
Invasion of Privacy		
Victim found nude	NOCLOTH; NUDE	1 if yes on either
Obstruction of Movement		
Victim seized (kidnapped or held hostage)	KIDNAP; HOSTAGE	1 if yes on either
Victim ambushed (ambushed, defendant lurking)	AMBUSH	1 if yes
Victim body concealed (disposed or hidden)	CONCELBD; HIDEBOD	1 if yes on either
Collapse of Relational Space		
Victim Stranger	STRANGER	1 if yes

Table 3.3 investigates whether death sentences are influenced by the movement of social time. Focusing on vertical time in Panel A and relational time in Panel B, the data disclose strong linear patterns. Ascending from the minimum movement of vertical time (score of 1) to the maximum movement of vertical time (score of 5 or more), the chance of a death sentence increases by about 40 percentage points – from 0% to 42%. Ascending from the minimum movement of relational time (score of 1) to the maximum movement of relational time (score of 6 or more), the chance of a death sentence increases by more than 50 percentage points – from <1% to 55%. Because the legal system responds to each case as a single entity, we combined vertical time and relational time into the overall movement of social time in Panel C (by summing the constituent indicators). Doing so reveals a rare phenomenon in social science: perfect prediction. Of the 545 defendants who scored a 2 for the overall movement of social time – meaning none of the additional circumstances occurred – nobody was sentenced to death. The same cannot be said of the defendants who scored a 10 or more, as 70% were sentenced to death. All the models are statistically significant ($p <$ 0.001).

TABLE 3.3 Death Sentences by the Movement of Social Time ($n = 2,483$)[1,2]

	Death Sentences	
	Number	*Percent*
Panel A: Movement of Vertical Time[3]		
Sum of 1	0/718	0.0%
Sum of 2	15/806	1.9%
Sum of 3	32/625	5.1%
Sum of 4	39/233	16.7%
Sum of 5 or more (5 to 7)	42/100	42.0%
Panel B: Movement of Relational Time[4]		
Sum of 1	11/1,455	0.8%
Sum of 2	26/558	4.7%
Sum of 3	18/230	7.8%
Sum of 4	20/104	19.2%
Sum of 5	22/80	27.5%
Sum of 6 or more (6 to 10)	31/56	55.4%
Panel C: Overall Movement of Social Time[5]		
Sum of 2	0/545	0.0%
Sum of 3	5/673	0.7%
Sum of 4	5/501	1.0%
Sum of 5	15/297	5.1%
Sum of 6	18/159	11.3%
Sum of 7	12/125	9.6%
Sum of 8	15/86	17.4%
Sum of 9	20/44	45.5%
Sum of 10 or more (10 to 14)	38/54	70.4%

Notes:

1 The number of cases sums to 2,482 in Panel A and 2,484 in Panel C because the sampling weights produce rounding error.

2 As discussed in Appendix 2, chi-square is an omnibus test of statistical significance. Thus, the p values for Panels A, B, and C indicate the probability of committing a Type I error if one rejects the null hypothesis of equal treatment across categories. The p values do not indicate whether specific differences are significant. But the logistic regression model in Table 3.4 (below) estimates the effect of a one-unit change in the movement of social time on death sentences.

3 $p < 0.001$; chi-square = 237.165 with 4 DF (percentages are based on the weighted data, but chi-square is based on the unweighted data because it assumes independent observations).

4 $p < 0.001$; chi-square = 268.617 with 5 DF (percentages are based on the weighted data, but chi-square is based on the unweighted data because it assumes independent observations).

5 $p < 0.001$; chi-square = 384.967 with 8 DF (percentages are based on the weighted data, but chi-square is based on the unweighted data because it assumes independent observations).

It is important to ask whether support for Black's theory of moral time remains after controlling for confounding variables. Perhaps the most egregious murders are accompanied by the strongest evidence against the defendant, as detectives and prosecutors work harder than usual to establish guilt. The most culpable

TABLE 3.4 Odds Ratios from the Weighted Logistic Regression of Death Sentences on the Movement of Social Time ($n = 2{,}483$)

	Odds Ratios Model 1	Odds Ratios Model 2
Social Time		
Movement of Vertical Time	2.5★★★	
Movement of Relational Time	1.9★★★	
Overall Movement of Social Time		2.1★★★
Controls (Baldus variable name)[1]		
Defendant deliberated (DTHINK)	2.0★	2.1★
Defendant did not kill (NOKILL)	0.46	0.46
Number of types of evidence against defendant (EVINDX2)	4.9★★★	4.4★★★
Sentenced 1974 (LDF4B)	5.1	4.9
Sentenced 1975 (LDF4B)	4.8	4.5
Sentenced 1976 (LDF4B)	3.5	3.3
Sentenced 1977 (LDF4B)	4.5	4.3
Sentenced 1978 (LDF4B)	2.3	2.0
Sentenced 1979 (LDF4B)	4.4	4.1
Sentenced 1980 (LDF4B)	2.3	2.2

Note:
1 The reference category for year is 1973.
★$p < 0.05$; ★★ $p < 0.01$; ★★★ $p < 0.001$

defendants also plan the crime and kill the victim (as opposed to those who act spontaneously or those whose involvement falls short of killing). But as Table 3.4 demonstrates, controlling for confounding variables does not change the underlying pattern: each unit-increase in the movement of vertical time, the movement of relational time, and the overall movement of social time roughly doubles the odds of a death sentence ($p < 0.01$).

Focusing on the subset of defendants who were sentenced to death, we also examined whether the overall movement of social time predicted executions. Of the 120 defendants who were condemned, 24 were executed. Given such small numbers, we simplified our measurement strategy. Specifically, the overall movement of social time ranged from 3 to 14 for condemned defendants, with a mean of 8 and a standard deviation of 2.8. So we treated cases that were at least one standard deviation above the mean as the "most extreme" movements of social time (a score of 11 to 14), and the remaining cases as the "least extreme" movements of social time (a score of 3 to 10). Table 3.5 reveals a stark pattern: an execution was carried out in 50% of the most extreme cases, compared to just 12% of the least extreme cases. Remarkably, the overall movement of social time explains legal outcomes in the penultimate stage of a capital case – death sentences – and the ultimate stage of a capital case – executions.

TABLE 3.5 Executions by the Movement of Social Time ($n = 120$)[1]

	Executions	
	Number	*Percent*
Overall Movement of Social Time[2]		
Least Extreme	11/94	11.7%
Most Extreme	13/26	50.0%

Note:
1 We do not present a test of statistical significance because the calculation is based on population data (for a discussion, see Appendix 2).
2 The "most extreme" cases are one standard deviation above the mean for the overall movement of social time.

Notes

1 Rendon, Ruth. 1998. "6 charged in death of mentally impaired man / Police say broken ornament led to fatal beating," *Houston Chronicle*, August 28, p. 29.
2 All five remaining defendants in the Musso case were convicted. Two received life sentences, one 80 years, one 60 years, and one 20 years.
3 Now known as the National Crime Victimization Survey (NCVS).
4 Black argued that the authors' reliance on a single stage of the process underestimated support for the theory, as social geometry influences whether an incident is defined as a crime that could be reported to police (e.g., a woman shoved by her husband is less likely to define the incident as an "assault" than if she had been shoved by a stranger). In response, Gottfredson and Hindelang (1979b) and another duo, John Braithwaite and David Biles (1980), argued that Black was backtracking – the theory claimed to explain the quantity of law at every stage of the legal process independent of every other stage. Our position is that while single-stage tests are valid provided there are enough cases to compare the outcomes along geometrical lines, better tests of the theory will address several stages of the legal process (as our analysis of the Baldus data does). For example, the geometrical effect at an earlier stage might be so strong that it results in a null effect at the next stage, though the overall effect is still quite strong. For an example, see Appendix 4, Table 4.5 (Penalty Trial and Death Sentence by Victim Law Enforcement Officer).
5 Research conducted elsewhere, including Canada, Norway, Puerto Rico, and Taiwan, largely replicated the rank ordering of seriousness found by Sellin-Wolfgang (Wolfgang et al. 1985).
6 A conflict also occurs if a person defines their own behavior as wrong; it is not unusual for people to have a grievance with themselves.
7 Angela Barlow (2019) tested this part of the theory in a study of sexual harassment. She found that students at a large southeastern university rated minor movements of relational time (e.g., squeezing biceps or rubbing shoulders) as less offensive than greater movements (e.g., staring at body parts or requesting a sexual encounter via email). And they rated the most intrusive actions (e.g., touching and sexual propositioning) as the most offensive. Offensiveness ratings also varied with the relational distance of the parties: for coworkers who were friendly and often socialized outside work the mean rating was 3.30; that increased to 3.56 when they were friendly but did not socialize

outside work, and to 3.63 when they had just met. One qualification is that offensiveness ratings do not necessarily translate into greater or lesser overt conflicts.

8   For additional thoughts on how the new theory of moral time relates to the original geometrical theory, see Black (2015: 387–389).

9   Black maintains that vertical, relational, and cultural movements of social time are each zero-sum. A change for one person or group necessarily means a change in the opposite direction for some other person or group. If you go up in the world, you necessarily increase your status relative to those who did not. If you go down in the world, you fall below those who stayed still or moved up. If you start an intimate relationship with A, some of your other relationships will become less close. If you break off an intimate relationship with A, your intimacy with some other person (or perhaps just yourself) will increase. If you adopt one culture you necessarily reject another (though you may tolerate it). If you reject one culture, you necessarily adopt another.

10   Prior studies, including tests of Black's theory, have often treated gender as an indicator of social status. But not all men are high status and not all women are low status. Gender is a complex multidimensional concept. For example, compared to women, men traditionally earn more money, own more property, and participate more in governmental and corporate affairs while women are more integrated into family life than are men (e.g., taking care of the young and the elderly) and are less involved in criminal conduct. But these factors can vary significantly from one setting and person to another. Greater physical vulnerability, however, is closer to being a universal social experience of women. Similar to how we treat race as an indicator of conventionality, we therefore treat gender as an indicator of physical vulnerability.

11   In the Basso case discussed at the beginning of the chapter, Basso's daughter, Christianna Hardy, hugged the prosecutor after the sentence of death was announced and said,

> We got a victory! She's off the streets for good. This is wonderful. Justice has finally been served! She's off the streets! She can't hurt anybody. Let the inmates kill her. I don't care. She was never a mother. She doesn't have any mothering instincts,

Hardy said. "She threw us away and left us out there to fend for ourselves. Now, let her do a little fending for herself." She added that she probably wouldn't attend her mother's execution: "I might just sit at home and pop a bottle of champagne when the lethal injection is given" (Brewer, Steve. 1999. "Basso weeps at hearing death sentence / Daughter cries tears of joy over punishment in mother's plot to kill," *Houston Chronicle*, September 2, p. 1).

12   One difference from our coding of the Baldus data was that we coded interracial murders as movements of cultural time. We found that the execution of an interracial murderer generated more posts than the execution of an intraracial murderer.

13   The new understanding of conduct seriousness stems from a new understanding of conduct in general. Social time encompasses everything humans do and say. That is why Black (2011: 154, n.18; 2015: 19–21) claims that, theoretically speaking, social time is "the death of the act." So, too, with the application of legal sanctions – arrest, prosecution, conviction, and punishment – all are changes in law, or movements of legal time. The movement of legal time is known by change in the quantity or style of law. Formulated in this new way, the proposition might read: *Legal time is a function of social time.*

References

Barlow, Angela. 2019. "'Can I Take Out My Penis'? Navigating Sex and Intimacy in the Workplace: An Empirical Test of Black's Theory of Conflict." *Deviant Behavior* 40: 621–634.

Baumer, Eric, Steven F. Messner, and Richard B. Felson. 2000. "The Role of Victim Characteristics in the Disposition of Murder Cases." *Justice Quarterly* 17: 281–307.

Black, Donald. 1976. *The Behavior of Law*. New York: Academic Press.

Black, Donald. 1979. "Common Sense in the Sociology of Law." *American Sociological Review* 44:18–27.

Black, Donald. 2010. "How Law Behaves: An Interview with Donald Black." *International Journal of Law, Crime and Justice* 38:37–47.

Black, Donald. 2011. *Moral Time*. New York: Oxford University Press.

Black, Donald. 2015. "The Beginning of Social Time: An Interview with Myself." *International Journal of Law, Crime and Justice* 43:382–395.

Black, Donald. 2018. "Domestic Violence and Social Time." *Dilemas: Revista de Estudos de Conflilto e Controle Social* 11:1–27.

Braithwaite, John and David Biles. 1980. "Empirical Verification and Black's *The Behavior of Law*." *American Sociological Review* 45:334–338.

Campbell, Bradley. 2013. "Genocide and Social Time." *Dilemas: Revista De Estudos De Conflito E Controle Social* 6 :465–388.

Cooney, Mark. 2009. *Is Killing Wrong? A Study in Pure Sociology*. Charlottesville: University of Virginia Press.

Cooney, Mark. 2014. "Family Honor and Social Time." *The Sociological Review* 62:87–106.

Dawson, Myrna. 2016. "Punishing Femicide: Criminal Justice Responses to the Killing of Women over Four Decades." *Current Sociology* 64:996–1016.

Estrich, Susan. 1987. *Real Rape*. Cambridge: Harvard University Press.

Gottfredson, Michael R. and Michael J. Hindelang. 1979a. "A Study of the Behavior of Law." *American Sociological Review* 44 :3–18.

Gottfredson, Michael R. and Michael J. Hindelang. 1979b. "Theory and Research in the Sociology of Law." *American Sociological Review* 44:27–37.

Manning, Jason. 2015. "Suicide and Social Time." *Dilemas: Revistas de Estudos de Conflicto e Controle Social* 8:97–126.

Myers, Martha A. and John Hagan. 1979. "Private and Public Trouble: Prosecutors and the Allocation of Court Resources." *Social Problems* 26:439–451.

Nagel, Illene H. 1982–1983. "The Legal/Extra-Legal Controversy: Judicial Decisions in Pretrial Release." *Law & Society Review* 17:481–516.

Phillips, Scott and Mark Cooney. 2015. "The Electronic Pillory: Social Time and Hostility toward Capital Murderers." *Law and Society Review* 49:725–759.

Sellin, Thorsten and Marvin E. Wolfgang. 1964. *The Measurement of Delinquency*. New York: Wiley.

Tasca, Melinda, Nancy Rodriguez, Cassia Spohn, and Mary P. Koss. 2012. "Police Decision Making in Sexual Assault Cases: Predictors of Suspect Identification and Arrest." *Journal of Interpersonal Violence* 28:1157–1177.

Warr, Mark. 1989. "What is the Perceived Seriousness of Crimes?" *Criminology* 27:792–822.

Wolfgang, Marvin E., Robert M. Figlio, Paul E. Tracy, and Simon I. Singer. 1985. *The National Survey of Crime Severity*. Washington D.C.: United States Department of Justice, Bureau of Justice Statistics.

4

SPACE AND TIME

Third Parties

Houston, Texas: March 23, 1995

Eric Charles Nenno was born and raised in a small town in northern Pennsylvania. After high school, he joined the Navy and qualified as a ventilation and plumbing systems technician. While in the Navy, he picked up a misdemeanor marijuana charge in California in 1980. After leaving the Navy, he relocated to Blytheville, Arkansas, where his mother and sister had moved after his father's death in Pennsylvania. He got a job working in his uncle's plumbing supply business. Nenno looked after his ailing mother, helping her with her portable oxygen bottle and taking her to the local Baptist church. According to his uncle, Nenno "was very friendly with people" and "got along with everyone" in the church. In 1992, Nenno's sister, by then married and living in the Houston area, called to ask her brother to house-sit the couple's small ranch-style home. The sister, her husband, and her husband's son by another marriage were going to Scotland and wanted someone to keep an eye on their property for the approximately four years they would be absent. Nenno agreed and moved into the Houston house. One resident described him as "the best neighbor anybody could ask for."

On the fateful day, Buddy Benton, a neighbor of Nenno's, was celebrating his birthday by playing country-western music with his band. His 7-year-old daughter, Nicole, was playing with other children. Nenno approached Nicole and suggested that they fetch his guitar from his house so that he could come back and play in her father's band. Nicole complied, following Nenno to his house. Nenno attacked Nicole, who tried to fight him off. In the struggle, Nenno killed the little girl, and then raped her twice before disposing of her naked body in his attic. While neighbors joined forces to search for the missing child, Nenno met with detectives to share his theories on who did it, why, and how the culprit deserved

DOI: 10.4324/9781003176633-5

to die for his crimes. Detectives became suspicious of Nenno after someone in the neighborhood reported that he had snatched a child years earlier and pulled down her underwear. Three days after the murder, Nenno led detectives to the corpse.

At his trial for capital murder, Nenno's confession was read to the jury. He admitted to long battling fantasies about fondling girls Nicole's age. Nenno also stated that the evening he lured Nicole to his house he had consumed six beers and was in a dream-like state. His attorneys pointed to his good reputation. A psychologist testified that his brain showed signs of abnormalities that either existed from birth, or resulted from a bicycle wreck when he injured his head at age 5, and that could contribute to his attraction to young girls. He said Nenno showed no significant signs of a personality disorder and was not mentally unstable. Nenno's fantasies were non-violent, but clearly were consistent with those of a pedophile.

Mahmudiya, Iraq: March 12, 2006

Steven Green joined the Army when he was 19 years old, although he had to be granted a "morals waiver" because of his convictions for drug and alcohol offenses. After being deployed to Iraq, two of his comrades were killed in December 2005 at a checkpoint when an Iraqi who had previously been friendly with American troops drove up and opened fire. Green said the deaths "messed me up real bad." Describing his feelings about Iraqis, Green stated in an interview, "There's not a word that would describe how much I hated these people." He added, "I wasn't thinking these people were humans." Green was seen by a military stress counselor, who indicated that he had homicidal thoughts about killing Iraqi civilians. She prescribed Seroquel, an anti-psychotic medication.[1]

One night, after playing cards and drinking bootleg Iraqi whiskey, Green and three other soldiers discussed raping an Iraqi girl. The soldiers chose the home of 14-year-old Abeer Qassim Hamzah Rashid al-Janabi because it would be an easy target – an isolated farmhouse about 20 miles south of Baghdad with just one male in the house. The house was several hundred meters away from the checkpoint where the soldiers were stationed. The four men wore black long underwear and ski masks as "ninja suits." After arriving at the home, Green herded Abeer's mother, father, and 6-year-old sister into a bedroom. With Green holding the family hostage, two of the men raped Abeer in the living room, while the remaining member of the group "stood guard in the hall."[2] As Abeer was being raped, Green killed her mother, father, and little sister. Green then raped Abeer, before putting a pillow over the teen's face and shooting her two to three times with the family's AK-47. To cover their tracks, the soldiers poured kerosene on Abeer's body and used blankets to fuel the fire. The soldiers left Abeer's home and made it back to the checkpoint without being detected.

A soldier who heard about United States involvement in the crime came forward as a whistle-blower. Because the other three members of the group were still in the military at the time the crime came to light, they were convicted in military court and sentenced to lengthy terms of imprisonment (with the possibility of parole) at a military prison in Fort Leavenworth, Kansas. Green had been discharged from the Army for a personality disorder before he was linked to the crime. He was therefore charged under the Military Extraterritorial Jurisdiction Act (a law originally created to prosecute military contractors operating in war zones). He was convicted of rape and murder in the United States District Court (federal court) on May 7, 2009. Prosecutors sought death. Defense attorney Scott Wendelsdorf drew attention to Green's disadvantaged upbringing in Midland, Texas: his mother called him "a demon spawn"[3] and his older brother, who was in charge of him and their sister while their mother worked in a bar at night, beat his two siblings regularly. His mother kicked him out of the house when he was 14 and he dropped out of high school during tenth grade, though he went on to obtain a General Education Degree (GED). Wendelsdorf argued that "The United States of America failed Steven Green" by keeping Green on the front lines despite knowing that he was obsessed with killing Iraqi civilians.[4]

One of these two defendants was sentenced to death, the other to life imprisonment. Which one? Both murders were extreme. Both involved the rape and killing of a minor. Both killed defenseless victims. Green's rape was clearly pre-planned; Nenno's rape may or may not have been. Green's victim was a teenager; Nenno's victim was a child. But Green had been abused as a child and traumatized by the killing of his comrades in a war zone while serving his country; Nenno's life had been relatively stress free (though he may have suffered from brain damage).

To predict the likely outcomes of these two cases, it is necessary to go beyond what we have discussed to this point. We have seen that the location, direction, and distance of a case in social space – as known by the social characteristics of the defendant and victim – influences who winds up being sentenced to death and ultimately executed. We know that incorporating the movement of social time – as known by who did what, to whom – significantly boosts our ability to distinguish cases that result in a death sentence or execution from those that do not. But we will do even better if we extend out gaze still further, to include the other people involved in the case – police officers, lawyers, witnesses, judges, and jurors. These "third parties" can profoundly affect the direction cases take. For example, how thoroughly will the police investigate the Green and Nenno cases? Will any witnesses turn up and testify? If they do, will they be believed? And who will the jury side with? Steven or Abeer? Eric or Nicole?

Third parties are actors, other than the principals, who know of a conflict (Black and Baumgartner 1983). They include supporters, opponents, and anybody who remains neutral. Although *The Behavior of Law* (1976) focuses almost exclusively on the principal parties, Black soon began to extend his theory to these additional actors. Since previous theory provided very little guidance, Black and a co-author, M.P. Baumgartner (1983), began by mapping out the full range of third-party behavior. They distinguished two main types of third parties: *partisans* who enter a case on behalf of one side (e.g., witnesses), and *settlement agents* (e.g., judges, jurors) who enter a case neutrally. Partisanship and settlement can occur at every stage of the criminal justice process. Indeed, the same individual can serve as both a partisan and a settlement agent, even in the same case. Take capital jurors, for instance. They enter a case as settlement agents (neutral parties) but eventually become partisans by voting for guilt/innocence and death/life (taking sides). We will come back to this point.

Fact-Finding

To describe the role of third parties, we analyze the stages of a case in rough chronological order. The initial stage involves fact-finding. When police become aware of an incident (whether by the victim, a member of the public, or through their own efforts), they must first try to figure out what happened. Was there, in fact, a crime? How was it committed? Who might have done it? The preliminary conclusions police come to are often revised, even reversed, as the case progresses through the system and more information comes to light. At all points, fact-finding typically depends heavily on third parties.

Black (1993a: chapter 7) advanced a theory of partisanship in a paper titled "Taking Sides." His theory predicts when third parties will support others in a conflict and how strongly they will support their chosen side. Treating partisanship as a form of "social gravitation" by which one party is attracted to another, he proposes that partisan attraction increases with a third party's (1) social closeness to one side and distance from the other side; and (2) social inferiority to one side and social superiority to the other side. (The terms "inferiority" and "superiority" do not imply any value judgment; they are simply short hand ways of saying "lower relative status" and "higher relative status," respectively.) More simply: people are drawn to support their intimates and superiors.

Mark Cooney (1994) applied and extended Black's theory, arguing that findings of fact made by legal officials are not determined solely by the underlying reality of what happened. Rather, partisanship shapes the story of what took place. This has an important implication: the same set of *actual facts* can generate very different *legal facts* depending on the social geometry of the case, including its third-party geometry. Consider the investigation of cases.

Investigation

When a body is discovered under suspicious circumstances, it falls to the coroner or medical examiner (depending on the jurisdiction) to determine whether the deceased person was a victim of homicide. Coroners work closely with the police and so when police mortally wound a civilian, the coroner is socially closer to the police officer than to the victim. Coroners are therefore slow to declare the case a homicide. A researcher who observed a coroner's office reports that in officer-involved deaths, "If any natural disease might allow for an alternative explanation, it will likely weigh heavily. Unless there are extraordinary circumstances, law enforcement officials will receive a generous benefit of the doubt" (Timmermans

2006: 183).[5] Just how generous was revealed by a national study comparing official records of death certificates to information in private sources (e.g., *The Guardian* newspaper). The research team found that more than half (56%) of all deaths the outside sources attributed to police violence were officially recorded as being due to some other cause (GBD 2019 Police Violence Subnational Collaborators 2021). Moreover, even if the case is ruled a homicide, it will usually be further investigated by members of the same police department. Again, close ties ensure that all ambiguities are typically constructed in favor of the officer.

Partisanship in the opposite direction is evident when the roles are reversed – when a citizen kills a police officer. In these cases, the police department throws virtually everything they have into finding the killer. The case jumps the queue, becoming a top priority. Multiple officers are assigned to the case, the crime scene is meticulously examined, all witnesses are followed up and interviewed, fingerprints are taken, DNA analyzed, and other forensic leads relentlessly pursued (see, e.g., Cooney 2009: 65).

Compare the thoroughness of the investigation of police victims to the killing of a homeless stranger whose body is discovered in a ditch bearing signs of violence. Assuming the police mount an investigation, it will almost certainly not be anything as exhaustive as that launched when one of their fellow officers is killed. Were the police case to be investigated like the homeless person case, fewer witnesses would be located and much less evidence generated. Conversely, were the homeless case to be investigated like the police case, the official file would be much thicker, the "facts" more comprehensive.

Police killings attract thorough investigations not just because the victims are socially close to the investigators (belong to the same occupational group and often the same department), but also because the victims enjoy organizational status as state officials. Wealthy and well-connected civilian victims similarly call forth extra effort from the state. The suspicious death of a corporate executive or a prominent doctor, for example, will be treated as an investigative priority. Homeless strangers, by contrast, are neither high status nor close to police officers and, consequently, their deaths are a lower priority. Likewise, victims with low normative status in the form of a long criminal record are unlikely to generate much investigatory zeal among the police (see, e.g., Simon [1991: 177]). Claims by officials that they did not pursue a case for lack of evidence therefore cannot be taken as invariably true: lack of effort might be a better explanation.

In the Baldus study, some cases included scientific evidence, but others did not. Detecting, collecting, and analyzing such evidence – fingerprints, footprints, tire tracks, and trace evidence such as blood or hair – requires more police work, especially decades ago. Whose death justified the effort? Higher status victims, as illustrated in Figure 4.1 (see Chapter 2 for a description of our measure of victim status). Among cases with the highest status victims, 28% included scientific evidence. Among cases with the lowest status victims, none had scientific evidence.

The pattern in Figure 4.1 is strong, but it could be caused by other factors. Perhaps cases with higher status victims were, on average, more serious than those

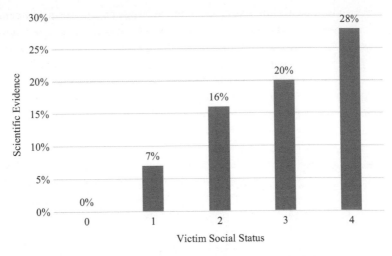

FIGURE 4.1 Scientific Evidence by Victim Social Status ($n = 2{,}483$)

with lower status victims. To check, we controlled for the movement of social time. Larger movements of social time should generate more partisanship from law enforcement than smaller movements (Campbell and Manning 2018: 56–58). Indeed, we found that victim status and the overall movement of social time each help to predict the production of scientific evidence. With the movement of social time held constant, a one-unit increase in victim status increases the odds of scientific evidence by 40%. With the victim's status held constant, a one-unit increase in the overall movement of social time increases the odds of scientific evidence by 56% (see Appendix 4).

On the defense side, too, investigation can make or break a case. The more time and effort the defense team invests in digging into what happened, the more likely they are to find evidence that casts doubt on the prosecution's case (see, e.g., Mann 1984). Clive Stafford-Smith discovered this through bitter experience. Early in his career, Stafford-Smith volunteered to represent Edward Earl Johnson, a Black man on death row in Mississippi. He writes, "I did not expect to lose. I had been to a prestigious law school and was sure that some clever legal wheeze would see him safe." However, lose he did, and Johnson was executed in May 1987. Only later did Stafford-Smith discover vital alibi testimony that might have made the difference. Reflecting on "the grandest failure of my life," he writes, "what was needed was a vigorous factual investigation to prove his innocence, rather than a series of legal theories I'd digested from a dusty law library" (2020: 20–21). Vigorous investigations are more common when the defendant is of high status. When the celebrity O.J. Simpson was accused of double murder in Los Angeles in 1994, his high-powered defense team (nicknamed "the dream team") spent months tracking down and interviewing witnesses, checking records, and analyzing forensic evidence. Eventually, they stumbled across an audio tape on which one of the police investigators used racial epithets. Since he had previously denied on the witness stand having done so, the defense was able to suggest that he had planted crucial evidence against the defendant, a Black man. A case that once appeared to be a slam dunk for the prosecution wound up with an acquittal for the defendant (Toobin 1996: 324, 326, 390–408).

Investigations by both sides look for any relevant evidence helpful to their cause or harmful to the opponent's. As we have seen, detectives will sometimes gather forensic clues, such as swabs for DNA tests, fingerprints, and ballistics analysis. Occasionally, they discover a video or audio recording of the incident. However, most cases hinge on the testimony of witnesses. What David Simon (1991: 446) observed of homicides is true of cases more generally: "the surest way for a cop to solve a murder is to get his ass out on the street and find a witness."

Witnesses

It is difficult to exaggerate the importance of witnesses in legal cases. It is equally difficult to exaggerate how little systematic information there is about them. Witnesses largely fly under the research radar. They are usually ordinary civilians whose input is more easily overlooked than that of the high-status professional insiders who staff the legal system.

Finding witnesses often requires considerable time and effort, particularly in large cities where people are frequently on the move. Once located, getting them to testify is the next hurdle (see Leovy 2015: chapter 8). Just because somebody witnesses a crime does not mean that person will wind up being a witness in the legal case arising out of the crime. The lawyers might decide that the witness lacks credibility. Or the witness might not agree to come forward and testify. It is not unusual for homicides to be committed in public places before scores of people, not even one of whom is prepared to testify in court (see, e.g., Cooney 1994: 843). Their reasons vary. Sometimes onlookers just do not want to insert themselves into other people's conflict; sometimes they have ties to both sides of the case and want to remain neutral; and sometimes they are afraid of retaliation if they testify (see Leovy 2015: 74–79). Whatever the reason, the party or the attorney can try to persuade reluctant witnesses to testify (e.g., appealing to their sense of justice). If that fails, the attorney can issue a subpoena to compel their testimony. But attorneys often shy away from issuing subpoenas, realizing that they may backfire: forcing a witness to testify can breed resentment that results in weak or even antagonistic testimony which winds up hurting, rather than helping, the client's case.

Who is prepared to testify is not random. Family members, friends, and other socially close third parties are likely to come forward when they have helpful testimony (and stay back if the testimony is unhelpful). In a Virginia case, for instance, the only individual out of approximately one hundred witnesses who saw the public confrontation that resulted in a killing and was prepared to testify for the state was the victim's girlfriend. Parties with close occupational ties also have an advantage in making their case: police officers, for example, are notorious for backing each other up on the witness stand (e.g., Hunt and Manning 1991: 61–62). High status helps, too. The defense team representing Claus von Bulow, a wealthy socialite who was accused of the attempted murder of his wife, received several unsolicited offers from total strangers prepared to testify to anything that might help the defendant (Dershowitz 1986: 225). It is difficult to imagine what these "witnesses" could have attested to without lying – a particularly strong form of partisanship since it carries the risk of a perjury charge.

Some testimony is more valuable. The testimony of higher status people tends to be treated as more credible – believable – than that of lower status people, all else the same. For instance, a police officer's word will nearly always be accepted over a citizen's. In experimental studies, witnesses who spoke confidently and assertively – as is typical of wealthy and highly educated people – were rated to be more convincing than witnesses who spoke in a more halting and tentative manner replete with hedges and qualifiers (O'Barr 1982). Higher status people are particularly credible when they testify about lower status people (and those of lower status are less credible testifying about those of higher status) (Black 2000: 350). Credibility also increases with social distance. Intimacy can therefore be a disadvantage. While intimates can be counted on to show up, they are not particularly convincing witnesses. The tendency of intimates to present their testimony in a light favorable to their own side, or a light unfavorable to the opposing side, is well known. If your brother insists in court that you did not commit the crime, will he be believed? But distant witnesses are harder to recruit. High status helps, as do indirect ties: A knows B who knows C, a stranger to A. A's chance of recruiting C is boosted by the mutual connection to B. Litigants who know many people, especially those from different walks of life, therefore enjoy a form of social wealth that can prove very useful should they find themselves embroiled in a legal conflict.

But credibility – being believed – does not necessarily mean veracity – being honest or accurate. Factual untruths may be just as credible as factual truths. Scott Phillips and Jamie Richardson (2016) encountered this when they analyzed a national database of defendants exonerated from death row. They discovered that murder cases that were larger movements of social time were more likely to have had flawed evidence, such as a false confession, untrue jailhouse inmate testimony, forensic evidence that failed to meet proper scientific standards, and official misconduct that contributed to the wrongful conviction. Extremely serious homicides, then, draw out extra efforts from police and prosecutors to secure a conviction, even to the point of generating evidence that can be later overturned. As the authors (2016: 448) state, "'the worst of the worst crimes' appear to produce the 'worst of the worst evidence.'" And since this evidence is produced and presented by or on behalf of the state, it tends to be accepted as true.[6]

The "Facts"

From the initial investigative stage and beyond, then, legal officials seek to determine the facts of the case. What actually happened between the parties matters in the construction of the legal facts, but so does the location, direction, and movement of the parties in social space – the case geometry. Facts do not simply fall from the sky. The wealthy, those with jobs and families, members of ethnic and racial majorities and other high-status parties are able to shape the facts in their favor as they elicit more partisanship from third parties: detectives and defense teams investigate their cases more thoroughly and witnesses are more prepared to come forward on their behalf. They are more likely to attract high-status support – the kind that carries more weight. Close ties to third parties also generate partisanship, though weaker ties are an advantage in attracting more credible support. The result is that different case structures elicit different legal facts for the same events. Hold the underlying reality constant but change the social status and distance of the parties, and different facts will be legally produced. Legal reality is thus geometrical (compare Frank 1949). To what degree is extremely difficult to measure. Researchers are rarely able to take cases from their very beginning – when a killing occurs – right through to their ultimate disposition to show the variety of ways in which the facts might have been constructed differently. The Baldus data set, for all its strengths, is no different. As we have seen, cases with higher status victims were more likely to generate scientific evidence. In addition, Baldus and colleagues found that cases in which the primary witness was a police officer or a civilian with no credibility problems were significantly more likely to result in a death sentence (Baldus, Woodworth, and Pulaski 1990: 625). Apart from that, the data set contains few hints about how the facts of the cases were established. That limitation is worth bearing in mind. The absence of information on the fact-finding process means that the effects of social geometry on the cases are almost certainly even greater than we can demonstrate. Ours is necessarily a conservative estimate of how strongly social geometry affected the handling of the Georgia capital cases.

Lawyers

What about defense lawyers? Do they matter? In the United States, there is no right to legal representation in civil cases. Many civil litigants go unrepresented and it hurts their cause. Research shows that litigants represented by lawyers do better in housing disputes, employment discrimination suits, and civil cases more generally (Seron et al. 2001; Berrey et al. 2017; Sandefur 2010). By contrast, American criminal defendants have a constitutional right to legal counsel. Hence, the issue is not whether there is representation but the nature of that representation. Some defendants are able to pay a lawyer to advocate for them; most defendants are not and must rely on public defenders or court-appointed attorneys. Do the defendants who retain their own lawyer fare better than defendants who rely on a lawyer assigned to them?

The answer is not immediately obvious. Perhaps taking a public lawyer is better both because the public lawyer will often have considerable experience in that area of law and because those who pay may not be able to afford the most effective lawyers. Or perhaps paying gets you a better lawyer because you can choose which lawyer to hire and do not have to rely on someone who, as has often been the case, turns out to be lazy or incompetent (see, e.g., Stevenson 2014: 77, 150, 152, 158, 190, 197–198, 258). Unfortunately, we cannot examine the issue. The Baldus study attempted to document whether the defendant had retained counsel but is missing information on a sizeable number of cases, preventing us from conducting a sound analysis. Scott Phillips (2009) was able to examine the issue in his Houston study.[7] He divided the 504 defendants indicted for capital murder into three groups: those who had been appointed counsel for the entire case, those who had hired counsel for the entire case, and those who had a combination. (A combination meant the person either hired someone and ran out of money, or took an appointment, realized it was going badly, and scraped together some money.) Among those with appointed attorneys, 23% were sentenced to death. Among those with hired attorneys, 0% were sentenced to death. Among those with both, 14% were sentenced to death. So being able to hire an attorney for even a portion of the case makes a difference, though probably not in the way most people think. Hired attorneys did not save their clients with soaring rhetoric in the punishment phase. Instead, they were much less likely to let the case go to trial in the first place, perhaps because the District Attorney was more willing to make a deal rather than face a more formidable adversary.[8]

Extra-Legal Partisanship

Before moving on to the prosecution stage, a word about partisanship beyond the law. Favorable publicity toward one's own side or negative publicity toward the other side can greatly influence the course a case takes. This is especially true in our highly connected electronic age. Many people now carry phones with powerful, high-resolution cameras and can quickly publish photographs, videos, and commentary on social media sites which other users can then repost to still other users. Information relevant to a legal case circulating widely can have a powerful galvanizing effect. The killing of George Floyd in Minneapolis in 2020 by police officer Derek Chauvin provides an example. At the outset, it appeared unlikely that Chauvin would be punished for the homicide. Floyd was a lower income Black man with a criminal record; Chauvin was a White officer with 19 years of experience (though he had 18 complaints against him). Distantly upward cases do not normally succeed: police officers are rarely even indicted for, let alone convicted of, the murder of civilians (see, e.g., Cooney 2009: 63–77).

But Chauvin's case was different. Chauvin knelt on Floyd's neck for over nine minutes, ignoring Floyd's increasingly desperate pleas that he could not breathe. Bystanders urged Chauvin to let Floyd stand, but he refused. This large murderous movement of social time (prolonged domination of a subdued suspect) was captured on security and civilian videos that were posted to the Internet and went viral. The publicity immediately sparked street protests denouncing the killer and urging justice for the victim not just in America but many other countries as well. The most prominent, but far from the only, partisan was the Black Lives Matter organization, which attracted supporters and resources in large numbers. The case became a rallying point for those seeking greater police accountability, especially for violence against minorities. The continued protests appear to have worked. The District Attorney's office charged Chauvin with murder and formed a team of highly experienced prosecutors and investigators to handle the case. The prosecutorial team prepared meticulously for months. The trial attracted enormous amounts of publicity, including the gathering of a large crowd outside the courthouse, most of whom demanded a murder conviction. The prosecutors pulled out all the stops, calling a total of 38 witnesses. Among them were many high-status witnesses such as medical and police experts including Chauvin's own Chief of Police who testified that Chauvin's actions were against departmental policy. The jury convicted Chauvin of murder, and the judge sentenced him to more than 20 years in prison, outcomes that were almost certainly influenced by the large movement of social time and the ocean of extra-legal support.

Prosecuting

Once the "facts" of a capital murder are established, a second stage arises in which the critical question is whether to advance, or not advance, the case to a penalty trial upon conviction.[9] This decision falls to the prosecutor – the District Attorney. In the Baldus study, prosecutors did so in 242 of the 2,483 cases. Which cases did they advance?

Slow Partisanship

Prosecutorial decisions involve a review of the evidence. In modern capital cases, the available evidence is usually substantial: larger movements of social time attract investigations that are more thorough. The prosecutor must sift through the witness statements and other evidentiary material, such as ballistic, fingerprint, fiber, medical, and DNA evidence. The defense attorneys' arguments – often centered on mitigation rather than innocence – have to be considered as well. Having reviewed the case file, and perhaps solicited the opinions of assistants, the prosecutor must elect whether to advance the case. The decision can go either way. In deliberating and deciding, the prosecutor is acting as a settlement agent, passing judgment on the case. Not a final judgment, but an essential one: if the prosecutor does not advance the case, the death penalty is off the table. Yet the prosecutor is not just a settlement agent.

Recall that the same person can be both a settlement agent and a partisan. The prosecutor is an example. The prosecutor's zero-sum decision to advance or not advance the case inevitably favors one party at the expense of the other. If the case is advanced, the prosecutor is siding with the victim; if it is not advanced, the prosecutor is siding with the defendant. Putting the awesome power of the state behind one party is an act of partisanship. Yet it differs from everyday partisanship, such as a person testifying for a spouse, child, or sibling. Relatives tend to support each other quickly and without much hesitation; the prosecutor's partisanship is less automatic, more deliberate, more evidence based. It exemplifies what Black (1993a: 138–139) calls slow partisanship. Since this is an unfamiliar idea, it is worth quoting Black's (2002: 111) words on the matter:

> Legal scholars normally describe law as a nonpartisan process – autonomous and neutral. They say law is functioning normally and properly only when it is completely impersonal and impartial. But my view is that law is inherently partisan. It is partisan whenever a legal official or jury decides who is right and who is wrong – who wins and who loses – in a particular dispute… But law rarely takes sides from the beginning. A legal trial determines the state's partisanship. Law takes sides only after the adversaries make arguments and present evidence about their dispute. These arguments and presentations might take minutes, hours, days, or weeks… Yet everywhere the process by which law takes sides typically takes time. It is slow. So I call it "slow partisanship"

Black is not arguing that legal officials are biased, consciously or unconsciously, in favor of certain parties. He is describing the observable behavior of legal officials, not their subjective experience. As he says,

> I do not know what they think – what they perceive or what they want. All that matters sociologically is what they actually do. And what do they actually do? They take sides.

If Black is correct, prosecutorial partisanship ought to be most evident where there are closer social ties between prosecutors and one of the parties.

Law Enforcement Officers

Prosecutors and law enforcement officers (LEOs), such as police, prison guards, and probation officers work for the same mega-sized organization – the state. That puts them on the same side in the great majority of criminal cases. Although

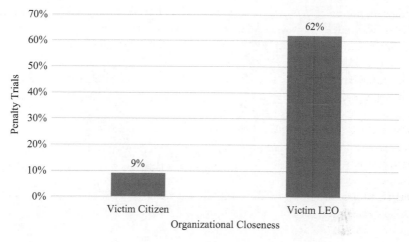

FIGURE 4.2 Penalty Trial by Victim Law Enforcement Officer ($n = 2,483$)

prosecutors have higher official status, they depend heavily on police to provide them with the evidence they need. As Nicole Gonzales Van Cleve (2016: 149) observes, "police offices are prosecutors' star witnesses, making police officers central to the prosecutors' ability to earn the convictions that are so essential to their promotion." In short, prosecutors and LEOs are organizationally close while jurors and LEOs are not (jurors with ties to LEOs would almost certainly be struck). Geometrical theory would lead us to expect that prosecutors are (1) more severe in LEO cases than non-LEO cases and (2) more severe than jurors in LEO cases. We can test these hypotheses with the Baldus data. Doing so reveals a strong pattern (Figure 4.2).

Prosecutors advance six out of ten cases to a penalty trial when the victim is a LEO, compared to one out of ten when they are not. In the cases that make it to a penalty trial, however, jurors are somewhat less likely to impose a death sentence in LEO cases (probably because the prosecutors have advanced LEO cases that are less legally serious than those they normally advance) (Figure 4.3). Combining both stages of the case, the probability of a death sentence is still significantly higher when the victim is a LEO (28%) rather than a private citizen (5%) because prosecutors seek death so often in such cases. Note that a study addressing only juror decisions would conclude that a death sentence is less likely if the victim is a LEO, illustrating the danger of studying a single stage of the legal process (see Appendix 4).

Sentencing

Once the prosecutor announces an intention to seek the death penalty, the case goes forward and the defendant may or may not be convicted. Since the Baldus

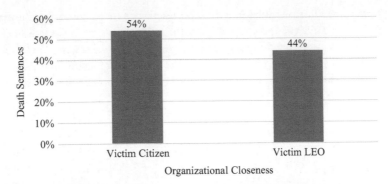

FIGURE 4.3 Death Sentences at Penalty Trial by Victim Law Enforcement Officer ($n = 242$)

data only includes defendants convicted of murder or voluntary manslaughter, we cannot analyze the decision to convict. But the next stage we can scrutinize: the sentence. Should the defendant be sentenced to death or to life imprisonment? This question falls to the jury.

Race and the Jury

Geometrical theory predicts, as we have seen, that third parties who are socially closer to one side will tend to favor that side. Cultural closeness is one form of social closeness. Measures of cultural closeness include whether people share a religion, language, belief system, or ethnicity. If the theory of partisanship is correct, jurors should favor their own culture over that of other cultures. Gay jurors should be somewhat biased in favor of gays, men in favor of men, English-speakers in favor of English-speakers, and so on. Most of the research addresses race.

Racial and ethnic groups, by definition, share a common culture – a collective history, language, set of customs, and the like. The theory predicts that in inter-racial cases, jurors should tend to side with the party of their own race. When a White person harms a Black person, Black jurors who are closer to the victim should favor more severe punishment than White jurors who are closer to the defendant. When a Black person harms a White person, the theory predicts the opposite: White jurors, being closer to the victim, should be more severe than Black jurors who are closer to the defendant. In intra-racial cases – Whites hurt Whites or Blacks hurt Blacks – we would not expect to see sharp differences in severity, as the White and Black jurors are either close to both parties or distant from both parties and hence not strongly drawn to either side.

An experiment conducted by Denis Chimaeze Ugwuegbu (1979) illustrates many of these patterns. The researcher had 244 White students read a description of an aggravated campus rape case and then rate the culpability of the defendant. The defendant was described as either Black or White, and so was the victim;

the "jurors" read just one version each. The researcher then repeated the exercise with 196 Black undergraduates. Strikingly, the culpability ratings were the mirror opposite of each other. Cases that White jurors considered the most culpable – Black on White rape – were rated by Black jurors as the least culpable. And cases that Black jurors considered the most culpable – White on Black rape – were rated by White jurors as the least culpable.

The Ugwuegbu paper is fascinating but, as with many experimental studies conducted at universities, it has an important limitation: the "jurors" were undergraduates. While the researcher went to some pains to ensure that the participants were all of an age to serve on a local jury, the mock jurors were younger than most people who sit on real juries. In addition, they rated their case free of many of the constraints and conditions under which actual jurors operate (e.g., they did not deliberate as a group). Thus, we cannot be sure that the racial partisanship revealed by the study operates in the more complex setting of real-world cases. But several high-profile cases suggest that it does.

In a 1987 incident that was widely publicized at the time, Bernhard Goetz, a White man, shot four Black teenagers who asked him for $5 on the New York subway. Three years previously, Goetz had been mugged by Black teenagers and had suffered permanent damage to his chest. To protect himself against becoming a repeat victim, he began to carry a gun (Rubin 1986: 56–57). A predominately White jury in Manhattan acquitted Goetz of all charges except carrying an unlicensed weapon in public. Subsequently, Goetz was sued in a Bronx civil court by one of the men, Darrell Cabey, who was now confined to a wheelchair because of the incident. Goetz had reportedly shot Cabey as he lay on the floor, saying "You don't look so bad – here's another." This time, a Black and Latino jury ordered Goetz to pay Cabey $43 million in damages (*New York Times* April 24, 1996, section A, p. 20).[10] A sharp divergence in jury decisions arising out of the same set of facts was evident in another pair of high-profile cases, though this time the defendant was Black and the victims were White. O.J. Simpson, a Black former professional football star, was charged in 1995 with murdering two White people in Los Angeles (his ex-wife, Nicole, and a waiter, Ron Goldman, who was returning to her a pair of glasses left at his restaurant). A jury consisting of nine Blacks, two Whites, and one Latino acquitted Simpson of both charges. However, in a civil case for wrongful death brought by the waiter's family, a jury of 11 Whites and one Asian-American found against Simpson and awarded the plaintiff $33 million in damages (see Black 2002: 122–123). In both pairs of cases, the predominately White jury favored the White party (Goetz, Nicole Simpson, and Goldman) and the predominately Black jury favored the Black party (Cabey, O.J. Simpson).

Returning to the Capital Jury Project (CJP) data, recall that CJP staff conducted lengthy interviews with about 1,200 men and women who had served on capital juries in 14 states. About one-half of the cases had ended with a death sentence; the other half resulted in a sentence of life imprisonment. Unfortunately, the data do not enable us to test for racial partisanship. The vast majority (87%) of CJP jurors are White. There are simply too few Black, Latino, or Asian jurors to compare to White jurors once we divide the cases according to the race of the defendant and victim.[11] Collapsing non-White jurors into a single category makes no theoretical sense as there is a good deal of cultural distance between racial and ethnic minorities.[12] We would not expect, for example, Asian jurors to strongly favor a Black victim over a White killer. However, we do have sufficient information on the status of jurors.

Juror Status

Jurors are a cross-section of the population. They have different jobs, levels of education, wealth, family and community involvement, and so forth. Geometrical theory proposes that variation in social status among jurors helps to explain variation in the decisions they make. In sentencing defendants, jurors are acting as settlement agents. (Recall that settlement agents enter a case neutrally, working to bring about a resolution or settlement). Black (1993b: chapter 8) proposed his theory of settlement in a paper titled "Making Enemies." The theory has several parts; for our purposes, the relevant prediction is that, all else the same, higher status settlement agents will be more punitive than lower status settlement agents.[13] This theory applies, in principle, to prosecutors, judges, and jurors, all of whom make decisions about the merits of a case as it progresses through the criminal justice system. We cannot test the prediction for prosecutors or judges, but we can for jurors.

The CJP provides reasonably good measures of juror status for the vertical, radial, organizational, and cultural dimensions, though not the normative dimension (presumably, because people with criminal records do not get to sit on capital juries). Table 4.1 lists the indicators we used. We scored each juror as a yes (1) or no (0) on nine variables: annual family income above $75,000, full-time employment, home ownership, married, children, college degree, Protestant or Catholic (the most common religious affiliations in the United States), White (the most common race/ethnicity in the United States), and veteran.[14] By summing the scores for each juror, we arrived at their overall social status.

Jurors take two votes on sentencing in capital cases: an initial vote when deliberations begin and a final vote when deliberations conclude. Figure 4.4 reports the final vote and reveals that, as predicted, high-status jurors are more severe in that they more often vote for death. The effect is linear and strong. Where jurors with the lowest status score vote for death in about four out of ten cases, those with the highest status score vote for death in seven out of ten cases. (Interestingly, the final vote difference was somewhat greater than the first vote difference; see Appendix 4).

Robust results, but do they disappear when we consider the nature of the murder? Could high-status jurors happened to have served on cases that are more

TABLE 4.1 Measuring Juror Social Status: The CJP Data

Dimensions				
Vertical Status:	*Radial Status:*	*Cultural Status:*	*Normative Status:*	*Organizational Status:*
Wealth	Integration in Social Life	Education and Conventionality	Respectability	Capacity for Collective Action

Measurement of Juror Social Status using Data from the CJP

Family income, employment, home ownership	Marital status, children	College degree, Protestant/ Catholic, White	No indicator	Military veteran

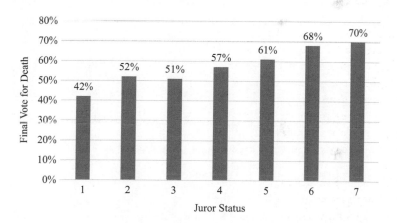

FIGURE 4.4 Final Death Vote by Juror Status ($n = 1,003$)

serious? To find out, we measured the murderous movement of social time. We used the same categories as previously: vertical time and relational time. However, because the CJP is less comprehensive than the Baldus study our measure of social time is less extensive, though still informative (see Table 4.2). Since murder is a large movement of social time, we assigned every case a starting score of 1. Cases acquired additional points if: the defendant killed multiple victims; the defendant injured someone beyond the murder victim; the victim was a child, an elderly person, or a woman; the victim was admired and respected in the community; the victim was maimed after death; or the victim was a stranger.[15]

Figure 4.5 reveals that the larger the movement of social time, the more likely jurors were to vote for death. Jurors opted for death in about one-quarter of the least egregious murders (one movement) compared to almost three-quarters of the most egregious murders (five or more movements). Between such extremes, the differences are more modest.

TABLE 4.2 Measuring the Movement of Social Time in a Capital Murder: The CJP Data

Panel A. Indicators of Vertical Time
  Devastation: defendant killed multiple victims
  Devastation: defendant injured someone other than the murder victim
  Devastation: victim was admired/respected in the community
  Abuse of Physical Power: victim was child (12 or younger), elderly (65 or older), or female

Panel B. Indicators of Relational Time
  Violation of Bodily Integrity: victim maimed after death
  Collapse of Relational Space: victim stranger

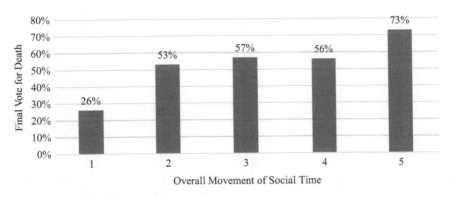

FIGURE 4.5 Final Death Vote by the Overall Movement of Social Time ($n = 902$)

To probe further, we conducted a multivariate analysis, examining the effect of juror status and social time on voting for death, while controlling for several other factors that might affect juror decisions. For jurors, we controlled for age, sex, and whether the juror had lingering doubts about the defendant's guilt (we did not control for the juror's race because it is part of the measure of juror status). For defendants, we controlled for age, sex, whether the defendant acted alone, and whether the defendant was remorseful. We found that both geometrical variables behave as the theory predicts. Each unit-increase in juror status increases the odds of a final death vote by 18%. The effect of social time is even more dramatic, with each unit-increase raising the odds of a final death vote by 42% (see Appendix 4 for details).[16]

To summarize, the CJP data strongly support geometrical theory. Higher status jurors are more likely to vote for death, and larger movements of social time attract more death sentences.

Conclusion

Third parties profoundly shape the outcome of many conflicts. Legal cases are no exception. Who supports whom? How strong is the support? Who decides the case? Black and Baumgartner took up these questions in their 1983 paper, "Toward a Theory of the Third Party." They developed a typology of third parties, distinguishing between types of partisans and settlement agents. In two later papers, "Taking Sides" and "Making Enemies," Black pushed on, proposing a theory of partisanship and settlement, respectively. These overlapping theories were significant advances, adding powerful new variables to his theory of law. The concept of social time provided even more explanatory power. Yet third-party theory has rarely been tested, perhaps because the information necessary to do so is difficult to obtain (but see Phillips and Cooney 2005). In this chapter, the excellent data gathered by Baldus and colleagues and by the CJP allowed us to test some, though not all, third-party effects.

Black's theory of settlement predicts that higher status settlement agents are more severe than are their lower status counterparts. Using the measures of status in the CJP, we found clear evidence in support of Black's theory: the higher the juror's status the more likely they were to vote for death. This was true even controlling for the movement of social time and several other factors that could influence the behavior of jurors.

The theory of partisanship is critical in understanding several aspects of cases, in particular, how legal truth is generated. The facts of the case are derived from the evidence, which begins accumulating with the investigation. Higher status and socially close parties should attract investigations that are more thorough. Analysis of the Baldus data provides some support for that claim: the higher the status of the victim the more likely the state is to generate scientific evidence. So too with the seriousness of the murder: the greater the movement of social time, the more scientific evidence the case attracts.

Witness testimony is the most important evidence in the great majority of cases. The participation, credibility, and truthfulness of witnesses cannot be taken for granted. The social location of the potential witness is important: those who are close to one side and distant from the other are usually reliable but not particularly credible – they are more likely to show up, but less likely to be believed. The same is true of witnesses who are lower in status than the principal: they too can usually be relied upon to participate though their credibility is not of the first order. To maximize both participation and credibility, a litigant should seek to have both close and distant witnesses and high and low-status witnesses. Although we could not test these ideas with our data, if correct, they imply that the impact of social geometry is even greater than we could document.

Partisanship is also evident in how prosecutors and jurors handle the killing of police and corrections officers. The close ties prosecutors have to the police and other legal officials are reflected in the much higher rate at which they seek a death sentence when a LEO is killed. Jurors who do not have the same close ties to law enforcement are more even-handed in imposing a death sentence.

Yet juries are not exempt from displays of partisanship. Jurors can be biased for or against people because of their race, religion, sexual orientation, gender, nationality, or other cultural characteristics.[17] While we cannot test these effects with

CJP data, it is clear that they can powerfully influence the outcome of cases. As an example, consider again the Green and Nenno cases we described at the beginning of the chapter. Nenno raped and killed 7-year-old Nicole Belton. Green raped and killed 14-year-old Abeer Qassim Hamzah Rashid al-Janabi as well as three members of her family. In both cases, the defense team introduced evidence that their clients suffered from psychological abnormalities. But the murders they committed were not equally egregious. If you had to guess which man was sentenced to death, it would surely be Green. His crime was a greater movement of social time: it included four victims (two of whom were minors), a rape, a kidnapping, and the burning of bodies. In fact, Green was spared while Nenno was dispatched to death row and subsequently executed. What saved Green was the jury. Green had a jury that was culturally closer to him than to his victims; Nenno did not. An American jury tried Green for killing Iraqis in Iraq; an American jury tried Nenno for killing an American in America. Nenno's jury was unmoved by his attorney's argument for mercy, but Green's jury did as Green's attorney urged when he pleaded with them in his final statement: "America does not kill its broken warriors! Spare this boy. For God's sake, spare him."[18]

Sources for the Eric Nenno Case

Milling, T.J. 1995. "Hunt for girl ends in tragedy/Neighbor arrested after body of 7-year-old found in attic," *Houston Chronicle*, March 27, p. 1.

Bardwell, S.K. 1995. "Girl wasn't the first, murder suspect says," *Houston Chronicle*, March 28, p. 1.

Kliewer, Terry. 1995. "Arrest of Nenno comes as 'shock' to Arkansas kin," *Houston Chronicle*, April 2, p. 1.

Liebrum, Jennifer. 1996. "Man convicted of killing girl, 7/Punishment phase starts today," *Houston Chronicle*, January 19, p. 29.

Flynn, George. 1996. "Girl's father sues murderer, family," *Houston Chronicle*, January 23, p. 14.

Liebrum, Jennifer. 1996. "Nenno's brain is called abnormal," *Houston Chronicle*, January 31, p. 14.

Liebrum, Jennifer. 1996. "Nenno jury deliberating over sentence," *Houston Chronicle*, February 1, p. 17.

Liebrum, Jennifer. 1996. "Nenno given death – just as he advised," *Houston Chronicle*, February 2, p. 1.

Staff. 1998. "Death sentence upheld," *Houston Chronicle*, June 25, p. 22.

Sources for the Steven Green Case

www.cnn.com/2014/02/18/us/soldier-steven-green-suicide/index.html Retrieved September 21, 2018.

www.bbc.com/news/world-us-canada-26265798 Retrieved September 21, 2018.

www.nbcnews.com/id/40739938/ns/us_news-crime_and_courts/t/ex-soldier-talks-about-slaying-iraqi-family/#.W6WyYXtKiT8 Retrieved September 21, 2018.

www.reuters.com/article/us-usa-iraq-murder-idUSN2037158220070221 Retrieved September 21, 2018.

www.nytimes.com/2009/05/21/us/21soldier.html Retrieved September 21, 2018.

www.huffingtonpost.com/gail-mcgowan-mellor/the-death-of-abeer-in-ira_b_205603.html Retrieved September 21, 2018.

http://content.time.com/time/nation/article/0,8599,1900389,00.html Retrieved September 21, 2018.

http://content.time.com/time/nation/article/0,8599,1960824,00.html Retrieved September 21, 2018.

Appendix 4

In this chapter, we used the Baldus data and the CJP data to investigate the role of third parties in death penalty cases. Specifically, we analyzed whether the behavior of police officers, prosecutors, and jurors conformed to Black's theoretical predictions.

To begin, we examined whether police effort – a form of partisanship on behalf of the victim – depends on the social status of the victim.[19] Drawing on the Baldus data, police effort is measured by the presence of scientific evidence in a case. Did police take the time to collect and analyze fingerprints, footprints, tire tracks, or trace evidence such as blood and hair?[20] Doing so requires additional work, especially in cases that were investigated 50 years ago. Following the procedure we established in prior analyses of the Baldus data, the status of the victim is operationalized as the sum of five dichotomous indicators: whether the victim had a professional job; whether the victim worked as a state official (police officers, corrections employees, and active-duty military personnel); whether the victim was a parent supporting children; whether the victim was White; and whether the victim had a clean criminal record.[21]

Table 4.3 reveals that police labor is a function of the victim's social standing. Indeed, the effect is linear and significant ($p < 0.001$). Among cases with the lowest status victims (a score of 0), no case had scientific evidence. Among cases with the highest status victims (a score of 4), 28% of the cases had scientific evidence.

But it is possible that high-status victims were killed in an especially gruesome manner. If so, the heinousness of the murder might explain the drive to collect and analyze scientific evidence. Table 4.4 examines the relationship between victim status and scientific evidence, controlling for the movement of social time (the model also includes the roster of control variables used in prior analyses of the Baldus data).[22] Both geometrical variables matter: for each unit-increase in victim

TABLE 4.3 Scientific Evidence by Victim Social Status ($n = 2{,}483$)

	Scientific Evidence[1]	
	Number	*Percent*
Victim Social Status		
0	0/34	0.0%
1	83/1,234	6.7%
2	138/879	15.7%
3	61/300	20.3%
4	10/36	27.8%

Notes:

1 $p < 0.001$; chi-square = 40.466 with 4 DF (percentages are based on the weighted data, but chi-square is based on the unweighted data because it assumes independent observations).

2 As discussed in Appendix 2, chi-square is an omnibus test of statistical significance. Thus, the p value indicates the probability of committing a Type I error if one rejects the null hypothesis of equal treatment across categories. The p value does not indicate whether specific differences are significant. But the logistic regression model in Table 4.4 estimates the effect of a one-unit change in victim social status on scientific evidence.

TABLE 4.4 Odds Ratios from the Weighted Logistic Regression of Scientific Evidence on Victim Social Status ($n = 2{,}483$)

	Odds Ratio
Social Geometry[1]	
Victim Social Status	1.40★★
Overall Movement of Social Time	1.56★★★
Controls (Baldus variable name)[2]	
Defendant Deliberated (DTHINK)	0.74
Defendant Did Not Kill (NOKILL)	1.63
Number of Types of Evidence Against Defendant (EVINDX2)	1.73★
Sentenced 1974 (LDF4B)	3.78★
Sentenced 1975 (LDF4B)	2.77★
Sentenced 1976 (LDF4B)	2.04
Sentenced 1977 (LDF4B)	2.48★
Sentenced 1978 (LDF4B)	3.29★
Sentenced 1979 (LDF4B)	2.26
Sentenced 1980 (LDF4B)	3.55★

Notes:

1 In this model, the overall movement of social time does not include whether the victim was high status.

2 The reference category for year is 1973.

★$p < 0.05$; ★★$p < 0.01$; ★★★$p < 0.001$.

status, the odds of scientific evidence increase by 40% ($p < 0.01$); for each unit-increase in the movement of social time, the odds of scientific evidence increase by 56% ($p < 0.001$). Bottom line: police officers work harder on behalf of high-status victims.

We next examined whether prosecutors were more likely to advance a case to a penalty trial if the victim was a LEO killed in the line of duty.[23] As representatives of the state, prosecutors and LEOs are allies in the fight against crime. According to Blackian theory, organizational closeness should produce partisanship. Drawing on the Baldus data, Table 4.5 provides strong support for the geometrical prediction. Prosecutors were about seven times more likely to advance a case to a penalty trial if the victim was a LEO, as compared to a citizen (Panel A). But jurors had no such allegiance. Among the subset of cases that advanced to a penalty trial, jurors were slightly less likely to impose a death sentence if the victim was a LEO (Panel B). In short, prosecutors "back the blue."

Having examined partisanship, we turn to settlement. Specifically, are high-status jurors more punitive? To test the theoretical proposition, we used the CJP data. Because we are shifting to a different data set, a brief recap of the CJP is in order. Recall that the CJP includes interviews with 1,198 capital jurors who served in more than 350 trials across 14 states: Alabama, California, Florida, Georgia, Indiana, Kentucky, Louisiana, Missouri, North Carolina, Pennsylvania, South Carolina, Tennessee, Texas, and Virginia.[24] Cases with death sentences and life sentences were chosen in equal numbers. Directed by William Bowers and supported by the National Science Foundation, the purpose of the CJP was to answer a constitutional

TABLE 4.5 Penalty Trials and Death Sentences by Victim Law Enforcement Officer

	Panel A: Prosecutor Advanced Case to a Penalty Trial[1] (n=2,483)		Panel B: Death Sentence Given Penalty Trial[2] (n=242)		Panel C: Overall Death Sentences[3] (n=2,483)	
	Number	Percent	Number	Percent	Number	Percent
Victim Regular Citizen	224/2,454	9.1%	120/224	53.6%	120/2,454	4.9%
Victim LEO	18/29	62.1%	8/18	44.4%	8/29	27.6%

Notes:
1 $p < 0.001$; chi-square = 49.634 with 1 DF (percentages are based on the weighted data, but chi-square is based on the unweighted data because it assumes independent observations).
2 We do not present a test of statistical significance because the calculation is based on population data. The Baldus data include the universe of penalty trials for the place and period in question (EJDP, p. 429).
3 $p < 0.001$; chi-square = 13.799 with 1 DF (percentages are based on the weighted data, but chi-square is based on the unweighted data because it assumes independent observations).

question (Did legislative reforms eliminate arbitrariness in capital punishment?) and support future litigation. In contrast, we use the CJP to test geometrical ideas. Since the CJP interviews were conducted for a different purpose, the data provide naïve evidence – evidence that is not biased for or against Black's theory.

Returning to the question of whether high-status jurors are more punitive, it is important to recall that Black treats social status as a multidimensional concept comprised of vertical status (wealth), radial status (integration in social life), cultural status (education and conventionality), organizational status (the capacity for collective action), and normative status (respectability). The CJP data include indicators of all the dimensions except normative status. As detailed in Table 4.6, juror status was operationalized as the sum of nine dichotomous

TABLE 4.6 Indicators of Juror Social Status

Dimension of Social Space	Description	Indicators	Codes	CJP Variable Name
Vertical	Wealth	Annual Family Income	1 = >$75,000 (highest bracket)	Q98
			0 = ≤ $75,000	
		Full Time Employment Outside Home	1 = yes 0 = no	Q97
		Home Owner	1 = yes	Q917
			0 = no	
Radial	Integration	Married (married once and still together)	1 = yes 0 = no	Q93, Q94
		Children (includes own, step, and foster)	1 = yes 0 = no	Q95
Cultural	Education	College Degree	1 = yes	Q96
			0 = no	
	Conventionality	Modal Religion in United States	1 = Protestant/ Catholic	Q912
			0 = Jewish/None/ Other	
		Modal Race in United States	1 = White 0 = non-White	Q91B
Organizational	Capacity for Collective Action	Military Veteran	1 = yes 0 = no	Q915

Note:
The CJP variable name refers to the section of the interview instrument and the question number within that section. For example, the CJP variable "annual family income" (Q98) can be found in section IX, question 8.

indicators: whether the juror had an annual family income above $75,000 (the highest income bracket); whether the juror was employed full-time; whether the juror owned a home; whether the juror was married; whether the juror had children; whether the juror had a college degree; whether the juror was Protestant or Catholic (the most common religions in the United States); whether the juror was White (the most common race/ethnicity in the United States); and whether the juror was a military veteran.

Table 4.7 considers whether the juror's social status predicts voting for a death sentence, including the person's first vote and final vote.[25] Juror status ranges from 1 (lowest) to 7 (highest). The data reveal a linear pattern: as juror status increases, so too does the chance of voting for death. Comparing the lowest status jurors to the highest status jurors, the magnitude of the relationship is substantial: the probability of initially voting for death increases by 20 percentage points (from 50% to 70%) and the probability of ultimately voting for death increases by 28 percentage points (from 42% to 70%). Both models are significant ($p < 0.01$).

Before concluding that high-status jurors are more punitive, we must consider an alternative explanation for the pattern: such jurors served in the most horrific cases. Table 4.8 describes how we measured the movement of social time using the CJP data. Although the Baldus data provided numerous indicators of vertical time and relational time, the CJP data provided just a few. Thus, we combined the

TABLE 4.7 Death Vote by Juror Status ($n = 1,003$)

	First Vote for Death[1]		Final Vote for Death[2]	
	Number	Percent	Number	Percent
Composite Juror Status[3]				
1	13/26	50.0%	11/26	42.3%
2	37/81	45.7%	42/81	51.9%
3	70/149	47.0%	76/149	51.0%
4	154/283	54.4%	161/283	56.9%
5	147/241	61.0%	147/241	61.0%
6	98/157	62.4%	106/157	67.5%
7	46/66	69.7%	46/66	69.7%

Notes:
1 $p < 0.01$; chi-square = 19.170 with 6 DF.
2 $p < 0.01$; chi-square = 17.321 with 6 DF.
3 Composite juror status originally ranged from 1 to 9. But categories 1 and 9 did not have enough cases. Thus, categories 1 and 2 were combined (now category 1) and categories 8 and 9 were combined (now category 7).
4 As discussed in Appendix 2, chi-square is an omnibus test of statistical significance. Thus, the p value indicates the probability of committing a Type I error if one rejects the null hypothesis of equal treatment across categories. The p value does not indicate whether specific differences are significant. But the logistic regression model in Table 4.10 estimates the effect of a one-unit change in juror social status on voting for death.

TABLE 4.8 Indicators of the Movement of Social Time in a Capital Murder: The CJP Data

Panel A. Indicators of Vertical Time

	Codes	*CJP Variables*
Devastation: defendant killed multiple victims	1 = yes 0 = no	Q2a4a1
Devastation: defendant injured someone other than murder victim	1 = yes 0 = no	Q2a4a2
Devastation: victim was admired/respected in the community	1 = yes (admired/respected in the community describes victim "very well" or "fairly well") 0 = no	Q2c1a
Abuse of Physical Power: victim was child (12 or younger), elderly (65 or older), or female	1 = yes 0 = no	Combination of victim age (Q2a4cv1a through Q2a4cv6a) and victim sex (Q2a4cv1s through Q2a4cv6s)

Panel B. Indicators of Relational Time

	Codes	*CJP Variables*
Violation of Bodily Integrity: victim maimed after death	1 = yes (describes "very well" or "fairly well") 0 = no	Q2a2l
Collapse of Relational Space: victim stranger	1 = yes 0 = no	Q2a5f

CJP indicators into a single or overall measure of the movement of social time. Following the same procedure as before, we assigned a baseline score of 1 to each case; all murders are extreme movements of social time. The murder was even more egregious if: the defendant killed multiple victims; the defendant injured someone beyond the murder victim; the victim was a child, an elderly person, or a woman; the victim was admired and respected in the community; the victim was maimed after death; or the victim was a stranger.

Table 4.9 reveals that jurors are influenced by the movement of social time. Consider the juror's first vote for a death sentence. As the movement of social time climbs from a minimum of 1 (none of the above circumstances occurred) to a maximum of 5 (four or more of the above circumstances occurred), the chance of initially voting for death increases from 31% to 63% ($p < 0.01$). Consider, too, the juror's final vote for a death sentence. As the movement of social time climbs

TABLE 4.9 Death Vote by the Overall Movement of Social Time ($n = 902$)

	First Vote for Death[1]		Final Vote for Death[2]	
	Number	Percent	Number	Percent
Overall Movement of Social Time[1 2 3]				
1	12/39	30.8%	10/39	25.6%
2	69/137	50.4%	72/137	52.6%
3	177/330	53.6%	189/330	57.3%
4	157/254	61.8%	143/254	56.3%
5	90/142	63.4%	103/142	72.5%

Notes:

1 The overall movement of social time originally ranged from 1 to 7. But categories 6 and 7 did not have enough cases. Thus, categories 5, 6, and 7 were combined.

2 Movement of social time and first vote for death: $p < 0.01$; chi-square = 19.208 with 4 DF.

3 Movement of social time and final vote for death: $p < 0.001$; chi-square = 30.815 with 4 DF.

4 As discussed in Appendix 2, chi-square is an omnibus test of statistical significance. Thus, the p value indicates the probability of committing a Type I error if one rejects the null hypothesis of equal treatment across categories. The p value does not indicate whether specific differences are significant. But the logistic regression model in Table 4.10 estimates the effect of a one-unit change in the overall movement of social time on voting for death.

from minimum to maximum, the chance of ultimately voting for death roughly triples from 26% to 73% ($p < 0.001$).

The unadjusted models suggest that geometrical variables – juror status and the movement of social time – predict voting for death. Table 4.10 investigates whether the relationships hold true after controlling for confounding variables, including: juror age, juror sex, whether the juror had lingering doubts about the defendant's guilt, defendant age, defendant sex, whether the defendant acted alone, and whether the defendant was remorseful. The models provide an affirmative answer. Consider the juror's final – and most fateful – decision. For each unit-increase in juror status, the odds of voting for death increase by 18% ($p < 0.05$). The heinousness of the murder is also critical. For each unit-increase in the movement of social time, the odds of voting for death increase by 42% ($p < 0.01$).

TABLE 4.10 Odds Ratios from the Logistic Regression of Death Vote on Juror Status and the Movement of Social Time ($n = 733$)[1]

	First Vote for Death	Final Vote for Death
Social Geometry		
Juror Status	1.19**	1.18*
Overall Movement of Social Time	1.35**	1.42**
Controls		
Juror Age	0.98*	0.99
Juror Male	1.16	1.03
Juror Has Lingering Doubts About Guilt	0.17***	0.33***
Defendant Age	1.02	1.04*
Defendant Male	1.23	1.61
Defendant Acted Alone	1.19	1.11
Defendant Remorseful	0.16***	0.18***

Note:
1 Robust standard errors were estimated in Stata to adjust for the clustering of jurors within cases.
*$p < 0.05$; **$p < 0.01$; ***$p < 0.001$

Notes

1 www.nbcnews.com/id/40739938/ns/us_news-crime_and_courts/t/ex-soldier-talks-about-slaying-iraqi-family/#.W6WyYXtKiT8.
2 www.nbcnews.com/id/40739938/ns/us_news-crime_and_courts/t/ex-soldier-talks-about-slaying-iraqi-family/#.W6WyYXtKiT8.
3 http://content.time.com/time/nation/article/0,8599,1960824,00.html.
4 http://content.time.com/time/nation/article/0,8599,1900389,00.html.
5 Independent autopsies are rare but not unknown. After George Floyd died while being restrained by police in Minneapolis in June 2020, an autopsy ordered by his family and conducted by two independent pathologists came to a different conclusion as to the cause of death than that of the Medical Examiner. (www.cbsnews.com/news/george-floyd-death-autopsies-homicide-axphyxiation-details/).
6 Phillips and Richardson (2016: 444–445) also found that the more evidentiary flaws a case had, the longer it took to have the defendant exonerated.
7 Texas does not have a statewide public defender office. Instead, the indigent defendants in Phillips's (2009) study received a court-appointed defense attorney – a system that has been heavily criticized. In other states, an indigent capital defendant would be represented by an experienced public defender who specializes in capital litigation. Whether capital defendants who hire a lawyer fare better might depend on the state in question.
8 Another issue we would like to have been able to pursue, but could not, is whether attorney effort differs by the social status of the client and the attorney–client relationship. Do lawyers try harder for higher status clients or for family members and friends? The Baldus data do not shed light on these questions. In her ethnography of a Chicago

criminal court, Nicole Van Cleve (2016: 174–176) describes several cases in which defendants whose status was clearly superior to that of the typical low-status defendant received more support from their public defender. But because of the small number of cases, strong conclusions cannot be drawn.

9   Defendants who plead guilty are not advanced. Of the 2,483 Baldus defendants: 1,187 had a jury trial; 3 had a bench trial; and 1,274 (52%) entered a plea of guilty (information was missing for 19 cases).

10   We thank Dan Boches for drawing our attention to this example.

11   The best we can do is compare the decisions of White and Black jurors, but even there we do not have enough White-on-Black killings (only 22 jurors, 19 of whom were White, sat on such cases). We find that in Black-on-White killings, White jurors were more likely to vote for death than were Black jurors. At first vote, 65% of White jurors opted for death compared to 14% of Black jurors – a 51 percentage point gap. At final vote, 56% of White jurors opted for death compared to 35% of Black jurors – a 21 percentage point gap. In the intraracial cases, the gap in final death votes is, as expected, smaller: 11 percentage points in White-White and 10 percentage points in Black-Black cases. Full details are available on request.

12   We thank Bradley Campbell for emphasizing this point.

13   Black (1993b) also proposes that settlement varies in how authoritative (or decisive), formalistic (reliance on explicit rules), and coercive (use of force) it is. We do not consider these dimensions of settlement here (but see Cooney 2009).

14   Our findings are the same regardless of whether race is included in the measure of juror status. Models available upon request.

15   The CJP data also includes subjective indicators of social time. Specifically, jurors were asked if the murder made you sick, made the victim suffer, or was bloody, depraved, gory, repulsive, or vicious. We also created an overall measure of the movement of social time in each case using the subjective indicators. Our substantive findings remained the same (models available upon request). But we do not present the subjective indicators because an objective concept – the movement of social time – should be measured by objective indicators.

16   Two control variables attained statistical significance. One is having lingering doubt about guilt, which reduces the probability that a juror will vote for death. Lingering doubt could be interpreted through a geometrical lens: if the defendant did not commit the murder then he is not responsible for the movement of social time suffered by the victim, and therefore should not suffer a reciprocal and proportional movement of social time – being sentenced to death and executed. The second was remorse on the part of the defendant. Again, this could be interpreted geometrically: defendants who said they were sorry for what they had done were, in effect, partially reversing the movement of social time. An expression of remorse involves self-criticism. That lowers the status of the person issuing it and modifies the increased status gap between the parties that resulted from the killing.

17   The Ugwuegbu study, for instance, found that female jurors rated the defendant more culpable of rape of a female victim than did male jurors.

18   http://content.time.com/time/nation/article/0,8599,1900389,00.html.

19   We conducted two distinct analyses of scientific evidence. Consider each in turn. Black argues that partisanship should be greater if the victim is higher in status than the defendant (1993a, p. 127, including footnote 10). The data are supportive: 20% of downward cases produced scientific evidence, compared to 9% of the remaining cases ($p < 0.001$). The relationship remains after controlling for confounding variables

(model available upon request). Black also argues that partisanship should increase as the status of the victim increases, noting: "Those with the most intimacy and social stature attract the most support" (1993a: 127). Again, the data are supportive as demonstrated in Figure 4.1. Both analyses provide a strong test of Black's theoretical argument. But the latter analysis hews closer to the idea that status effects are a matter of degree. As Black notes, "The greater the differences, the greater the effects" (1993a: 127). Thus, we present the latter analysis.

20   The Baldus data include a variable called scientific evidence (SCIEVID). SCIEVID is coded 1 if LDF451 = 1 (see CSS codebook, p. 99). Despite the name, Baldus's variable for scientific evidence includes non-scientific evidence (such as whether the defendant's personal belongings were found at the scene). We created a new variable for scientific evidence (y_SCIENTIFIC_EV) coded 1 if the police analyzed fingerprints, footprints, tire tracks, or trace evidence (such as blood or hair). Thus, we excluded non-scientific evidence. Our revised measure of scientific evidence is coded as follows: scientific evidence = 1 if LDF452, LDF453, LDF454, LDF455, LDF456, or LDF457 is coded 1, 2, 3, 5, 5A, or 6 (for details see EJDP 1990, p. 543).

21   See Appendix 2.

22   In Table 4.4, the overall movement of social time does not include victim status (because it is analyzed separately).

23   The Baldus variables for the analysis are LDF38 (whether the case advanced to a penalty trial; recoded 1 = 1, else = 0) and LDFB8 (whether the victim was a police officer or corrections officer killed in the line of duty).

24   See: What is the Capital Jury Project? www.albany.edu/scj/13189.php. Retrieved 8/26/2019.

25   The CJP variable for the juror's first vote (q414) includes codes for death, life, undecided, and missing. We began by recoding the juror's first vote into two categories: death = 1 and non-death = 0 (including life and undecided). Next, we reduced the number of missing values on first vote from 105 to 49. To do so, we compared the juror's final vote (finvfiz) to whether the juror's first vote and final vote were the same (q415). That strategy worked to correct missing values unless: (1) the data were missing on whether the juror's first vote and final vote were the same (the CJP includes complete data on final vote), or (2) the juror's final vote was for life, but the juror's first vote was different (meaning the juror's first vote could have been for death or undecided which are coded differently). We restricted our analyses to the 1,149 cases where we knew the juror's first vote and final vote, as doing so provides a consistent set of cases.

References

Baldus, David C., George Woodworth, and Charles A. Pulaski. 1990. *Equal Justice and the Death Penalty: A Legal and Empirical Analysis.* Boston: Northeastern University Press.

Berrey, Ellen, Robert L. Nelson, and Laura Beth Nielsen. 2017. *Rights on Trial: How Workplace Discrimination Perpetuates Inequality.* Chicago: University of Chicago Press.

Black, Donald. 1976. *The Behavior of Law.* New York: Academic Press.

Black, Donald. 1993a. "Taking Sides." Chapter 7, pp. 125–143 in *The Social Structure of Right and Wrong.* Orlando: Academic Press.

Black, Donald. 1993b. "Making Enemies." Chapter 8, pp. 144–157 in *The Social Structure of Right and Wrong*. Orlando: Academic Press.

Black, Donald. 2000. "Dreams of Pure Sociology." *Sociological Theory* 18:345–367.

Black, Donald. 2002. "The Geometry of Law: An Interview with Donald Black." *International Journal of the Sociology of Law* 30:101–129.

Black, Donald and M.P. Baumgartner. 1983. "Toward a Theory of the Third Party." Pp. 84–114 in *Empirical Theories about Courts*, edited by Keith O. Boyum and Lynn Mather. New York: Longman.

Campbell, Bradley and Jason Manning. 2018. *The Rise of Victimhood Culture: Microaggressions, Safe Spaces, and the New Culture Wars*. New York: Palgrave Macmillan.

Cooney, Mark. 1994. "Evidence as Partisanship." *Law & Society Review* 28:833–858.

Cooney, Mark. 2009. *Is Killing Wrong? A Study in Pure Sociology*. Charlottesville: University of Virginia Press.

Dershowitz, Alan M. 1986. *Reversal of Fortune: Inside the Von Bulow Case*. New York: Random House.

Frank, Jerome. 1949. *Courts on Trial: Myth and Reality in American Justice*. Princeton: Princeton University Press, 1973.

GBD. 2019. Police Violence Subnational Collaborators. 2021. "Fatal Police Violence by Race and State in the USA, 1980–2019: A Network Meta-Regression." *The Lancet* 398:1239–1255.

Hunt, Jennifer and Peter Manning. 1991. "The Social Context of Police Lying." *Symbolic Interaction* 14:51–70.

Leovy, Jill. 2015. *Ghettoside: A True Story of Murder in America*. New York: Spiegel & Grau.

Mann, Kenneth. 1984. *Defending White-Collar Crime: A Portrait of Attorneys at Work*. New Haven: Yale University Press.

O'Barr, William M. 1982. *Linguistic Evidence: Language, Power, and Strategy in the Courtroom*. New York: Academic Press.

Phillips, Scott. 2009. "Legal Disparities in the Capital of Capital Punishment." *Journal of Criminal Law and Criminology* 99:717–756.

Phillips, Scott and Mark Cooney. 2005. "Aiding Peace, Abetting Violence: Third Parties and the Management of Conflict." *American Sociological Review* 70:334–354.

Phillips, Scott and Jamie Richardson. 2016. "The Worst of the Worst: Heinous Crimes and Erroneous Evidence." *Hofstra Law Review* 45:417–449.

Rubin, Lillian B. 1986. *Quiet Rage: Bernie Goetz in a Time of Madness*. Berkeley: University of California Press.

Sandefur, Rebecca. 2010. "The Impact of Counsel: An Analysis of Empirical Evidence." *Seattle Journal for Social Justice* 9:51–95.

Seron, Carroll, Gregg Van Ryzin and Martin Frankel. 2001. "The Impact of Legal Counsel on Procedural Outcomes for Poor Tenants in New York City's Housing Court: Results of a Randomized Experiment." *Law and Society Review* 35:419–434.

Simon, David. 1991. *Homicide: A Year on the Killing Streets*. Boston: Houghton Mifflin.

Stafford-Smith, Clive. 2020. "No Steps Forward for Some: Edward Earl Johnson at Sixty." *The Times Literary Supplement* 6116, June 19:20–21.

Stevenson, Bryan. 2014. *Just Mercy: A Story of Justice and Redemption*. New York: Spiegel and Grau.

Timmermans, Stefan. 2006. *Postmortem: How Medical Examiners Explain Suspicious Death*. Chicago: University of Chicago Press.

Toobin, Jeffrey. 1996. *The Run of His Life: The People v O.J. Simpson*. New York: Random House.

Ugwuegbu, Dennis Chimaeze E. 1979. "Racial and Evidential Actors in Juror Attributions of Legal Responsibility." *Journal of Experimental Social Psychology* 15:133–146.

Van Cleve, Nicole Gonzales. 2016. *Crook County: Racism and Injustice in America's Largest Criminal Court*. Stanford: Stanford University Press.

5

THE DEATH PENALTY AND BEYOND

Winona, Mississippi: July 16, 1996

Shortly after Tardy's furniture store opened its doors for another day's business, the store's owner, Bertha Tardy, bookkeeper, Carmen Rigby, delivery man, Robert Golden, and a 16-year-old, Derrick "Bo Bo" Stewart, were shot in the head, execution style. There were no eyewitnesses to the murders in the store. Several victims' relatives suspected Curtis Flowers, who had worked at the store for three days earlier that summer delivering and fixing furniture. He had been let go after he stopped showing up for work. However, the police did not immediately charge Flowers, who shortly after moved to Texas to live with his sister. Some months later, though, the police arrested Flowers and charged him with four counts of capital murder.

The state claimed Flowers was a disgruntled former employee who had vented his anger on everybody in the store. Even though no fingerprints, murder weapon, or DNA evidence linked Flowers to the crime, a jury convicted him in less than an hour. At the penalty stage, he was sentenced to death. Flowers appealed his conviction and it was overturned. He was retried again, thus beginning a long sequence of retrials. In total, the same prosecutor, Doug Evans, tried Flowers six times for the crimes. He was found guilty in trials 1, 2, and 3 but those convictions were overturned by the Mississippi Supreme Court. In trials 4 and 5, the jury split along racial lines and could not reach a decision. He was found guilty in trial 6 and sentenced to death. The United States Supreme Court overturned that conviction. However, the Court gave the state the option of re-trying him a seventh time. Following the Court's decision, Evans removed himself from the case and the state Attorney General took over. Flowers was released from prison on bail after nearly 23 years (of which 20 were spent on death row). Several months later, in

DOI: 10.4324/9781003176633-6

September 2020, the Attorney General of Mississippi dropped all charges against Flowers.

Being tried six times for the same crime is unprecedented in U.S. legal history. What explains the zeal with which the DA pursued Curtis Flowers? One important factor was race. Three of the four murder victims were White; the defendant was Black. The Supreme Court agreed that the prosecutor had impermissibly excluded Blacks from the jury. Consider the racial dynamics:

- In the first four trials, the DA used all 36 peremptory strikes to exclude Black jurors.
- In the six trials combined, 61 of the 72 jurors were White even though 53% of Winona's residents are Black.
- Of the 61 White jurors, all voted to convict. Of the 11 Black jurors, five voted to convict.
- At the sixth trial, Evans struck five of the six prospective Black jurors, leaving just one Black juror to serve. The DA also asked potential Black jurors more questions: Evans asked the Black jurors who were struck a total of 145 questions, compared to just 12 total questions for the 11 White jurors who were seated.

Important though race was, other factors mattered too. Indeed, the case illustrates the importance of considering the entire case geometry, a point to which we shall return. For now, let us review where we are. In the previous chapters, we presented and tested the three principal components of the geometrical theory of law formulated by Donald Black. Here we assemble those components into a single theory, summarize our findings, discuss several additional applications of the theory, and outline issues for future investigation.

We begin by reviewing the theory. Black developed the theory in several principal phases, publishing first, *The Behavior of Law*, then the third-party papers, and finally *Moral Time*. Our presentation is a little different: we summarize the theory in the sequence exhibited by the life course of conflicts rather than the sequence in which the ideas saw the light of day. In describing the theory, we will expand on our previous description, revealing several of its additional elements – particularly those related to social time. But, first, we summarize the paradigm in which the theory is packaged: pure sociology.

Pure Sociology

Three broad types of scientific laws govern human behavior: the laws of the body, the mind, and the social world. The laws of the body are the province of biology, the laws of the mind the province of psychology, and the laws of the social world the province of sociology. Of these, the laws of the social world are the least developed, in part because our habitual, common sense way of thinking is to combine psychological and sociological elements. Pure sociology is that branch of science dedicated to discovering the laws of the social world as such: sociology without psychology or biology.

The social world is created through social interaction – between people, groups, corporations, states. Black calls this reality social space, and it has several dimensions. The five principal dimensions that have been discovered to date are: the vertical (wealth), horizontal (connectivity), symbolic (culture), normative (social control), and corporate (organization). People and groups occupy positions or locations in each of these dimensions. Those locations are statuses. A wealthy person has high vertical status, a married person high horizontal or radial status, and a college professor high cultural status. An individual has low organizational status, and a criminal record confers low normative status. When actors at the same status level, whether high or low, interact we say their interaction is lateral. Between unequal parties, interaction is vertical – either downward (from high status to low status) or upward (from low status to high status). Interaction also varies across horizontal distances, such as relational and cultural distance. Relational distance is the degree of involvement in the life of others – are people intimates, acquaintances, or strangers? Cultural distance is the degree of cultural diversity between actors – do they speak the same or different languages, adhere to the same or different cultures, worship the same or different gods?

The location, direction, distance, and movement of actors in social space constitutes their social geometry. Pure sociology is a broad theoretical system that, in principle, can be applied to explain any type of human behavior. Geometrical explanations have two principal components: temporal and spatial. The temporal component is dynamic: an alteration or change in social space constitutes a movement of social time. Social time explains, for example, why conflict occurs and how severe or serious the conflict will be. The spatial component is static: a snapshot of the relative position of the parties in social space. Social space explains the handling of conflict. (Since the temporal component includes some elements of social space, there is some overlap between the two branches of geometrical theory.) Third-party theory combines the spatial and temporal components to make predictions about partisanship and settlement.

The Geometrical Theory of Law

Recall that Black's geometrical theory explains the quantity and style of law.[1] The quantity of law is the amount of governmental social control that enters a conflict. The four styles of law are the penal, compensatory, therapeutic, and conciliatory. The death penalty is a severe form of punishment and so falls squarely within the penal style. Since our data are confined to the penal style, our analysis focuses only on variation in the quantity of law, and specifically on two issues: who gets the death penalty, and who gets executed.

For our purposes, then, the theory consists of a series of testable propositions linking variation in the quantity of law to variation in social geometry. Below we briefly describe each theory, present ten core propositions, outline how we tested them with capital punishment data, and summarize what we found.

Social Time

Social space is constantly fluctuating as people's circumstances improve or worsen, as they become closer or more distant from others, and as they encounter or reject other cultures. Most of these movements are small, barely noticeable. Even so, they can cause irritation, especially if they are repeated. And some movements of social time are larger and faster – and more prone to trigger overt conflict.

Homicide is a particularly large movement of social time: it violates the victim's physical space and bodily integrity and deprives the victim of something of great value – life itself. The negative consequences of homicide may radiate outward as family members lose loved ones, neighbors lose friends, and coworkers lose colleagues. Some homicides are even larger movements of social time. When the victim is physically vulnerable, robbed, or killed in a humiliating manner, for example, the movement of vertical time is greater. When the victim is kidnapped, raped, or tortured, the movement of relational time is greater. Homicides that are larger movements of social time are larger movements of legal time: they trigger more detailed investigations, more serious charges, more vigorous prosecutions, and more severe sentences. Where the death penalty is available, larger movements of social time increase the probability that the defendant will be charged with capital murder, convicted of that crime, sentenced to death, and executed.

The concept of social time provides a solution to the long-standing problem of conduct seriousness. The movement of vertical, relational, and cultural time entailed by an action provides a factual, value-free criterion for assessing the amount of law that different actions – beating, killing, trespassing, breaking promises, and so forth – are likely to attract. Fortunately, the Baldus data set includes multiple measure of the movement of vertical time, including the number of victims killed, the vulnerability of the victims, and the degree of domination of the killing itself (Baldus, Woodworth, and Pulaski 1990). Also included are variables measuring the movement of relational time, such as whether the victim was raped, tortured, or held hostage. With these measures in hand, we tested this proposition: *Law increases with social time.* We found that:

- The larger the movement of vertical time, the more likely a death sentence.
- The larger the movement of relational time, the more likely a death sentence.
- The larger the movement of social time (vertical and relational time combined) the more likely a death sentence.
- The larger the movement of social time, the more likely an execution.

Social Space

The conduct of the parties is important but so too is who those parties are. Social time incorporates some aspects of social space: the murder of a high-status person is a greater movement of vertical time and the murder of a stranger a greater movement of relational time. However, Black's original theory presented in *The Behavior of Law* and elaborated in *Sociological Justice* provides a more comprehensive spatial theory. The theory's core claim is the quantity of law varies with the location, direction, and distance of cases in a multidimensional social space or, more simply, the social status and distance of the parties. We reduced Black's theory to four core propositions and tested each one.

To test the theory's status predictions, we located indicators of vertical, radial, cultural, normative, and organizational status in the Baldus data and combined them to create an overall measure of defendant social status and victim social status. Doing so allowed us to test the proposition, *Downward law is greater than upward law.*

We found that:

- Downward cases are more likely to result in a death sentence than upward cases.
- Given a death sentence, downward cases are more likely to end in an execution than upward cases.[2]

A second proposition states: *In a downward direction, law increases with vertical distance.*[3] We found that:

- The more downwardly distant the case, the more likely a death sentence.

A third proposition states: *Law increases with social status.* We found that:

- Cases between higher-status parties are more likely to result in a death sentence than cases between lower-status parties.
- Given a death sentence, cases between higher-status parties are more likely to end in an execution than cases between lower-status parties.

A fourth proposition states: *Law increases with relational distance.* We found that:

- Stranger cases are more likely to result in a death sentence than nonstranger cases.
- Given a death sentence, stranger cases are more likely to end in an execution than nonstranger cases.

Third Parties

The theory of the third party supplements the theory of law. Third parties fall into two main categories: partisans who provide support to one side, and settlement agents who work to settle the case. The theory of partisanship predicts how thoroughly the prosecution and defense investigate cases, whether witnesses appear, how strongly witnesses present their testimony, how credible witnesses are, how adversarial lawyers are in representing their clients, and with whom jurors side. The theory of settlement predicts several variable aspects of settlement behavior, the most important of which for our purposes is its severity. To impose a death sentence is clearly more severe than to pass a sentence of life imprisonment; the theory of settlement, if valid, should therefore help to predict the decisions of capital jurors.

Using a combination of the Baldus data and the Capital Jury Project (CJP) data, we were able to test several aspects of third-party theory, beginning with possible partisanship on the part of prosecutors and jurors. The first principle of partisanship states: *Partisanship increases with social closeness to one side and social distance from the other.* We found that:

- Prosecutors are far more likely to advance a case to a penalty trial when officers of the law are killed.
- At the penalty trial, however, citizen jurors are somewhat more likely to impose a death sentence for the killing of a fellow citizen than for an officer of the law.

The second proposition states: *Partisanship increases with the social superiority of one side and the social inferiority of the other.* We found that:

- As the social status of the victim increases, the more likely scientific evidence is to be collected and analyzed.[4]

The third proposition states: *Partisanship increases with social time.* We found that:

- The larger the movement of social time, the more likely scientific evidence is to be collected and analyzed.

We tested two settlement propositions, the first being: *Settlement severity increases with third-party status.* We found that:

- As the status of jurors rises, the more likely they are to vote for death.

Finally, we tested the proposition: *Settlement severity increases with social time.* We found that:

• The larger the movement of social time, the more likely jurors are to vote for death.

In short, although some of our results support the theory more strongly than do others, all three parts of Blackian theory receive robust confirmation. We can safely conclude that the death penalty varies with its location, direction, distance, and movement in social space. But does law in general obey a geometrical logic? Can we generalize from the death penalty?

So What?

Black's geometrical theory successfully predicts which defendants in the Baldus and CJP data are most likely to be sentenced to death and executed. However, before the ball is spiked and victory declared, we must acknowledge that death sentences are, statistically, very rare. Of the millions of criminal cases filed every year, only a miniscule number are charged as capital crimes and, of those, only a minority result in a sentence of death. Even fewer end in an execution. Surely, such a rare event cannot be taken to represent the way law operates more generally. Actually, it can.

Our Findings in Context

Our study is a companion to Mark Cooney's (2009) book, *Is Killing Wrong?* Like the present work, *Is Killing Wrong?* addresses the response to homicide. But where the present work focuses on capital murder, Cooney's book analyzes homicide cases in general, drawing on contemporary, historical, and anthropological data and showing that the handling of homicide in human societies conforms closely to the predictions of geometrical theory. Cooney's book is broad in scope, but it is not a quantitative test. Here, we have done the opposite: we have taken a narrow class of cases and subjected it to extensive statistical analysis. In combination, we obtain a picture of the law of homicide that is both broad and deep.

Realize, too, that the death penalty probably provides the single most challenging test of geometrical theory. Modern death penalty cases generate high levels of judicial and public scrutiny. Since *Furman*, an appellate court automatically reviews a death sentence. Legislators, judges, and other legal officials have gone to considerable lengths to minimize the role of race, gender, and other sociological variables. If those factors continue to operate when the stakes are so high and the cases so public, they are surely no less important in run of the mill, less visible cases.

Moreover, as we saw in Chapter 2, there are some 30 good-quality explicit statistical tests, the bulk of which support the theory, either wholly or in part. These studies cover a range of topics, including the reporting of crimes to the police (Gartner and Macmillan 1995), the arrest of suspects (McCamman and Mowen

2018), pleading guilty in criminal cases (Auerhahn 2012), and the sentences of female defendants (Krutschnitt 1980–1981).

Additionally, there are studies from both modern and pre-modern societies that do not meet our criteria for a statistical test but are nonetheless strongly consistent with aspects of geometrical theory. Consider two of Black's own papers in his collection of essays on policing, *The Manners and Customs of the Police*. In the introductory chapter, Black (1980a) draws on (1) data gathered by the 1966 three-city (Boston, Chicago, and Washington DC) observation study of patrol officers, of which he was a key member, (2) his own observations of police behavior conducted in Detroit during 1964–1965, and (3) studies of policing by other researchers. He shows that his theory explains central features of patrol, investigation, the enforcement of traffic and vice law, the handling of juveniles, those on skid row, and those who resist police authority. In "Dispute Settlement by Police," he demonstrates, again with the three-city and Detroit data, how the social class, race, intimacy and other characteristics of the parties explain differences in the amount and style of law that the police apply to disputes between acquainted people (Black 1980b). Scott Phillips (2009) examined the cases of all 504 defendants indicted for capital murder in Houston, Texas 1992–1999. He found that, controlling for the characteristics of the defendant and the killing, death sentences were more likely to be sought and imposed for high-status victims – those who were married or widowed, were members of the two largest racial and ethnic groups (Whites, Latino), held a college degree, and had no criminal record. In a historical study, M.P. Baumgartner (1978) analyzed the courts records of the New Haven Town Court between the years 1639 and 1665. Baumgartner found that, despite being a minority of the population, high-status parties initiated more cases, civil and criminal, than low-status parties did. Downward complaints – typically criminal in nature – were more common than upward complaints – typically civil in nature. Winning followed the four-fold pattern: high versus low cases were the most likely to succeed, followed by high versus high, low versus low, and low versus high. Finally, James Tucker (2015) noted that some societies have criminalized suicide, penalizing it in various ways, such as allowing exposure and mutilation of the corpse and posthumous confiscation of property. Reviewing the historical record, Tucker reported that penalties for suicide tended to increase with the social superiority (centralization) of the state and the social inferiority of the self-killer (see also Mullis 1995).

Finally, as mentioned earlier, there is the wealth of evidence (much of it naïve evidence) marshaled in support of the theory by Black in *The Behavior of Law* and *Sociological Justice*, and by Baumgartner in "The Myth of Discretion" (1992a) and *The Social Organization of Law* (1999). The evidence stretches across time and place, from the small-scale preindustrial societies of Africa, Asia, and the Americas to the advanced, affluent Western societies of today, from the earliest stirrings of legal codes in Ancient Babylonia to the latest innovations in contemporary legal life. The evidence includes civil, criminal, and regulatory cases, spanning the entire life of legal conflicts, from the initial contacting of the police or an attorney through to the final disposition by a court or indeed an executioner.

In short, although our analysis is confined to the death penalty as it operated in late 20th-century and early 21st-century America, it does not stand alone. Ours is the most rigorous test of the theory to date, but it should be read in the context of a much broader range of evidence that, in combination, clearly demonstrates the unprecedented power of geometrical theory to explain law more generally. Even so, it does not end there: the theory has still more applications that are important. Consider three: the desocialization of cases, the decline of the death penalty, and the content of legal rules.

Desocialization

Social status predicts who lives and dies. That offends many people's sense of justice – their belief that legal penalties should reflect what we do, not who we are. Can these disparities be reduced or even eliminated? In *Sociological Justice*, Black (1989) argued that they can, that sociology can be used to negate sociology. One technique is the desocialization of cases through the removal of social information.[5] Underlying this strategy is a simple but powerful idea: if legal officials have no information about the social characteristics of the parties, those characteristics cannot influence the outcome of a case (1989: 64–72).[6]

The Death Penalty

Based on his study of Houston capital cases, Scott Phillips (2008b) described a series of steps by which the death penalty could be desocialized. In Houston, prosecutors prepare a Capital Murder Summary Memorandum for the District Attorney who decides whether to seek death. Although the DA's office already removed race from the memo, Phillips (2008a, 2012) found that race still mattered. He proposed four additional procedures to blind the process: (1) The DA's office hires an assistant to read the memo and remove any racial clues. Phillips argues that racial clues cannot be fully enumerated in advance. For example, the memo might contain information about schools (the defendant or victim might go to a school that is predominately Black or White) or drugs (the defendant or victim might have been using a drug that is thought to be more prevalent among one racial group). If racial clues are difficult to list in advance, then clues about social status more generally are impossible. Still, an algorithm might be created to take the first pass at removing social information and a human then double-checks the memo (see, e.g., Chohlas-Wood et al. 2020). (2) The prosecutors who prepare the memo know the race and social status of the defendant and victim, and therefore do not make a recommendation about whether to seek death. (3) The DA is sequestered from media reports about pending cases. Although sequestration might seem unreasonable, jurors often face the same demand. (4) If the DA happens to learn the social characteristics of the defendant or victim, then a designated alternate decides whether to seek death (such as the state Attorney General).

If the DA seeks death, the capital murder trial could also be desocialized. The guilt–innocence phase poses a challenge, as the defendant's physical presence reveals social information (e.g., gender, race). But virtually all defendants are found guilty.[7] The only mystery is the punishment phase – a hearing that is replete with revelations about social standing. Desocializing the punishment phase would require three changes:

- The convicted defendant would not appear in the courtroom.
- The prosecution and defense would empanel a new death-qualified jury to decide punishment.
- The prosecution and defense would be allowed to discuss aggravating and mitigating factors, but would not be allowed to mention (or even insinuate) the race and social status of the parties.

In this way, the new jury would only know the relevant legal facts and not the irrelevant social facts. This proposal is not as radical as it might sound. Death sentences are often overturned on appeal. In the current system, if the DA decides to seek death again then a new jury is seated for the new punishment phase. Thus, the only real changes are removing the defendant from the courtroom and eliminating information that is not supposed to matter anyway.

Desocializing the punishment phase would also require the elimination of a controversial practice: Victim Impact Statements (VIS). These statements provide an opportunity to describe the impact of the murder on the victim's family. But VIS inevitably highlight the social attributes of the victim: the loss of a loving father who coached little league, the loss of a devoted mother who expertly juggled work and family, the loss of a sister who was a leader in the church. Even if obvious social clues were removed, the status of the victim's family would be evident in vocabulary, grammar, sentence structure, and the eloquence of the speaker: education tends to shine through. VIS are the opposite of desocialization.[8] Experimental research by Paternoster and Deise (2011) suggests that VIS make a difference. The authors randomly assigned death-qualified jurors to two conditions. In the experimental group, jurors watched a video of the punishment phase of a real capital case including the VIS. The control group was identical with one exception – the VIS was edited out. Perhaps not surprisingly, the jurors who saw the VIS felt more anger toward the defendant, felt more sympathy toward the victim, and were more likely to vote for death. VIS would have no place in a desocialized capital murder trial.

Desocialization Versus the Alternatives

How does desocialization compare to the current system of guided discretion laws? Recall that guided discretion attempted to reduce disparities by narrowing the range of death-eligible offenses, separating the guilt and sentencing phases of a trial to facilitate more evidence, and guaranteeing appellate review. Thus, guided discretion doubled-down on law. Describing the legal system's default solution, Black (2002: 117) notes:

> The oldest recipe for better law reads as follows: To improve law, add more law. Is law unjust or ineffective? Then give legal officials more power and use law still more than before. Introduce new legislation, new grounds for lawsuits, new penalties, and so on.

Desocialization is different. Desocialization begins with the premise that social information cannot influence a case if such information is unknown. The job of a reformer would be to figure out how to apply the broad concept of desocialization in a specific legal setting. Phillips (2008b: 9) argues that, compared to other potential remedies, "…desocialization is procedural rather than revolutionary, logistical rather than utopian, affordable rather than exorbitant."

Desocialization would not eliminate all potential disparities. The legislative definition of capital murder might prioritize downward cases, such as robberies. The police might conduct a more thorough investigation in a downward case. Prosecutors might write a more comprehensive memo in a downward case. If so, the blinded memo that reaches the DA would be more compelling – more facts, more admissible evidence – in a downward case. Additionally, the line between legal information and social information is blurry. Assume, hypothetically, that the defendant's mother is a witness in the punishment phase: "Yes, my husband beat and sexually abused our son when we lived in government-subsidized housing." The statement contains mitigating evidence, but also betrays low social status. High profile cases also pose a challenge, and any murder in a small town is high profile. Some might also object to the possibility of "leveling up." In an experiment on desocialization, Kan and Phillips (2003) found that defendants in the blinded condition were treated the same as Black defendants who killed a White victim. The authors note: "Ironically, then, desocialization might appeal to both liberals and conservatives: it eliminates discrimination based on race and gets tough on crime at the same time – everyone is treated in an equally harsh manner."

We are not advocating desocialization – its adoption requires a moral decision outside the ambit of science. We recognize that people may believe that other values outweigh the benefits of deosocialization (e.g., the defendants' right to have their day in court). But on the issue of whether desocialization works, its advocates can legitimately argue that it does not have to be perfect; it just has to be better than the existing system. Although the stakes are much lower, the desocialization of grading illustrates the benefits of incremental advances in equal treatment. Blind grading allows the professor to grade student assignments and then match anonymous identification numbers to names. Students' grades are based on what students know rather than who they are. As professors who use blind grading know, the system breaks down occasionally. Sometimes students put their name on an assignment. Or a student might repeat a memorable comment from class. Extensions are also tricky. By the time a student turns in a late paper, the rest of the students' papers might have been graded and returned. Nonetheless, blind grading works in the vast majority of cases. It is truly rare to know which answer belongs to which student. If capital murder cases were desocialized, the result would likely be similar. Greater, yet imperfect, equality.

If not desocialization, what else might be done to reduce disparate outcomes based on race and other indicators of social status? Many people would like to see the American death penalty abolished. Given the historical decline of the death penalty and the modern trend toward abolition, that seems destined to happen. But complete abolition in all 50 states, the federal system, and the military system will probably not occur soon. The death penalty will likely continue to limp along with death sentences and executions remaining low, but nonetheless remaining. Given the failure of guided discretion, desocialization might be the way of the future.

The Decline of the Death Penalty

Capital punishment has been retreating for centuries. "For most of human history," as David Garland (2010: 73) has noted, "the death penalty was what anthropologists call a 'cultural universal,' forming an element of every organized society." But that has changed in several ways over time, albeit slowly.

Tracing the Decline

In Europe during the Middle Ages, a great number of defendants were sentenced to death and executed. Manuel Eisner (2014) has calculated that from about 1300 to 1600, the execution rate in Europe ranged from 10 to 25 per 100,000. To put this in perspective, the United States executed 98 people in 1999 – the largest number since the reinstatement of the death penalty in 1976. If the United States had an execution rate of 10 per 100,000 – the most conservative estimate from the Middle Ages – 27,800 Americans would have been executed. In other words, the European rate of execution was 284 times higher than the US rate.[9] Even modern countries that lead the world in execution come nowhere close to the Middle Ages. During the 1990s, for example, China executed 10,000–15,000 people a year (Johnson and Zimring 2009). Taking China's highest estimate (15,000) yields an execution rate of about 1.25 per 100,000.[10] Even the lowest estimate for Europe in the Middle Ages is eight times greater than the highest estimate for modern China.

The retreat of the death penalty, then, is a long-term historical trend. Although exact numbers are elusive, Eisner (2014: 104–105) estimates that execution rates began to decline across most of Europe in the late 1300s, rose again during the

1500s, before beginning a long-term decline around 1590. The decline was steepest to about 1700 and then became more gradual. By the time the 20th century arrived, most European countries were using the death penalty sparingly, if at all. Abolition picked up pace after the Second World War. The Council of Europe – the continent's largest human rights organization – currently has 47 member countries, all but one of whom has abolished the death penalty (Belarus). Many other nations have done likewise (Hood and Hoyle 2008). Some countries, such as South Korea, retained the death penalty on the books, but have not executed anybody in 10 years and are therefore listed as abolitionist "in practice" by Amnesty International. Even countries that continue to execute prisoners do so less frequently. India, for example, averaged 140 executions a year in the 1950s; that declined to 2–3 a year in the 1980s and 1990s, and to the execution of just a single person between 1998 and 2007 (Johnson and Zimring 2009: 68, 18). By the end of 2017, over 70% of the world's countries had abolished the death penalty either formally or in practice.[11]

Along with the decline has come a narrowing of the range of offenses for which the death penalty could be imposed. Steven Pinker (2011: 149) observes that "in biblical, medieval, and early modern times, scores of trivial affront and infractions were punishable by death, including sodomy, gossiping, stealing cabbages, picking up sticks on the Sabbath, talking back to parents, and criticizing the royal garden." Gradually, fewer crimes became eligible for the death penalty. By the time Queen Victoria ascended the throne in 1838, the number of capital crimes had dropped in Britain from 200 to 15. By 1860, murder was the only common crime that could result in execution (Garland 2010: 105). Other European countries displayed a similar contraction over time.

As the death penalty became less frequent it also became less severe. In medieval and early modern Europe, for example, there were many forms of execution, all of them designed to inflict pain on the body of the condemned person. The most excruciating forms tended to be reserved for downward cases. After Charles II was restored to the British Crown in 1660, his regime sought out those who had signed the execution warrant of his father, Charles I, in 1649. 13 men were tried and executed, most having heard the following sentence passed upon them:

> The judgment of this Court is, and the Court doth award, that you be led back to the place, from whence you came, and from thence to be drawn upon a hurdle to the place of execution, and there you shall hang by the neck, and being alive shall be cut down, and your privy members be cut off, your entrails, to be taken out of your body, and (you living) the same to be burnt before your eyes, and your head to be cut off, your body to be divided into four quarters, and your head, and quarters, to be disposed of at the pleasure of the King's majesty.
>
> *Spencer 2014: 148*

A century later – toward the end of the 1700s – aggravated forms of execution began to disappear. Following a Parliamentary report, in 1866 the British government standardized its execution technique, introducing long drop hanging which sought to kill instantaneously by rupturing the spinal cord rather than by, as with short drop hanging, slow strangulation (Garland 2010: 110).

American capital punishment has followed a similar trajectory. In colonial America, a broad range of conduct could elicit a death penalty, including blasphemy, sodomy, and adultery (Bohm 2017: 1–2). Some capital crimes – such as destroying grain, preparing or administering medicine, or burning a house – only applied to slaves. Merely bruising a White person could lead to execution for a slave in some southern states in the 1700s (Banner 2002: 8–9). Over time, a narrower range of conduct became eligible for the death penalty. As a result, the percentage of executions for crimes other than murder fell from 75% in 1650 to close to 0% at present (Pinker 2011: 151–152). The execution rate per 100,000 also plummeted, as Figure 5.1 illustrates:[12]

Despite a slight increase in the 1990s, the downward trend is clear. In 2020, 17 people were executed in the United States, compared to 85 twenty years earlier.

As the American death penalty declined, it became less (intentionally) painful.[13] Making the condemned person suffer increasingly came to be seen as barbaric. Officials sought ways to reduce the physical pain inflicted on the person being put to death. The dominant form of execution therefore evolved from hanging to the electric chair or the gas chamber to lethal injection (Banner 2002).

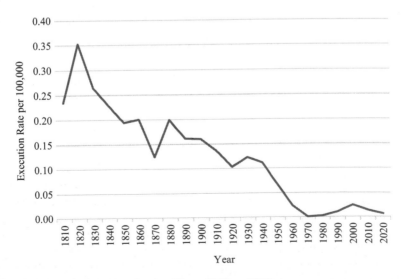

FIGURE 5.1 United States Execution Rate, 1810 to 2020

Explaining the Decline

What is driving this long-term retreat of capital punishment? Any trend sustained over several centuries is almost certainly propelled by multiple factors. Geometrical theory would look to changes in social space – movements of social time (Black 2011: 140–152). One important movement is the increased status of the individual brought about by modernity. With the huge growth in productivity, the wealth of the average person has risen considerably (vertical status). While individuals are less likely to be integrated into family and community, they are more likely to be linked into larger networks, networks that have come to span the entire globe (radial status). They are more likely to be employed by an organization (organizational status). And much more likely to be literate and to have received several years of schooling (cultural status). These changes help explain why, as Durkheim (1898) noted, modern societies have sympathy for all that is human. Because the individual has come up in the world, even the lowest status person is a human being deserving of respect. Although death row inmates remain low status, they too are individuals imbued with human rights. As a person's status rises, the death of that person is a greater movement of social time and causes more conflict. An execution today therefore generates vastly more resistance than an execution in 1400.

Some might object that the concept of "human rights" is a post-World War II creation and thus cannot explain a trend that unfolded across several centuries. But the concept of human rights has long been in the making. As Jouet (2022: 48) argues, citing Montaigne writing in the 1500s, "'a general duty of humanity' emerged in the Renaissance before progressing in the Enlightenment and onward." Today, that duty is evident in the moral claim that all lives are valuable, and that "each of us is more than the worst thing we've ever done" (Stevenson 2014: 17–18). This idea that every person matters regardless of status reflects the actual long-term rise in status of every person.

Individual worth is why painful punishments of all kinds, not just those that ended in death, retreated over the centuries. And it is why executions, once noisy, often raucous, public spectacles in which the condemned prisoner was paraded through the town, are now conducted indoors with solemnity before a small audience (e.g., Banner 2002: 10–12; Garland 2010: 107).

Elevated status depresses the death penalty for another reason: defendants attract more support. Sometimes partisanship comes from ordinary people who, objecting to the state killing those who kill, put pressure on legislators to curb or abolish the death penalty. At the case level, the most impactful partisanship comes from lawyers. It was not always so. Not until the 1730s were lawyers in Britain allowed to represent defendants accused of murder and other felonies. For the first 100 years, they operated under strict limitations that forbade them, for example, from addressing the jury on their client's behalf. Moreover, trials were often quick affairs, lasting no more than half an hour, including jury deliberations

(Beattie 1991). Today, not every capital defendant receives a vigorous defense. However, a cadre of highly trained lawyers has emerged who dedicate their careers to representing defendants who might be, or have been, sentenced to death (see e.g., Dow 2005; Stevenson 2014). This vigorous representation makes convictions, death sentences, and executions more difficult for prosecutors to secure.

Legal Rules

For a long time, as we have seen, legal sociology did not have a scientific theory of legal seriousness – the gravity of a crime. Rules govern conduct and any attempt to understand why some conduct attracted more law than other conduct bumped up against the problem of subjectivity: what you regard as more serious may not be what I regard as more serious. Social time solved that problem. However, there is a related issue: Why is some behavior illegal at all? This is the problem of the content of legal rules. And it is a thorny problem, if only because there are so many rules, governing so many types of behavior. The concept of social time appears to have the capacity to explain this variation. We cannot demonstrate the point fully here. But we can sketch the potential of social time by considering how it can explain differences in legal rules across time and place. Compare briefly, for example, colonial America with contemporary America.

Colonial Versus Contemporary America

In Colonial America, there were laws against murder, assault, and theft as there are today. There were also a host of laws that appear strange to modern sensibilities (Chapin 1983). Sumptuary laws, for example, regulated consumption, especially what people could wear. Laws of this kind go back at least as far as ancient Greece and Rome. They formed part of the rules of medieval and early modern Europe as well, typically forbidding lower status people from wearing silks, furs, velvets, or other clothing indicating elevated social status. Sumptuary laws crossed the Atlantic with the colonists. A Connecticut order of 1641, for example, targeted people "who dressed in such a way as to 'exceed their conditions and ranks'" (Chapin 1983: 139). A decade later, Massachusetts outlawed "luxury items such as gold or silver lace, gold or silver buttons, silk hoods or scarves, and 'great boots' to those with an annual income of less than £200" (Hunt 1996: 39). Sumptuary laws kept the lower classes lower.

Colonial America also outlawed a broad range of expressive behavior that the law tolerates today. Massachusetts and the other colonies proscribed non-attendance at Sunday church. A Virginia law of 1611 authorized the death penalty for those who repeatedly broke the Sabbath (Bonomi 2003: 16). The colonists took a dim view of many forms of sexual behavior as well. Homosexuality was not permitted and two men were executed for sodomy, one in Virginia, the other in New Haven (Chapin 1983: 127). Adultery was criminalized as was fornication (sex between unmarried people). Severe penalties could be inflicted on those who offended, such as branding, imprisonment, fines, or public whippings (Sweeny 2014: 133). Despite the potentially harsh sanctions, "fornication charges were the most frequent charges brought against women in New England in the 1600s" (Sweeny 2014: 134). Fornication, "filthy dalliance" (i.e., other heterosexual conduct outside marriage), and "lewdness" (other prohibited sexual behavior) made up about a fifth of all criminal cases heard by the court of the Puritan New Haven colony, 1639–1665 (Baumgartner 1978). Even outside the Puritan colonies, fornication and adultery charges were common (Sweeny 2014: 134).

If all of this seems strange to us today, how odd many of our laws would appear to the colonists. Modern legal systems generate an enormous volume of rules and regulations. Even so, a few themes underlie many of these rules. One is anti-discrimination. Many laws today forbid people and organizations from negatively discriminating in housing, education, employment, and other activities against people on multiple grounds, including race, religion, gender, national origin, disability status, and sexual orientation. A related set of laws prohibit hate crimes so that punishments are increased for crimes committed against persons because of their social identity (e.g., race, religion). These laws were unknown in colonial America.

A second theme in modern law is the curbing of inequality. Anti-trust law prevents corporations from dominating a market and becoming too powerful. Insider trading rules prohibit people from using confidential information to make money trading stocks and thereby surge ahead of others. Many modern laws prevent people from falling too far below others by, for example, providing economic and social assistance for the unemployed, disabled, and poor, and by making education compulsory.

The freedom of the individual is a third theme running through the laws of modern legal systems. Laws that restrict the liberty of individuals to do as they wish have been cast aside. Adultery and homosexuality have been decriminalized. Privacy rights have been given legal recognition. But freedom is not unlimited because harming others undermines their freedom. Rules directed against stalking and sexual harassment have therefore expanded. So too have laws against child sex abuse and rape (e.g., repeal of the rule that a man could not be guilty of raping his wife) (Frank et al. 2010).

Other themes and examples could be cited but the point is clear: modern law is directed against many different behaviors than was colonial law. Why? True, values have changed. People now treasure things like privacy much more than colonial Americans did. However, to explain the changes with values is not very satisfactory because it raises the question: What caused the values to change? Here is where social time can help (Black 2011: 140–152).

Do Not Disturb

Black's theory of moral time proposes that law tends to prohibit disturbances of social space and thereby preserve its current shape (2011: 11–12). In unequal settings, law preserves inequality; in more equal settings, law preserves equality. In intimate settings, law preserves intimacy; in less intimate settings, law preserves distance. In homogeneous settings, law preserves cultural uniformity; in less homogenous settings, law preserves cultural diversity. In other words, law preserves the status quo.

Over the centuries, the shape of social space has changed drastically and, with it, the movements of social time prohibited by law. Agrarian societies like colonial America were extremely stratified along multiple dimensions: the rich versus the poor, the highborn versus the lowborn, the rulers versus the ruled, the landowners versus the landless, the master versus the slave or servant. Over time, these inequalities have moderated: the aristocracy has disappeared, a middle class has emerged, ordinary people have become citizens who participate in the political process, and an economy has emerged that caters to an ever-wider range of tastes and talents. Laws now mitigate inequality whereas previously law consolidated inequality (e.g., sumptuary laws). At the same time, relational distance has increased. Families have become smaller and more temporary. Communities are now larger and more transitory and strangers are ubiquitous. As people become, on average, more distant from one another, laws protecting distance expand (e.g., privacy laws). Simultaneously, laws protecting intimacy contract. Adultery creates as much relational distance as it ever did, but the chasm is no longer a crime. Greater relational distance and an emphasis on equality – in all possible forms – have combined to create legal rules that protect free adult choices that do not harm others. Rather than legally enforced closeness – one heterosexual partner for life – people are free to have sex with any consenting partner, and so laws against fornication and homosexuality have disappeared. But behaviors that have existed since time immemorial – such as sexual harassment and stalking – have now been named and criminalized, as greater relational distance created a strict zone of personal privacy: the right to be left alone. Finally, cultural distance has widened. A wide array of beliefs and nonbeliefs has replaced the religious homogeneity of earlier times. Attendance at church is now optional and atheism is no longer a crime. Modern societies have become increasingly multicultural, home to people of many different ethnicities, national origins, and opinions, and their laws prioritize the prevention and punishment of discrimination.

The diversity of modern societies means, however, that not all its parts are equally modern. Institutions that retain the social geometry of earlier times should have laws that reflect that geometry. Consider the military (Schlueter 2008: chapter 2). The military is a highly stratified social system with members occupying a series of well-defined ranks from private to general. Military law carefully preserves this stratification, prohibiting conduct unbecoming an officer, insubordination, disrespecting an officer, fraternizing between members of different ranks, and the wearing of the wrong uniform (sumptuary). In addition, the military has a relatively high degree of intimacy: many members work and live together and solidarity is encouraged. Consequently, military law restricts certain individual freedoms, such as desertion, being absent without authorized leave, and, something no longer prohibited by civilian law, adultery. The modern military is, however, a culturally diverse institution, its personnel belonging to every race, religion, and social background. Military law therefore shares with civilian law a strong concern with non-discrimination.

Why the Resistance?

Before closing, we must revisit an issue raised in Chapter 1: the reception of geometrical theory. If the geometrical theory of law is so powerful, and it has no serious case-level competitors, why has it run into such resistance? Over time, as we saw previously, the theory has moved to the margins of legal sociology, increasingly omitted from scholarly reviews of the field. What happened?

Geometrical theory can illuminate its own marginalization. Since criticism and exclusion are responses to conflict, they fall within the jurisdiction of the theory of moral time. At least three movements of social time help explain the reception of the geometrical theory of law: a vertical, relational, and cultural movement. Consider each.

Geometrical Theory as Social Time

Recall that *The Behavior of Law* advanced the first, and still the only, general sociological theory of law. Since theory is the heart of any scientific field, Black's book, if successful, must be the most important publication in legal sociology. To rise above others is a movement of vertical time. Specifically, it is a form of what Black (2011: 60–71) calls oversuperiority, a common cause of conflict among people everywhere. We might think that success is always celebrated, but reality suggests otherwise. Those who move ahead are often resented by those left behind. Examples abound. In many societies, successful people have been accused of witchcraft. Alternatively, they have been mocked and insulted. And some groups, like Jews at many times and places, have been persecuted, banished, and killed. By adopting a modest and self-effacing mien, successful people can sometimes blunt the hostility of others. Black has not taken that path, however. On the contrary, he has forcefully argued for the preeminence of his theory (Black 1995; 2015). Black's own theory suggests that doing so would lead to hostility.

A second disturbance of academic space occurred when, after publishing his theory of law, Black began to think systemically about the larger universe of conflict management: "The more we study law, the more we realize how little people use it to handle their conflicts" (1984: 3). Black's work on conflict management beyond law led to a series of papers collected in a 1993 book, *The Social Structure of Right and Wrong*. Since then, Black has continued to publish on other topics, including developing theories of terrorism (2004a), weapon lethality (2004b), and domestic violence (2018). Sociologists employing pure sociology have done likewise, producing theoretical work on the response to mental illness (Horwitz 1982) as well as the management of conflict in suburbia (Baumgartner 1988), child day care centers (Baumgartner 1992b), Alcoholics Anonymous (Hoffmann 2006), and corporations (Morrill 1995; Tucker 1999). Pure sociologists have paid particular attention to several types of violence, including criminal homicide (Cooney 1998; Phillips 2003; Phillips and Cooney 2005), suicide (Manning 2020), lynching (Senechal de la Roche 1997), collective violence (Senechal de la Roche 1996), family honor violence (Cooney 2019), and genocide (Campbell 2015). Black (1979; 1995; 2000) has even extended pure sociology beyond moral conflict to topics such as medicine, art, religion, and ideas (see also Jacques 2014). All of this comes with a price. By moving on from law, Black and those working within his tradition have drifted away from the core network of law and society scholars. Rarely participating in the annual conference of the Law and Society Association, they have had fewer of those encounters, formal and informal, that help to keep ideas in front of fellow scholars. Publishing only occasional items in legal sociology has left the pages of journals to be filled by other perspectives. This reduction in intimacy (underintimacy) has created additional conditions favorable to the theory's neglect.

But the most telling movement of social time is cultural. While Black is by no means the first to adopt a sociological perspective on law, he has done so in a manner increasingly at odds with the prevailing orthodoxy. As legal sociology has become more applied, activist, and humanistic, Black's insistence on an uncompromisingly scientific approach has come to be a form of intellectual deviance (Black 1997). Were *The Behavior of Law* to be published for the first time now, it is quite possible that it would be received much less warmly than it was in 1976.

Black's theory is not just different. More tellingly, it is radically new (see Baumgartner 2002). The theory introduces the idea that law consists of a system of behavior, not a body of rules. It contains a wealth of innovative imagery and concepts, such as "vertical distance," "organizational direction," "normative status," "centrifugal law" (law directed against more marginal actors), and "sociological litigation" (lawyers employing social geometry to further their practice). It rests on a definition of law ("governmental social control") with surprising implications. Technically illegal actions can be instances of "law" in this sense (Black 2002: 112, 123–124). Thus, just as law responds to crime, it can itself be a crime. When a police officer kicks a homeless man, for example, the officer is simultaneously exercising governmental social control and breaking the formal law. Moreover, for Black (2002: 111), law is an inherently partisan process. As such, it can be predicted with more general principles of partisan behavior (Black 1993: chapter 7). Beyond all this, the theory has additional novel features, including the claims that:

- Law is a quantitative variable.
- Social life has five co-equal spatial dimensions, each of which represents a major theoretical tradition in sociology.
- Law is geometrical, varying with its location, direction, and distance in social space.
- Geometrical theory explains all stages of all legal systems at all times and places.
- Human behavior can be explained without reference to psychology, purposes, or even people as such.

Originality of this magnitude inevitably meets with resistance. In *Moral Time*, Black coined the term "overinnovation" to describe the creation of something new, and proposed that *Conflict is a direct function of overinnovation* (109). In other words, the more something deviates from existing culture, the more conflict it generates: too much creativity is unacceptable. That is largely why, for example, the early Christians were martyred, why most contemporaries were hostile to Mozart's music, why the poets John Keats and Emily Dickinson were mainly ignored or scorned during their lives, and why Impressionist and early abstract painters were frequently ridiculed. Science is by no means immune from overinnovation conflict as the persecution of Galileo, the opposition to Darwin, and the hostility that greeted Einstein's most important ideas attests. Black (2011: 115) writes:

> Resistance to scientific innovation is so commonplace that physicist John Barrow sarcastically describes three stages in the life cycle of every new scientific idea later recognized as important: "Stage 1. It's a pile of shit and we don't want to hear about it. Stage 2: It's not wrong but it certainly has no relevance whatsoever. Stage 3: It's the greatest discovery ever made and we found it first."

At least for some, Black's theory is still in stage 1 of the cycle. In this sense, it is still ahead of its time (see Cooney 2002). It will not always be. Young people enter a field with a fresh eye, largely indifferent to the conflicts of their elders. It may take time, but quality inevitably rises to the top.

Conclusion

Geometrical theory provides a uniquely powerful, novel, and testable explanation of the handling of legal conflicts. It applies across time and place, as much to imperial China, precolonial Africa, and early modern Europe as to contemporary America. A question has hovered over it, however: can it survive a confrontation with a rigorous set of quantitative data? To answer this question, we tested the geometrical theory of law with the highest quality case-level data ever collected by legal sociologists – the Baldus data. Supplementing that with the CJP data, we have come up with a clear answer: yes, it can.

The strong support for geometrical theory that emerges from our test does not imply that all questions have been answered. Far from it. Plenty of research remains to be done on the conditions underlying legal behavior. For example, while many, perhaps most, criminal and civil cases that could be brought to law are not brought, clearly people will sometimes call the police or file a lawsuit. When? Family members rarely invoke the law against one another, but sometimes they will initiate domestic violence complaints, inheritance suits, or other legal actions. When? Lower status people are slow to bring cases against their social superiors, but sometimes they will launch and even win legal actions against employers, governments, or other high-status actors. When? Partisanship usually occurs among those who are socially close, but sometimes people will provide money, advice, or testimony to support complete strangers in their legal battles. When?

We also need better measures of the theory's concepts (Black 1979). In Chapter 3, for instance, we assigned a score of one to each indicator of the movements of vertical and relational time in the data. But is each movement simply a one? Do some movements deserve a higher score? Is a rape-murder a greater movement of social time than a murder in which the victim is mutilated either before or after death? How would we go about assigning those scores? These complex issues will require considerable thought.

As we work more on geometrical theory, anomalous findings will surely emerge. Some will be errors. Of those findings that are not erroneous, some will be explained by other parts of the theory. A full geometrical analysis of a case requires a consideration of all three strands of the theory – social time, social space, and third parties. But some cases may turn out to be exceptions, stubbornly resisting geometrical explanation. In that case, the theory may need to be further developed. The challenge then will be to extend the theory while remaining faithful to its core logic and resisting the temptation to introduce ad hoc assumptions (e.g., those based on the motivations of the parties).

Much remains to be done. But much has already been accomplished. We have a scientific theory of law that is both highly general and highly specific. Consider again the Curtis Flowers case. Curtis was tried six times for the quadruple murder in Winona, Mississippi. He spent 23 years in prison before finally being released. What explains the District Attorney's extraordinary and unprecedented effort to secure a conviction and death sentence? Geometrical theory predicts that extreme quantities of law are a product of extreme social geometries. That is certainly true of the Flowers case.

Earlier, we mentioned the racial dimension of the case – three of the four victims were White, the defendant was Black, and the District Attorney, a White man, consistently picked White jurors. All the White jurors voted to convict, but the Black jurors were split. But there were other aspects of the case that played a part as well. There were four victims, and all were shot execution style. The murders were accompanied by a robbery. The victims were high status. One was the owner of a well-established furniture business, the other three were her employees. All had some organizational status by virtue of being employees of a corporate entity. All were socially integrated, being members of local churches. Bertha Tardy, the owner of the store, had an especially high degree of social integration based on all kinds of community involvement. According to her obituary,

> Mrs. Tardy was owner and operator of Tardy Furniture Company since 1985. She graduated from Winona High School and was also a graduate of the New York School of Interior Design. She was an active member of Moore Memorial United Methodist Church where she formerly served as chairperson of the finance committee for five years, as a teacher of children and youth, as chairperson of its Commission on Education, and as treasurer of the United Methodist Women. Mrs. Tardy was a past president and member of the board of directors, and chairperson of the selection committee for the Montgomery County Habitat for Humanity. She was a past treasurer and president of the Montgomery County Economic Council and was a member of Leadership Mississippi. Named 1989 Retail Person of the Year, she also served as president of the Downtown Merchants Association in which she spearheaded obtaining grant money to renovate Downtown Winona.

The obituary of the 16-year-old victim describes a multi-talented young man who was popular with his peers:

> Bo Bo attended Shiloh Baptist Church near Vaiden. He played short stop and pitcher for the Winona High School baseball team and was their leading hitter. He was a member of FCA, VICA and the Gifted Art Club. He attended Winona Academy as a freshman and was voted Most Handsome, Most Athletic and Mr. Junior Winona Academy. At Winona Academy he played Junior High football and was moved to the high school team during the year.

The defendant, by contrast, was of lower status – an unemployed Black man. Although he had no criminal record and was a member of a church choir, his integration and respectability had been compromised somewhat by his failure to show up for work and being let go after three days. In addition, he was not particularly intimate with any of the victims. In sum, the Flowers case was a distantly downward case involving multiple movements of social time. If an unusually high degree of prosecutorial zeal were ever to occur, it is in this type of case that geometrical theory predicts we would find it.

A successful theory is a rare and valuable thing. As such, it should be treated with care. Black (2010: 42) puts the case well:

I believe that because theory – especially testable, general, simple, and original theory – is extremely rare in science, we should strive to nourish and protect any conceivably valuable theory that might appear. We should thus normally be gentle with new theories, not heavy-handed or brutal... We should cherish what we have, and be careful not to reject any new idea prematurely or recklessly. We should look first not for what might be less than perfect about a theory, but for what might be useful or worthy of further testing or development. A theory is too precious to waste or damage with faulty tests or questionable claims about its shortcomings. And anything that claims to be a test or other assessment of a theory should be subject to the same standards as we apply to any other scientific work. We should discredit anyone who unjustifiably criticizes a theory, much as we discredit those who are, say, sloppy or otherwise incompetent in their research. Theory, after all, is the lifeblood of science. It is the means by which science makes its greatest progress.

When so much social science, now and in the past, is ideological, Donald Black demonstrates what can be accomplished by scientific, value-free sociology. His theoretical ideas address what is the case, not what should be. Unrestricted by time or place, his propositions describe and explain social reality – no more, no less. And they do so successfully. Focusing on the death penalty in America, we demonstrate that who lives and dies turns on the social geometry of the case, including the movement of social time. Justice is indeed geometrical.

Sources for the Curtis Flowers Case

https://features.apmreports.org/in-the-dark/season-two/ Retrieved November 14, 2021.

www.nytimes.com/2020/09/04/us/after-6-murder-trials-and-nearly-24-years-charges-dropped-against-curtis-flowers.html Retrieved November 14, 2021.

www.nytimes.com/2019/12/16/us/curtis-flowers-murder.html Retrieved November 14, 2021.

www.nytimes.com/2019/06/21/us/politics/curtis-flowers-supreme-court-in-the-dark-podcast.html Retrieved November 14, 2021.

www.nytimes.com/2020/01/07/us/doug-evans-curtis-flowers.html Retrieved November 14, 2021.

www.nytimes.com/2021/02/16/briefing/winter-storm-adam-kinzinger-pelosi-congress.html Retrieved November 14, 2021.

www.nytimes.com/2018/05/20/opinion/mississippi-curtis-flowers-trial.html Retrieved November 14, 2021.

www.cbsnews.com/video/curtis-flowers-in-the-dark-60-minutes-2021-07-25/#x Retrieved November 14, 2021.

www.npr.org/2019/06/21/732159330/supreme-court-strikes-down-conviction-of-mississippi-man-on-death-row-for-22-yea Retrieved November 14, 2021.

www.reuters.com/article/us-usa-mississippi-deathrow-idUSKBN0FQ29Q20140721
  Retrieved November 14, 2021.
https://en.wikipedia.org/wiki/Winona,_Mississippi Retrieved November 14,
  2021.

Notes

1 The theory also addresses variation in liability (see e.g., Black 1987).
2 However, high lateral cases were slightly more likely to result in an execution than downward cases (25% versus 21%).
3 The theory also predicts that: *In an upward direction, law decreases with vertical distance.* Because so few upward cases resulted in a death sentence, we were unable to test this proposition.
4 For details regarding how we tested the proposition in question, see endnote 19 in Appendix 4.
5 Two other techniques are legal cooperatives (which would confer organizational status on everyone) and delegalization (which would reduce disparities by reducing law) (1989: chapters 3, 5).
6 Blinding decision to ensure greater equality of treatment appears to be gaining traction. Chohlas-Wood et al. (2020) created an algorithm that masks five pieces of information that could reveal the race of the suspect and victim: explicit mentions of race, physical descriptions, names, locations and addresses, and the police officer's name (as the prosecutor might know the officer's beat).
7 In the Phillips (2008a) study of the Houston death penalty, the DA sought the death penalty in 129 cases. Only one defendant was acquitted.
8 In *Booth v. Maryland* (1987), the US Supreme Court ruled that VIS are not allowed in capital cases, concluding that the statements would shift the jury's focus from the defendant's culpability to the victim's worth. But the Court reversed course in *Payne v. Tennessee* (1991). The Court reasoned that VIS describe harm, and harm is part of culpability. Additionally, VIS counterbalance the defendant's right to present any form of mitigating evidence.
9 According to the Census Bureau, the US population in 1999 was approximately 278 million. Conducting 98 executions in a population of 278 million people yields an execution rate of 0.03525 per 100,000 (10/0.03525 = 284).
10 In 1995, the population of China was about 1.2 billion. (see: www.statista.com/statistics/263765/total-population-of-china/).
11 https://deathpenaltyinfo.org/policy-issues/international/abolitionist-and-retentionist-countries.
12 In Figure 5.1, annual execution counts were drawn from the Espy file (1800–1967) and the Death Penalty Information Center (1976 to 2020). https://deathpenaltyinfo.org/. Population data were drawn from the US Census (Social Explorer). To illustrate the calculation of the execution rate, consider an example. In 2000, the US population was 282,162,411. From 1996 to 2005, 691 executions were carried out – an average of 69.1 per year. Thus, the execution rate for 2000 was calculated as: (69.1 / 282,162,411) ★ 100,000 = 0.02449. Averaging the number of executions for each decade smooths the trend. Data available upon request.
13 Some argue that lethal injection only masks excruciating pain. For our purposes, the attempt to eliminate pain represents a change in the evolution of the death penalty regardless of whether the attempt succeeded.

References

Auerhahn, Kathleen. 2012. "'Social Control of the Self' and Pleading Guilty in Criminal Court." *International Review of Sociology* 22:95–122.

Baldus, David C., George Woodworth, and Charles A. Pulaski. 1990. *Equal Justice and the Death Penalty: A Legal and Empirical Analysis*. Boston: Northeastern University Press.

Banner, Stuart. 2002. *The Death Penalty: An American History*. Cambridge: Harvard University Press.

Baumgartner, M.P. 1978. "Law and Social Status in Colonial New Haven, 1639–1665." Pp. 153–174 in *Research in Law and Sociology: An Annual Compilation of Research*, Volume 1, edited by Rita J. Simon. Greenwich, CT: JAI Press.

Baumgartner, M.P. 1988. *The Moral Order of a Suburb*. New York: Oxford University Press.

Baumgartner, M.P. 1992a. "The Myth of Discretion." Pp. 129–162 in *The Uses of Discretion*, edited by Keith Hawkins. Oxford: Clarendon Press.

Baumgartner, M.P. 1992b. "War and Peace in Early Childhood." Pp. 1–38 in *Virginia Review of Sociology*, Volume 1: *Law and Conflict Management*, edited by James Tucker. Greenwich, CT: JAI Press.

Baumgartner, M.P. 2002. "The Behavior of Law, Or How to Sociologize with a Hammer." *Contemporary Sociology* 31:644–649.

Beattie, J.M. 1991. "Scales of Justice: Defense Counsel and the English Criminal Trial in the Eighteenth and Nineteenth centuries." *Law and History Review* 9:221–267.

Black, Donald. 1976. *The Behavior of Law*. New York: Academic Press.

Black, Donald. 1979. "A Note on the Measurement of Law." *Informationsbrief für Rechtssoziologie, Sonderheft* 2:96–106 (reprinted as Appendix A in *The Manners and Customs of the Police*).

Black, Donald. 1980a. "Introduction." Chapter 1, pp. 1–40 in *The Manners and Customs of the Police*. New York: Academic Press.

Black, Donald. 1980b. "Dispute Settlement by the Police." Chapter 5, pp. 109–192 in *The Manners and Customs of the Police*. New York: Academic Press.

Black, Donald. 1984. "Social Control as a Dependent Variable." Pp. 1–36 in *Toward A General Theory of Social Control*, Volume 1: *Fundamentals*, edited by Donald Black. Orlando: Academic Press.

Black, Donald. 1987. "Compensation and the Social Structure of Misfortune." *Law and Society Review* 21:563–584.

Black, Donald. 1989. *Sociological Justice*. New York: Oxford University Press.

Black, Donald. 1993. *The Social Structure of Right and Wrong*. San Diego: Academic Press.

Black, Donald. 1995. "The Epistemology of Pure Sociology." *Law and Social Inquiry* 20:829–870.

Black, Donald. 1997. "The Lawyerization of Legal Sociology." *Amici* 5:4–7.

Black, Donald. 2000. "Dreams of Pure Sociology." *Sociological Theory* 18:343–367.

Black, Donald. 2002. "The Geometry of Law: An Interview with Donald Black." *International Journal of the Sociology of Law* 30:101–129.

Black, Donald. 2004a. "The Geometry of Terrorism." *Sociological Theory* 22:14–25.

Black, Donald. 2004b. "Violent Structures." Pp. 145–158 in *Violence: From Theory to Research*, edited by Margaret A. Zahn, Henry H. Brownstein, and Shelly L. Jackson. Newark: Lexis-Nexis/Anderson Publishing.

Black, Donald. 2010. "How Law Behaves: An Interview with Donald Black." *International Journal of Law, Crime and Justice* 38:37–47.

Black, Donald. 2011. *Moral Time*. New York: Oxford University Press.

Black, Donald. 2015. "The Beginning of Social Time: An Interview with Myself." *International Journal of Law, Crime and Justice* 43:382–395.

Black, Donald. 2018. "Domestic Violence and Social Time." *Dilemas: Revistas de Estudos de Confllicto e Controle Social* 11 :1–27.

Bohm, Robert M. 2017. *Death Quest: An Introduction to the Theory and Practice of Capital Punishment in the United States.* New York: Routledge.

Bonomi, Patricia. 2003. *Under the Cope of Heaven: Religion, Society, and Politics in Colonial America.* New York: Oxford University Press (updated edition; first edition, 1986).

Campbell, Bradley. 2015. *The Geometry of Genocide: A Study in Pure Sociology.* Charlottesville: University of Virginia Press.

Chapin, Bradley. 1983. *Criminal Justice in Colonial America, 1606–1660.* Athens: University of Georgia Press.

Chohlas-Wood, Alex, Joe Nudell, Zhiyuan Lin, Julian Nyarko, and Sharad Goel. 2020. "Blind Justice: Algorithmically Masking Race in Charging Decisions." *Stanford University Working Paper.* October 5:1 –11.

Cooney, Mark. 1998. *Warriors and Peacemakers: How Third Parties Shape Violence.* New York: New York University Press.

Cooney, Mark. 2002. "Still Paying the Price of Heterodoxy: The Behavior of Law a Quarter Century On." *Contemporary Sociology* 31:658–661.

Cooney, Mark. 2009. *Is Killing Wrong? A Study in Pure Sociology.* Charlottesville: University of Virginia Press.

Cooney, Mark. 2019. *Execution by Family: A Theory of Honor Violence.* New York: Routledge.

Death Penalty Information Center (DPIC): https://deathpenaltyinfo.org/

Dow, David R. 2005. *Executed on a Technicality: Lethal Injustice on America's Death Row.* Boston, MA: Beacon.

Eisner, Manuel. 2014. "From Swords to Words: Does Macro-Level Change in Self-Control Predict Long-Term Variation in Levels of Homicide?" *Crime and Justice* 43:65–134.

Durkheim, Emile. 1898. "Individualism and the Intellectuals." *Political Studies* 17:14–30, 1969 (Translated by Steven Lukes).

Frank, David John, Bayliss J. Camp, and Stephen A. Boutcher. 2010. "Worldwide Trends in the Criminal Regulation of Sex, 1945 to 2005." *American Sociological Review* 75:867–893.

Garland, David. 2010. *Peculiar Institution: America's Death Penalty in an Age of Abolition.* Cambridge: Harvard University Press.

Gartner, Rosemary and Ross Macmillan. 1995. "The Effect of Victim–Defendant Relationship on Reporting Crimes of Violence against Women." *Canadian Journal of Criminology* 31:393–429.

Hoffmann, Heath. 2006. "Criticism as Deviance and Social Control in Alcoholics Anonymous." *Journal of Contemporary Ethnography* 35:669–695.

Horwitz, Allan V. 1982. *The Social Control of Mental Illness.* New York: Academic Press.

Hood, Roger and Carolyn Hoyle. 2008. *The Death Penalty: A Worldwide Perspective.* Oxford: Oxford University Press (4th edition).

Hunt, Alan. 1996. *Governance of the Consuming Passions: A History of Sumptuary Law.* New York: St. Martin's Press.

Jacques, Scott. 2014. "The Quantitative-Qualitative Divide in Criminology: A Theory of Ideas' Importance, Attractiveness, and Publication." *Theoretical Criminology* 18:317–334.

Johnson, David T. and Franklin E. Zimring. 2009. *The Next Frontier: National Development, Political Change, and the Death Penalty in Asia.* Oxford: Oxford University Press.

Jouet, Mugambi. 2022 (forthcoming). "Death Penalty Abolitionism from the Enlightenment to Modernity." *American Journal of Comparative Law.*

Kan, Yee and Scott Phillips. 2003. "Race and the Death Penalty: Including Asian Americans and Exploring the Desocialization of Law." *Journal of Ethnicity in Criminal Justice* 1:63–92.

Krutschnitt, Candace. 1980–1981. "Social Status and Sentences of Female Defendants." *Law and Society Review* 15:247–265.

Manning, Jason. 2020. *Suicide: The Social Causes of Self-Destruction.* Charlottesville: University of Virginia Press.

McCamman, Michael and Thomas Mowen. 2018. "Does Residence Matter? Local Residency as a Predictor of Arrest." *Criminal Justice Studies* 31:128–142.

Morrill, Calvin. 1995. *The Executive Way: Conflict Management in Corporations.* Chicago: University of Chicago Press.

Mullis, Jeffrey. 1995. "Medical Malpractice, Social Structure, and Social Control." *Sociological Forum* 10:135–163.

Paternoster, Ray and Jerome Deise. 2011. "A Heavy Thumb on the Scale: The Effect of Victim Impact Evidence on Capital Decision Making. *Criminology* 49:129–161.

Phillips, Scott. 2003. "The Social Structure of Vengeance: A Test of Black's Model." *Criminology* 41:673–708.

Phillips, Scott. 2008a. "Racial Disparities in the Capital of Capital Punishment." *Houston Law Review* 45:807–840.

Phillips, Scott. 2008b. "Racial Disparities in Capital Punishment: Blind Justice Requires a Blindfold." Issue Brief for the *American Constitution Society.* www.acslaw.org/wp-content/uploads/2018/07/Phillips_Issue_Brief.pdf

Phillips, Scott. 2009. "Status Disparities in the Capital of Capital Punishment." *Law and Society Review* 43:807–837.

Phillips, Scott. 2012. "Continued Racial Disparities in the Capital of Capital Punishment: The Rosenthal Era." *Houston Law Review* 50:131–156.

Phillips, Scott and Mark Cooney. 2005. "Aiding Peace, Abetting Violence: Third Parties and the Management of Conflict." *American Sociological Review* 70:334–354.

Pinker, Steven. 2011. *The Better Angels of Our Nature: Why Violence Has Declined.* New York: Viking.

Schlueter, David A. 2008. *Military Criminal Justice: Practice and Procedure.* Newark, NJ: Lexis Nexis (seventh edition; first edition, 2003).

Senechal de la Roche, Roberta. 1996. "Collective Violence as Social Control." *Sociological Forum* 11:97–128.

Senechal de la Roche, Roberta. 1997. "The Sociogenesis of Lynching." Pp. 48–76 in *Under Sentence of Death: Lynching in the American South*, edited by W. Fitzhugh Brundage. Chapel Hill: University of North Carolina Press.

Spencer, Charles. 2014. *Killers of the King: The Men Who Dared to Execute Charles I.* London: Bloomsbury Paperbacks.

Stevenson, Bryan. 2014. *Just Mercy: A Story of Justice and Redemption.* New York: Random House.

Sweeny, JoAnne. 2014. "Undead Statutes: The Rise, Fall, and Continuing Uses of Adultery and Fornication Criminal Laws." *Loyola University Chicago Law Journal* 46:128–173.

Tucker, James. 1999. *The Therapeutic Corporation.* New York: Oxford University Press.

Tucker, James. 2015. "The Geometry of Suicide Law." *International Journal of Crime, Law and Justice* 43 :342–365.

INDEX